Christianity, Islam, and Liberal Democracy

Christianity, Islam, and Liberal Democracy

Lessons from Sub-Saharan Africa

Robert A. Dowd

OXFORD
UNIVERSITY PRESS

Oxford University Press is a department of the University of
Oxford. It furthers the University's objective of excellence in research,
scholarship, and education by publishing worldwide.

Oxford New York

Auckland Cape Town Dar es Salaam Hong Kong Karachi
Kuala Lumpur Madrid Melbourne Mexico City Nairobi
New Delhi Shanghai Taipei Toronto

With offices in

Argentina Austria Brazil Chile Czech Republic France Greece
Guatemala Hungary Italy Japan Poland Portugal Singapore
South Korea Switzerland Thailand Turkey Ukraine Vietnam

Oxford is a registered trademark of Oxford University Press
in the UK and certain other countries.

Published in the United States of America by
Oxford University Press
198 Madison Avenue, New York, NY 10016

Library of Congress Cataloging-in-Publication Data
Dowd, Robert Alfred, 1965– author.
Christianity, Islam and liberal democracy : lessons from Sub-Saharan Africa / Robert A. Dowd.
pages cm
Includes bibliographical references and index.
ISBN 978–0–19–022521–6 (cloth : alk. paper) 1. Democracy—Religious aspects.
2. Democracy—Africa, Sub-Saharan. 3. Democracy—Nigeria. 4. Christianity and politics—
Africa, Sub-Saharan. 5. Christianity and politics—Nigeria. 6. Islam and politics—
Africa, Sub-Saharan. 7. Islam and politics—Nigeria. 8. Cultural pluralism—Africa,
Sub-Saharan—Religious aspects. 9. Cultural pluralism—Nigeria—Religious aspects.
10. Political culture—Africa, Sub-Saharan. 11. Political culture—Nigeria. I. Title.
BL65.P7D69 2015
201.720967—dc23
2014037386

1 3 5 7 9 8 6 4 2
Printed in the United States of America
on acid-free paper

To my parents, my family, and others who have inspired me
with their courage, persistence, and patience.

Contents

List of Figures

List of Tables

Acknowledgments

We always learn from and with others, and I have learned immensely from several people without whom this book and the research it features would not have been possible. While all of the shortcomings are my own, any insightful contributions in the book are the result of the thoughtful input and important questions raised by generous, knowledgeable, and wise colleagues. William Evans read over countless drafts and provided indispensible advice on data analysis. Bill was absolutely tireless in his support and was always ready to offer constructive criticism, for which I am most grateful. Scott Mainwaring, Tim Scully, and Dan Philpott gave very thoughtful input at various stages of the book's development. I cannot thank them enough for their wise counsel and insightful comments. The Comparative Politics Reading Group at the University of Notre Dame provided a wonderful and enjoyable forum for sharing sections of this book, and I am most grateful for the advice offered by Jaimie Bleck, Sean McGraw, Monika Nalepa, Sarah Daly, and Guillermo Trejo. As Chair of the Political Science Department at Notre Dame, Mike Desch gave me just the right kind of encouragement and pushed me when I needed a push to complete this book. I am extremely grateful for Mike's guidance. I also want to thank David Nickerson, whose advice on survey development and analytical techniques at an early stage of this project was extremely valuable. Despite their busy schedules and their own important research as students at the time, Michael Driessen, Javier Osorio, and Michael Hoffman went beyond the call of duty as research assistants and I am very grateful to them. For her skilled help with graphics, I want to thank Judy Bartlett. I also owe a debt of gratitude to many others who, at different points in time and in various ways, encouraged and inspired me to complete this project or otherwise assisted me (sometimes without realizing it), especially Richard Warner, Lloyd Torgerson, Paul Kollman, Bill Lies, Dan Groody, Jim King, Bill Miscamble, Lou Delfra, Paulinus Odozor, Jim McAdams, Andy Gould, Eileen Botting, Michael Coppedge, Robert Fishman, Edmond Keller, Dan Posner, Richard Sklar, Don Miller, Mike Bratton, Carolyn Logan, Clark Gibson, Molly Lipscomb, Gabriela Ippolito-O'Donnell, John Paden, Timothy Shah, John Campbell, Ani Sarkissian, Ian Linden and Rachel Beatty Reidl. I am particularly grateful for the encouragement offered by the late and great Guillermo O'Donnell at the earliest stages of this project. Guillermo continues to be an inspiration to me and to so many others.

A great deal of fieldwork went into the making of this book, and such fieldwork would have been impossible without the assistance of and hospitality extended by wonderful colleagues in Nigeria, Senegal, and Uganda. I wanted to thank the countless research assistants and those who allowed themselves to be interviewed in all three countries. I am especially grateful to Nigerian Christian and Muslim religious leaders who were open to participation in this study. For their inspiring and courageous example, I wish to extend a special thanks to Cardinal John Onaiyekan, the late Sultan Muhammadu Maccido, Sultan Sa'adu Abubakar, and Archbishop Ignatius Kaigama. I would also like to thank many other local Christian and Muslim religious leaders whose cooperation made this book possible. Because of the sensitive nature of the subject matter and inter-religious tensions that exist at this writing in some parts of Nigeria, I do not mention them by name. However, my hope is that this book is somehow helpful to all of those who are interested in increasing the extent to which Christian and Islamic religious communities effectively promote civic engagement and religious tolerance. I also wish to thank Practical Sampling International, in Nigeria and Senegal, and Wilsken Agencies, in Uganda, for professional survey research support.

The field research presented in this book was made possible largely thanks to the Metanexus Institute's Spiritual Capital research initiative, which was supported by a grant from the John Templeton Foundation. I am very grateful for the opportunities that the grant made possible.

The Kellogg Institute for International Studies at Notre Dame offered financial support through its faculty grants program and a wonderfully conducive environment for research and writing. I want to especially thank the Kellogg Institute's leadership team, Paolo Carozza, Steve Reifenberg, Sharon Schierling, and Holly Rivers, for their encouragement and understanding. Additionally, I would like to express my gratitude to the entire staff of the Institute and that of the Institute's Ford Family Program in Human Development Studies and Solidarity. I served as director of the Ford Program while writing this book. This meant that other Ford Program staff, particularly Dennis Haraszko, Kristi Lax-Walker, Jackline Aridi, Ilaria Schnyder von Wartensee, Danice Brown, Tony Pohlen, and Lacey Haussamen, often had to pick up the slack. To them, I am very grateful. The Kroc Institute for International Peace Studies and its director, Scott Appleby, also provided support that helped make this book possible. I would like to thank Scott and everyone at the Kroc Institute for believing in this project.

Of course, I am also grateful to the editorial staff at Oxford University Press. I thank Theo Calderara for his thoughtful consideration of this project and his attentiveness to the book from its very first stages. Marcela Maxfield and Glenn Ramirez were extremely patient with me during the production phase. To both of them, I am very grateful.

Finally, I want to thank the members of the Congregation of Holy Cross, especially at the University of Notre Dame and in East Africa, and my family, particularly my parents, Norma and Harvey, my sister Mary, brother-in-law, Jim, and my nephews, Ryan and Eric. My dad has been a model of perseverance whose example continues to inspire. I am very grateful for the lessons in life he helped me to learn. Without doubt, the love of family and friends encouraged me to complete this project and to put it in proper perspective.

Christianity, Islam, and Liberal Democracy

1

Introduction
Christianity, Islam, and Liberal Democracy

"To be involved in politics is our Christian duty," declared James, a devout member of an Anglican church in the city of Jos located in Nigeria's Middle Belt. "If we do not speak up, we only have ourselves to blame for the immorality and corruption in our country," he continued.[1] In Enugu, a city in southeastern Nigeria, about seven hours by road from Jos, another religiously observant Anglican named Joshua calmly stated, "We should leave the dirty game of politics to the politicians. Christians should concern themselves with living a morally upright life and leave the rest to God."[2] It is clear that these two Nigerian Christians, both members of the Anglican Church, apply their Christian faith to politics in different ways. One applies Christianity in a way that encourages political activism and the other in a way that discourages such activism. Anglicans are not the only Christians in Nigeria who apply their faith to politics in different ways. Some Roman Catholics and Pentecostals draw on their faith to justify political activism, while others use their faith to excuse their political inactivity. Islam, too, is applied to politics in different ways. Some Nigerian Muslims believe that their faith requires that the Islamic religious law, the *Shari'ah*, must be enshrined as the law of the land, while other religiously observant Muslims believe that it would be a mistake to enshrine the Islamic religious law in the state's constitution.

While we know that Christians and Muslims apply religious ideas to politics in various ways in Nigeria, in sub-Saharan Africa as a whole, and in other regions of the world, we have yet to understand and explain this variation very well. Some theorists emphasize the importance of the religious tradition itself and argue that not every religious tradition includes the ideas or ideological resources to support a liberal democratic political culture. In their view, Western Christianity has the ideological resources to support liberal democracy but Islam does not (Huntington 1996; Kedourie 1994; Pipes 1983; Lewis 2003). Others suggest that the organizational structure of a religious institution matters at least as much as the ideological resources. They propose that hierarchically organized religious institutions, such as the Catholic Church, give ordinary believers fewer opportunities to exercise leadership and to develop the skills and confidence that would make them as civically engaged and politically active as ordinary believers in less hierarchically organized religious communities, such as many Protestant churches (Verba, Schlozman, and Brady 1995).

Theories that focus on the type of religion do not explain very well the various ways in which people apply religion to politics, or the different ways in which James and Joshua, both Nigerian Anglicans, apply their Christian faith to politics. Perhaps with people like James and Joshua in mind, other theorists suggest that the variation in the political impact of religious communities depends less on the type of religion in question than on the environment (Geertz 1973; Villalon 1995; Stepan 2000; Appleby 2000; Philpott 2007). They suggest that neither Christianity nor Islam is wholly compatible or incompatible with liberal democracy. Rather, they suggest that there is something about certain times and places that prompts people, regardless of faith tradition or denomination, to apply their religious traditions to politics in ways that are more or less conducive to liberal democracy. They propose that we compare social, political, economic, and religious conditions in Jos and Enugu to understand the different ways in which our two Nigerian Anglicans—James, in Jos, and Joshua, in Enugu—apply their Christian faith to politics. While these analysts suggest that there must be something about a certain time and place that makes the world's great religious traditions more or less encouraging of actions and attitudes that are conducive to liberal democracy, they do not point to that "something."

In this book, I point to evidence from sub-Saharan Africa to argue that religious diversity is that "something," though not the only thing, which affects how religious leaders and ordinary believers apply their faith to politics. Based largely on research I conducted in Nigeria, and to a lesser extent in other parts of sub-Saharan Africa, this book points to qualitative data (i.e., narrative accounts of events and in-depth interviews) and quantitative data (i.e., mass survey research) to advance an argument that Christian and Islamic religious communities become more conducive to actions and attitudes compatible with liberal democracy in religiously diverse and integrated settings than in religiously homogeneous settings or settings that are diverse but segregated along religious lines. While many analysts have thought that religious diversity in developing countries is most often an obstacle to liberal democracy, this book points to evidence that indicates just the opposite. I find that Christian and Islamic religious communities in sub-Saharan Africa have tended to contribute more effectively to the formation of a liberal democratic political culture in settings that have long been religiously diverse than in those settings that have long been religiously homogeneous.

In our examination of data from sub-Saharan Africa, we find evidence that religious diversity has prompted religiously inspired support for a liberal democratic political culture—a political culture that is characterized by social tolerance and civic engagement. This does not mean that the positive relationship between religious diversity and religiously inspired support for actions and attitudes conducive to liberal democracy has been automatic or instantaneous. In fact, as settings have become religiously diverse, we find that religious leaders, especially those who represent long-dominant religious majorities, have often discouraged the religious tolerance that characterizes liberal democracy in hopes of preserving or gaining a privileged place for their religious institutions. However, over time, religious leaders decided that they would be better off if they promoted the growth and influence of their own religious institutions by encouraging civic engagement, respect for religious freedom, and separation of religious and state authority than by seeking cultural and political dominance. In this way, Christian and Muslim religious leaders in religiously diverse and integrated settings have contributed positively to the prospects for liberal democracy.

This book assumes that Christian and Muslim religious leaders enhance the prospects for liberal democracy when and where they respect the freedom of other religious groups and individuals to disagree with them. They also contribute to the prospects for liberal democracy when and where they defend the separation of religious and state authority and reject the idea that there should be one established religion to the exclusion of others.[3] In other words, they promote a political culture conducive to liberal democracy where and when they encourage a "live and let live" ethic—when and where they seek to persuade rather than impose.[4] In this book, we find evidence to suggest that, without the experience of living in religiously diverse societies, religious leaders and ordinary religious people are less likely to learn to live and let live—or more likely to learn to live and let live more slowly than those in religiously diverse settings. Although more research is necessary, the findings presented in this book call into question attempts to enhance the prospects for political stability and liberal democracy that would create or reinforce religiously homogeneous neighborhoods, cities, and broader political units. The results suggest that such attempts may actually decrease the likelihood that Christian and Islamic communities encourage actions and attitudes conducive to liberal democracy, and that efforts to enhance the extent to which religious communities contribute to political stability and the prospects for liberal democracy may be better served by cultivating religious diversity and integration.

RELIGION AND POLITICAL CULTURE

Religion, which I define as a system of beliefs in the transcendent that communities develop and use to explain the world around them, is uniquely positioned to affect political culture or attitudes and behaviors concerning government.[5] In settings where poverty is widespread, secular civil society is weak, and political institutions are underdeveloped, religious communities are valued not only for the spiritual services they provide but also for the material needs they meet. As Inglehart (1988: 1221) argues, in most agrarian societies "religion is an overwhelmingly important force, filling the functions that educational and scientific institutions, the mass media, art museums, and philanthropic foundations now fill in advanced industrial societies." Where there are authoritarian regimes or where democratic institutions are not firmly established, religious institutions are often the only organizations capable of effectively challenging the state.[6]

Sub-Saharan African is arguably the most religiously vibrant region in the world. More people spend more time gathered in religious communities in sub-Saharan Africa than anywhere else on earth. Christianity and Islam have experienced tremendous growth in the region over the past century, so the religious communities in which most sub-Saharan Africans are actively involved are Christian and Islamic. Christians and Muslims in sub-Saharan Africa are more likely to turn to religious leaders when in need than to governmental officials and leaders of other non-governmental groups.[7] Given the growth and vibrancy of Christianity and Islam in sub-Saharan Africa, we cannot help but wonder whether and how Christian and Islamic religious communities are affecting the chances that liberal democratic institutions will emerge and survive in the region. Religious belief and communal participation may increase, decrease, or have no effect at all on participation in fragile democratic institutions, support for freedom of speech and association, and respect for freedom of religion.

Like many theorists, we might assume that the effects of religion on the prospects for and the quality of liberal democracy largely depend on the type of religion or religious community in question. We might assume that some faith traditions and religious communities are more compatible with and conducive to liberal democracy than others. For example, many argue that Western Christianity is typically more compatible with and conducive to liberal democracy than Islam, just as it has been assumed that Protestantism is more conducive to liberal democracy than Roman Catholicism (Huntington 1991, 1996; Crone 1980; Pipes 1983; Hall 1985; Woodberry and Shah 2004). After all, the first liberal democracies were in predominantly Protestant countries, and, as of this writing, most predominantly Protestant and Roman Catholic countries are liberal democracies, whereas most predominantly Muslim countries are not. However, it seems quite a stretch to expect that a religious institution will affect political culture in the same way always and everywhere.

Let us assume for a moment that the impact of a religious community on political actions and attitudes does depend on the type of religious community itself, whether it is Christian or Islamic, Roman Catholic or Protestant. We need to identify those characteristics of Christianity and Islam, Roman Catholicism and Protestantism, which promote or impede a political culture conducive to liberal democracy. The organizational structure and the political theologies espoused by religious faith traditions are thought to be very important to any explanation for how religious faith communities affect political culture. Religious communities that are "horizontally organized," open to "lay" participation in decision-making or make no distinction between laity and clerics, and tolerate many different points of view are thought to be more conducive to liberal democracy than religious communities that are "vertically organized," draw a clear distinction between the laity and clerics, reserve decision-making authority to the clerics, and do not tolerate dissent (Verba, Schlozman, and Brady 1995). According to Woodberry and Shah (2004), these are the distinctions that have tended to make many Protestant churches more conducive to liberal democracy than the Roman Catholic Church.[8] Hatch (1989) and Bruce (2006) note that certain Protestant sects in the United States were organized in such a way that they provided millions of ordinary people with training in public speaking, organizational skills, and group leadership. Further, Thompson (1848) notes,

> They [Secessionist Protestant Sects] insisted on the right of popular election in its full and scriptural extent—that every member of the congregation, of whatever sex or social status, should enjoy the right of choice. People have been trained to interest themselves in their own affairs, and in attending to their own

interests have acquired that habit of individual judgment, which stands closely associated with the continuance of ecclesiastical civil liberty.

Of course, the organizational attributes that characterized certain Protestant sects of the nineteenth century, as described above, were founded on ideas and theological convictions, such as the inherent equality of all believers before God. However, these organizational attributes concerned the internal life of the religious communities themselves. They did not necessarily correspond to explicit teachings about the place of the religious community in the wider social or political order and actions and attitudes vis-à-vis government. An internally democratic religious community may teach nothing about the ideal political system, the role of religion in the wider society, or what makes an individual believer a good citizen. In fact, such a religious community might discourage concern with politics and government and may encourage complete devotion to the inner life of the religious community that, if governed democratically, would require believers to devote considerable time and energy to the running of the religious institution itself.[9] If we are concerned with the effects of religious communities on political culture, we need to do more than analyze how decisions are made within religious communities. We need to study the political theologies or ideas about citizenship, representation, freedom, and the place of organized religion in the wider society that are espoused by religious communities.

In this book, I follow the lead of Philpott (2007: 7–10) and define a political theology as a set of ideas that a religious community holds about what constitutes legitimate political authority, the proper relationship between sacred and secular authority, and the responsibilities of the individual believer vis-à-vis government. Religious faith traditions and communities which teach that human beings must take responsibility for shaping the world around them, that respect freedom of association and speech, and that espouse separation between sacred and secular authority are most conducive to liberal democracy. Religious faith traditions and communities which teach that human beings do not have responsibility for shaping the world around them, that there should be strict limits to freedom of association and speech, and that there should be no separation between religious and secular authority are least conducive to liberal democracy. While not denying that the organizational structures of religious communities are important, this book focuses on the variation in the types of political theologies or ideas about politics espoused by Christian and Muslim religious leaders and their impact on the actions and attitudes of ordinary Christians and Muslims.

This book attempts to rise above the polemics that so often plague studies of religion and politics to show that it is possible to develop a systematic explanation for why religiously based ideas that are pro-democratic and respectful of basic freedoms, especially freedom of religion, are emphasized more (or less) than those that are anti-democratic and do not respect basic freedoms. As Steven Fish (2011) suggests, while there is a great deal that we do not know about religion and its impact on public life, what we do know indicates that the relationship between religion and politics is messy and more complex than most observers and commentators have recognized. It is difficult to know when religious factors are more important than other factors (e.g., ethnic identity and class) for explaining political behavior and attitudes. This is especially true when religious differences overlap with class differences or ethnic identities, as they do in a number of societies in both the developed and developing world. Further, there are many different expressions of Christianity and Islam. Christianity, in particular, has been prone to splits and splintering for much of its history. The denominations are many, and some new and rapidly growing religious expressions defy denominational categorization. Pentecostal Christianity is a case in point. It is not really a church, like the Roman Catholic, Anglican, Lutheran, and Presbyterian churches. Although Pentecostal churches share certain similarities and features in common (e.g., emotional style of worship, emphasis on healing, prohibition of alcohol consumption), they are different from and independent of each other (Anderson 2013).

While recognizing that political theologies espoused by religious faith communities are crucially important for understanding whether faith communities are compatible with and conducive to a liberal democratic political culture, this book argues that political theologies are fluid and not fixed.[10] Agreeing with Marshall (2009: 27), I propose that Christianity and Islam are not unchanging essences. They always have a locality in time and space, and their locality affects the way in which the religions are interpreted and appropriated. In short, political theologies are themselves the product of human beings who make decisions; they themselves have not dropped from the sky and they themselves beg explanation. The religious, economic, social, and political environment may prompt religious leaders and ordinary believers to amend social teachings and create new political theologies. Max Weber (1963) referred to this as the "practical religion of the converted." In other words, the political theologies promoted by religious communities change across time and place. When we look back in time and across the world today, it becomes apparent that, with varying degrees of effectiveness, Christianity and Islam are capable of generating political theologies that encourage or discourage actions and attitudes that are compatible with or conducive to liberal democracy.

For example, some churches within Western Christianity have been more supportive of liberal democracy than others (e.g., until recently, many Protestant churches as opposed to the Roman Catholic Church). It is also apparent that the same Christian denomination has often been more supportive of liberal democracy in one place than in another (e.g., during the 1980s, the Roman Catholic Church in Brazil as compared to the Roman Catholic Church in Argentina or, during the 1990s, the Anglican Church in Kenya as opposed to the Anglican Church in Uganda). Some churches have been more supportive of liberal democratic ideals at some points in time than others (e.g., the Roman Catholic Church after the Second Vatican Council as compared to before the Second Vatican Council).[11] Although the integration of sacred and secular authority and strict boundaries on freedom of expression are thought to be essential to Islam, I have already noted that different political theologies may be espoused and significant variation can be found among Muslims (Esposito and Voll 1996; Hefner 2005; Akyol 2011). For example, there is reason to believe that recently Islam has been more encouraging of actions and attitudes that are conducive to liberal democracy in countries such as Indonesia and Bosnia than in Saudi Arabia, Sudan, and Afghanistan. Yet, even within countries and within *Sunni* and *Shia* communities, Muslim religious leaders may vary a great deal in how they apply religious ideas to politics. For example, in Iran, Mulla Sadra, the spiritual mentor of Ayatollah Khomeini, abhorred coercion in religious matters and argued that it is forbidden in the Koran (Armstrong 2007). Nonetheless, as noted above, other *Shia* religious leaders have applied Islam in such a way so as to justify a political system in Iran that is coercive on matters of religion. So, we cannot say that all *Shia* apply Islam to politics in one way and all *Sunni* apply Islam to politics in another. *Sunni* religious leaders inspired by the ideas of Arabian Ibn al-Wahhab, Pakistani theorist Ayyid Mawdudi, and Egyptian literary critic Sayyid Qutb promote the complete integration of state and religious authority as the only way to be faithful to the Koran. Abu Bakr al Baghdadi, who presided over the growth of the Islamic State of Iraq and the Levant (ISIL), is one such leader. Yet, other *Sunni* leaders have been inspired by jurists who argue that it is wrong to harness God's law to the interests of the state and have espoused their separation (Soroush 2000).

Given the variation across time and place in how religion is applied to politics, the task at hand is to identify conditions that give rise to an application of religion to politics that is conducive to liberal democratic institutions. Certain social changes prompted Catholic leaders to apply the Christian faith so as to officially bless democracy and religious liberty at the Second Vatican Council after more than a century of appealing to the Christian faith to openly and vigorously condemn democratic forms of government and religious freedom. Social changes explain why Anglican Church leaders began to renounce the discrimination against Roman Catholics in England's institutions of higher learning after hundreds of years of justifying such an official policy. Due to changing social conditions, leaders of Pentecostal Christian communities in many parts of the world no longer appeal to the Bible to discourage participation in politics but instead appeal to sacred scripture to justify civic engagement and political activism. As one Pentecostal pastor in Nigeria told me, "We used to think the Bible called us to stay out of politics; you know, to give to Caesar what is his and to God what is His. We do not think that way now. Everything belongs to God and, through His holy prophets Isaiah, Jeremiah and others, I know that He is calling us to politics; to vote our faith, to vote for God-fearing Christians, and to bring this country back to Him."[12] The question is, what is it about time and place that helps us to understand and explain this change in the way religion is applied to public life?

THE ARGUMENT

In this book, I offer an argument to explain the variation in the extent to which Christian and Islamic religious communities encourage a political culture conducive to liberal democracy and test its explanatory power on evidence from sub-Saharan Africa. I argue that *religious diversity*, which varies across time and place, has a very significant effect on how religious leaders choose to apply their religious beliefs and doctrines to politics and helps explain the fluidity in political theologies that we observe throughout history and across the world today. I propose that Christian and Muslim religious leaders are typically more encouraging of political participation *and* respect for religious liberty in religiously diverse and integrated settings than in religiously homogeneous settings, or in religiously diverse settings where religious groups are segregated. In religiously diverse settings, as compared to religiously homogeneous settings, religious leaders are more likely to mobilize believers to make sure the voices of their religious communities are heard by politicians and by the wider society. Religious leaders in religiously diverse settings are likely to do all they can to ensure that the voices of the religious communities they lead are not drowned out by the voices of rival religious communities or the voices that seek to weaken and marginalize organized religion in general (Kymlicka and Norman 2000; Wald 2003).

While it may not be surprising to find that religiously motivated political participation is greater in religiously diverse settings than in religiously homogeneous settings, we may be surprised to find that religiously motivated support for religious tolerance and respect for religious liberty is greater in religiously diverse societies than in religiously homogeneous societies. This is because religious passions are thought to be an obstacle to political stability, let alone liberal democracy. And such religious passions are thought to run highest in religiously diverse, materially impoverished, and politically uncertain settings (Minkenberg 2007). In the most religiously diverse settings, particularly where poverty is widespread and the political system, including the relationship between the state and religious institutions, is up for grabs, we might assume that religious leaders will adopt defensive and aggressive strategies that are not conducive to liberal democracy. Religious leaders may promote outward displays of piety as a way of drawing well-defined boundaries between their religious communities and others. They may also negatively portray other religious faith traditions in order to discourage conversions to these rival religions. We might even expect leaders of historically dominant faith traditions to use the legislative process and the courts to limit the freedoms of new or different religious faith traditions and communities.[13] In fact, this is often what happens in religiously diverse settings *until* religious leaders realize that such efforts are futile and immensely costly for the religious institutions they lead.

While there is plenty of historical evidence to indicate that religious diversity in impoverished and politically unstable settings often gives rise to religious conflict initially, there is also evidence to suggest that such diversity eventually leads to the religious compromise and accommodation that are necessary for liberal democracy. I propose that Christian and Muslim religious leaders in religiously diverse settings are more likely than their counterparts in religiously homogeneous settings to learn that the best way to grow their religious institutions and influence the wider society is to promote civic engagement and respect for religious liberty. Unfortunately, the process of learning can be slow and painful. Sometimes the learning comes only after or as the result of repeated episodes of violence that clearly leave all religious institutions worse off. In religiously diverse settings, religious leaders are more likely to come to learn that it would be in the best interest of their religious communities if they would work to ensure that no religious institution has a privileged relationship with the state, rather than to persist in their efforts to maintain or achieve a privileged position for their religious communities over all others. Such a shift in the behavior of religious leaders, initially a strategic choice intended to protect the interests of their religious institutions in a religiously diverse setting, opens the way for religious integration or desegregation, including religiously mixed schools, workplaces, neighborhoods, and even families. In turn, religious desegregation decreases the likelihood that religious leaders ever discourage religious tolerance or call for the integration of religious and state authority. It increases the likelihood that religious leaders use their influence to promote respect for freedom of religion and separation of religious and state authority—necessary but insufficient conditions for liberal democracy.[14] The argument is illustrated in Figure 1.1.

This begs the question about the origins of religious diversity itself and raises the problem of endogeneity (Alesina et al. 2003). It is important to recognize that religious diversity, which we focus on as a causal variable here, is also a dependent variable. Something causes societies to become religiously diverse in the first place, and it is conceivable that liberal democracy precedes rather than follows religious diversity. We need to know whether religious diversity is the cause or the consequence of liberal democracy. Although Alesina et al. (2003) find that religious diversity is positively related to democracy and human rights, they suggest that religious diversity is simply greater in more tolerant and open countries. For example, it would appear that a relatively liberal democratic political culture is the cause rather than the consequence of religious diversity in the United States. Is it not true that millions of immigrants flocked to the United States in large part because of the religious liberty they expected to enjoy in America?

While many have argued that Protestantism itself is more conducive to liberal democracy than Roman Catholicism and point to the early Protestant colonists to explain the religious liberty, and hence the religious diversity, that came to prevail in the United States, upon closer examination, there is good reason to question this narrative of events. There is evidence to indicate that many of these early Protestant communities, where they enjoyed a significant majority over a territory, were quite

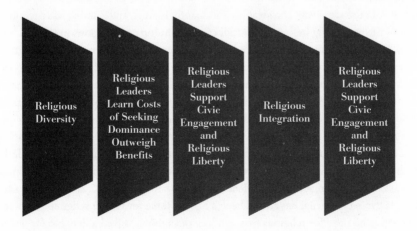

Figure 1.1 Religious Diversity and Religious-Based Support for Liberal Democratic Ideals

intolerant of dissent and sought to promote religious monopolies for themselves (Gill 2008; Trigg 2014).[15] These Protestant churches did not become champions of liberal democracy in the United States until the growth of other Protestant churches and waves of Catholic immigration made the country more religiously diverse (Fenton 2011). In the same way, Roman Catholicism was friendlier to liberal democracy in the United States, where the church formed either a minority or found itself in settings that were religiously diverse, than in many parts of Europe or Latin America, where the Roman Catholic Church included the vast majority of the population and had grown accustomed to a privileged relationship with the state (McGreevy 2003).

When we look to Europe and Latin America, we also find evidence to indicate that religious diversity preceded rather than followed religious-based support for liberal democratic ideals and the institutionalization of liberal democracy. The first liberal democracies in Europe were countries with significant Protestant populations, but these countries, such as Britain, the Netherlands, and Belgium, also included significant Catholic populations and were Europe's most religiously diverse countries. Gould (1999) notes that Catholic leaders were typically more encouraging of political participation and supportive of freedom of conscience, association, and speech where such freedoms curtailed the influence of Protestant monarchs over Catholic populations. He argues that such support was crucial to the development of liberal democracy in nineteenth century Europe. Gill (1998) argues that Catholic leaders were much more critical of authoritarian regimes in Latin America's most religiously diverse countries, such as Chile, Nicaragua, and El Salvador, than in the region's least religiously diverse countries, such as Argentina, Bolivia, and Honduras.

Evidence from sub-Saharan Africa is especially instructive. In sub-Saharan Africa, no country, except for Botswana, was even remotely democratic until multiparty elections were introduced or reintroduced during the early 1990s. Yet, dating from the colonial era, the region's authoritarian regimes allowed freedom of worship, and sub-Saharan African countries varied significantly in terms of how religiously diverse they were. Religious diversity preceded liberal democracy. For example, Nigeria was roughly half Christian and half Muslim well before its Fourth Republic was launched in 1999. In the same way, Mali was predominantly Islamic, and Zambia was predominantly Christian long before the introduction of multiparty elections in these countries. While it is impossible to have liberal democracy without freedom of religion, it is possible to have freedom of religion without liberal democracy. In many countries of sub-Saharan Africa, there was religious freedom and diversity without liberal democracy for several decades, and, if we are interested in how religious diversity affects the impact of Christian and Islamic communities on democratic transitions, sub-Saharan Africa is a good place to look. When we do look, we find that Christian and Muslim religious leaders have been more encouraging of liberal democratic ideals in the region's religiously diverse settings than in its religiously homogeneous settings. In sum, there is a great deal of evidence to support Roger Trigg's (2014: 157) assertion, "Diversity of belief has always been a driving force for greater religious freedom. Similarly, the need for religious freedom has inevitably involved a demand for wider political and economic freedoms."

Although there are several religiously homogeneous countries where liberal demo-cratic institutions have been established and sustained, I propose that, all else being equal, religious communities do not become great champions of liberal democracy unless there is crucial degree of religious diversity. Of course, there are conditions that increase the likelihood that religious leaders in a religiously homogeneous society pro-mote liberal democracy, such as when there is a hostile relationship between a religious institution and government leaders under secular authoritarian regimes. Toft, Philpott, and Shah (2011) refer to such situations as hostile separation. Examples include the Roman Catholic Church in Poland under Communist rule between the 1940s and the late 1980s, and Muslim groups in Indonesia under Suharto. In both cases, lead-ers of the dominant religion played leading or supporting roles in promoting liberal democracy. Nonetheless, there is evidence to suggest that dominant religions do not often remain great champions of the religious freedom necessary in a liberal democ-racy once they have won their own freedom from state control. With their newly won freedoms, leaders of dominant religious institutions often attempt to negotiate deals with governments that give their institutions state-sanctioned advantages over other religious communities, or that impede the entry of other religious institutions. For example, some Roman Catholic leaders believed that the church's contribution to the pro-democracy movement in Poland entitled the church to a privileged place vis-a-vis the state in the post-Communist era (Anderson 2003). Some Roman Catholic leaders failed to get all the privileges they wanted. However, the Taliban in Afghanistan and the followers of Ayatollah Ruhollah Khomeini in Iran, who sought more comprehen-sive privileges than Roman Catholic leaders in Poland would have ever attempted to achieve, were more successful. After having struggled for freedom of religion when Afghanistan and Iran were under secular-autocratic rule, they effectively imposed their own strict versions of Islam and severely restricted religious freedom for adherents of other faiths and Muslims who would rather not conform to the versions of Islam that were imposed.

This book does not propose that religious homogeneity is an impediment to liberal democracy. There are plenty of religiously homogenous countries with relatively lib-eral and democratic political cultures, such as Senegal, Spain, Italy, Portugal, Norway, and Sweden, just as there are religiously diverse countries with relatively illiberal and undemocratic political cultures (Gellar 2005; Fishman 2004; Putnam 1993). I do not argue that people in religiously homogeneous countries are condemned to live under illiberal and/or non-democratic political systems. First, conditions that favor liberal democracy may eventually overwhelm any illiberal or undemocratic influence that dominant religious institutions have in a society. These conditions may include education and income. I propose that education and income do not necessarily make people less religious, but they often change the ways in which people are religious and decrease the likelihood that Christians and Muslims are easily persuaded that freedom of religion and separation of religious and state authority are incompatible with their religious faith traditions. There is reason to think that educational advances increase the likelihood that people recognize that there is something special about their own faith tradition and, at the same time, reject the idea that their religious faith tradition (or any religious faith tradition) should enjoy monopoly status and a privileged relationship vis-à-vis the state. Where people are highly educated, leaders of dominant religious institutions are likely to promote more liberal and democratic political theologies, since to do otherwise would almost certainly undermine the credibility of their religious institutions. While educational advances may explain why religious leaders do not oppose basic freedoms and democratic ideals, by themselves they do not explain very well why religious leaders actively promote basic freedoms and liberal democratic ideals. The extent to which settings are religiously diverse and integrated is a key explanatory factor.

The argument that I make here is that Christian and Muslim religious leaders are typically more encouraging of actions and attitudes conducive to liberal democracy in religiously diverse and integrated settings than in religiously homogeneous settings or in religiously diverse settings where people are segregated along religious lines. If they do so at all, religious leaders in religiously homogeneous societies are typically slower to promote actions and attitudes that are conducive to liberal democracy than religious leaders in religiously diverse societies. In religiously diverse settings that are religiously segregated or where ethnic and religious differences overlap and reinforce each other, religious leaders are likely to encourage political activism but not as likely to promote religious tolerance as religious leaders in religiously diverse and integrated settings.

THE SIGNIFICANCE OF THE ARGUMENT AND THE FINDINGS

Why does it matter that sub-Saharan Africa's Christian and Muslim religious leaders have been more openly supportive of pro-democracy movements in religiously diverse countries than in religiously homogeneous countries, that religious communities tended to have a more positive effect on actions and attitudes conducive to liberal democracy in the region's most religiously diverse settings than in the region's more religiously homogeneous settings, and that Nigeria's Christian and Islamic communities were more conducive to civic engagement and religious tolerance in a religiously diverse and integrated city than in cities that were homogeneous or diverse but highly segregated? Does this book merely recognize an interesting relationship that existed at a particular point in time that has no practical or policy relevance within or beyond sub-Saharan Africa?

Although we cannot yet conclude that—just because religious diversity has tended to increase the extent to which sub-Saharan Africa's Christian and Islamic religious communities have effectively encouraged actions and attitudes conducive to liberal democracy—religious diversity will always and everywhere trigger the same effect, the findings reported in this book are important and far-reaching in that they call into question certain assumptions about how and why religious communities affect political culture. First, the findings reveal that we cannot easily predict how a religious community will affect political culture based solely on whether that religious community is Christian or Islamic. Second, results reveal the importance of digging down into countries rather than simply examining countries from a distance. From a distance, appearances are deceiving. For example, when we look at the case of Nigeria from a distance, we would likely conclude, as many have, that the country's religious diversity has led to inter-religious conflict and has been an obstacle to political stability and liberal democracy. However, when we dig down into Nigeria, as we do in this book, we find that religious communities have had the most positive effect on civic engagement and religious tolerance in the country's most religiously diverse and integrated settings. So, given these findings, we cannot very well conclude that religious diversity has been Nigeria's problem. It suggests that religious segregation, not religious diversity, has been Nigeria's problem. The lesson we learn is that religious diversity is not necessarily a bad thing in Nigeria and possibly elsewhere. In fact, religious diversity can be, as it has been in Nigeria, a good thing, even increasing the likelihood that Christian and Islamic communities promote a political culture conducive to liberal democracy. However, even if religious diversity and integration can be good things, gradually enhancing the likelihood that religious communities become champions of a political culture characterized by civic engagement and social tolerance, the question is, can religious diversity and integration be manufactured or created?

While religious diversity cannot be manufactured per se, policymakers often make decisions that affect the extent to which settings are religiously diverse and integrated. After the breakdown of an authoritarian regime (e.g., the former Yugoslavia), in the aftermath of war (e.g., Iraq), where there is intergroup tension and incidents of violent conflict (e.g., Israel, Lebanon, Nigeria, and Northern Ireland), policymakers often must draw or redraw political or social boundaries intended to promote peace and stability. They may do this in ways that segregate or integrate groups in conflict. Even without drawing or redrawing boundaries, policymakers may permit certain neighborhoods or localities to become socially and religiously homogeneous. In the name of promoting social harmony, they may allow discrimination to take place that prevents the emergence of more diverse neighborhoods and localities. While this may make destabilizing religious conflict less likely in the short term, the results suggests that this may increase the probability of religious conflict in the medium to longer term. There is reason to think that members of different religious groups, especially those in the same state, will eventually interact, despite the efforts of policymakers to prevent it. By attempting to prevent or put off the inevitable, policymakers increase the likelihood that different religious groups view each other as rivals competing for cultural and political hegemony. Religious institutions do not contribute positively to the emergence of liberal democracy where they are competing for cultural and political superiority over each other. Instead, religious leaders contribute positively to a liberal democratic political culture where they promote political participation in order to ensure that no religious institution enjoys cultural or political superiority over the others.

While many theorists have argued that social homogeneity is a prerequisite or at least a condition that is conducive to peace and stable democracy (Lipset 1959; Almond and Verba 1963; Dahl 1971; Easterly and Levine 1997), the evidence presented in this book suggests just the opposite: that religious diversity can enhance the prospects for peace and stable democracy. When and where policymakers have created or allowed religiously homogeneous political units, we often find that religious communities are least conducive to the political actions and attitudes that sustain liberal democracy. Although there may be certain conditions, such as protracted sectarian violence, that call for the temporary separation of ethnic, racial, and religious groups, I argue that, in the long run, religious homogeneity means that religious institutions are less likely to promote the political participation and support for freedom of association, speech, and religion that make liberal democracy feasible.

In this book I focus on political culture, beliefs, and attitudes that guide individual political behavior, and I consider culture to be fluid and dynamic rather than static and unchanging. Whereas Inglehart (1988: 53) suggests that "the publics of different societies are characterized by durable cultural orientations that have major political consequences," it is important to remember that culture is a consequence as well as a cause of political outcomes—a dependent and an independent variable. Every major society in the world has undergone changes in beliefs, norms, and values.[16] Societies have become more or less religiously observant, conservative, liberal, individualistic, and communitarian. At times, freedom is more or less valued over conformity. Culture not only varies from place to place, but across time within societies.

While religious diversity alone does not supply a complete explanation for why Christian and Islamic religious communities promote a political culture conducive to liberal democracy, explanations that ignore religious diversity fail to capture an important, often crucial, dimension affecting the impact of Christianity and Islam on political culture. Just as it would be wrong to assume that culture is fixed, we must avoid treating religion as immutable, static in its effect, and entirely independent of social context. Certain religious doctrines and organizational attributes of religious communities are subject to change. Thus, the way in which religion and religious communities affect political culture varies across time and place. This book is devoted to explaining such variation and is meant to shed light on what has been a blind spot in the study of political culture, the prospects for democracy where it is new and fragile, and the quality of democracy where it is firmly established.

WHY CHRISTIANITY AND ISLAM?

I focus on Christianity and Islam because they are the world's largest, most multinational, and fastest growing religions. There are approximately two billion Christians and 1.6 billion Muslims in the world today (Pew Research Center 2012). Christians and Muslims together account for one-half of the world's total population. It is important to know how the world's two largest religions are affecting the prospects for liberal democracy in the world.

Neither Christianity nor Islam is an ethno-national religion, but each is universalizing and cuts across nations, ethnic groups, and class in many countries. While there are certain regions of the world that are predominantly Christian, such as Western Europe and the Americas, or Muslim, such as the Middle East and North Africa, Christianity and Islam can be found in many different regions of the world. Although differences between Christians and Muslims do overlap or coincide with ethnic and class differences in some countries, such as in parts of northern and eastern Nigeria and in Sudan, in many others they do not. While religious affiliation in some countries has come to be thought of as an ethnic identity, as is the case with Muslims and Hindus in India, in most countries of Africa, Asia, Europe, Latin America, the Middle East, and North America, Christianity and Islam cut across ethnic differences. In many countries, we also find Christians and Muslims of various levels of wealth and of different socioeconomic backgrounds. The relatively universal and multinational span of Christianity and Islam not only makes the effects of Christianity and Islam on political culture an important subject for study, it also enables us to more effectively distinguish the effects of religion on political culture from the effects of ethnicity and class.

Christianity and Islam continue to grow at a faster rate than other world religions. The number of Christians in the world increased by more than one hundred million between 1995 and 2005, and the number of Muslims increased by more than two hundred million during the same period (Barrett, Kurian, and Johnson 2001: 4). Between 2005 and 2025, the number of Christians worldwide is expected to grow by six hundred million and the number of Muslims is expected to increase by seven hundred million (ibid.). Christianity's Evangelical and, more specifically, Pentecostal branches have recently experienced the most dramatic growth (ibid.). This in itself has potentially significant implications for inter-religious relations and the impact of Christianity and Islam on political participation and tolerance. Pentecostal Christians are reputed to be more aggressive in their efforts to convert mainstream Christians, such as Catholics and Anglicans, and Muslims. Where we find dramatic growth in Pentecostal Christianity, we might also find Christian and Islamic communities more mobilized than where we find a less pronounced Pentecostal presence. The growth of Islam and the brands of Christianity that are thought to be the most uncompromising and proselytizing, especially in parts of the world where the future of religion and state relations are uncertain, makes the impact of Christianity and Islam in the developing world a crucially important topic for study.

WHY FOCUS ON SUB-SAHARAN AFRICA?

Whether theories are born or survive depends crucially on the cases examined, and the first cases to be examined often have a disproportionate effect on the development of theory. Because most studies of religion and politics have begun in and/or have been confined to the United States, Europe, and Latin America, and, to a lesser degree, the Middle East, our understanding of the relationship between religion and politics is largely shaped by observations from these countries and regions. As Ellis and Ter Haar (2004: 15) put it:

The precepts of social science are based to a large extent on data drawn from Western societies and European and North American history, and influential theories have been based on more or less idealized readings of what actually happened in those areas. Therefore, models of social and political action that aspire to be universal in application are too often culturally specific. . .

If all or most of our studies of religion and politics begin in or are confined to North America, Europe, or any one country or region of the world, our understanding will remain less developed than it could be. This book uses sub-Saharan Africa as a starting point and focuses in a special way on the case of Nigeria because studies of religion and politics intended to build theory rarely include evidence from sub-Saharan Africa, let alone begin with observations from the region. The focus on sub-Saharan Africa promises to raise interesting questions and provide us with new insights concerning the impact of religion on political culture more generally. The book uses insights gained from contemporary sub-Saharan Africa to consider the political impact of religious communities in other parts of the world and at other points in time.

Sub-Saharan Africa is one of the most religiously diverse and diversifying regions in the world. Seventeen sub-Saharan African countries are predominantly Christian (i.e., over 65 percent Christian), seven are predominantly Muslim (i.e., over 65 percent Muslim), eight have significant Christian and Muslim populations (i.e., at least 20 percent Christian and at least 20 percent Muslim), and four have considerably large Christian and Muslim populations (i.e., at least 30 percent Christian and at least 30 percent Muslim) (Barrett, Kurian, and Johnson 2001; Pew Research Center 2010). Although there are twice as many predominantly Christian countries in sub-Saharan Africa as there are predominantly Muslim countries, the number of Muslims, even in many predominantly Christian countries of the region, is considerable. For example, in East Africa, more than 20 percent of the population is Muslim (Barrett, Kurian, and Johnson 2001; Pew Research Center 2010). In West Africa there are nearly 80 million Muslims, of which an estimated 58 million are Nigerians. In predominantly Christian Southern Africa there are approximately 4 million Muslims (ibid.).

Sub-Saharan Africa is also a good starting point for this study because in no other region have both Christianity and Islam spread more quickly as in sub-Saharan Africa. Between 1990 and 2000 the Islamic community in sub-Saharan Africa grew by between 30 and 40 million, from 120 million to more than 150 million (Quinn and Quinn 2003; Barrett, Kurian, and Johnson 2001). During the same period, the number of Christians grew by nearly 90 million, from 270 million to 360 million (Barrett, Kurian, and Johnson 2001). Although, at the time of this writing, the vast majority of sub-Saharan Africans are already either Christians or Muslims, both Christianity and Islam are expected to grow dramatically in sub-Saharan Africa in the coming decade. Much of this growth will be due to sub-Saharan Africa's relatively high birth rates, rather than conversions from Christianity to Islam or from Islam to Christianity. Due to population growth, as well as migration of Muslims into predominantly Christian areas and the migration of Christians into predominantly Muslim areas, Christians and Muslims are coming into contact with each other in sub-Saharan Africa like in few other regions of the world.[17] Therefore, it is important to learn whether, where, and why this contact results in extremism or tolerance and even collaboration. Poverty, disease, and weak states in sub-Saharan Africa make religious organizations very important. People turn to religious communities when they are in need. How does involvement in these religious communities affect how people define their social, economic, and political situation? We cannot help but wonder whether religious communities pacify, mobilize, moderate, or radicalize those who turn to them for solace and inspiration. Given the widespread poverty and the political transitions underway in the region, there is good reason to believe that sub-Saharan Africa is a potential breeding ground for religious extremism and recruitment pool for terrorist organizations. Groups like *Boko Haram* in West Africa and *al Shabab* in East Africa have become major concerns, as the deadly violence they perpetrate threatens to undermine regional stability, economic growth, development, and the prospects for liberal democracy. Religious extremism has raised its head in sub-Saharan Africa. However, before leaping to conclusions about the causes of such religious extremism and the best ways to discourage it, we would be wise to take a closer look at what is happening on the ground.

Sub-Saharan Africa also provides a good testing ground for hypotheses intended to explain the variation in religiously inspired support for liberal democracy because most authoritarian regimes that have existed in the region have not suppressed organized religion. In recent decades there are some notable exceptions, such as regimes in Sudan, Ethiopia, and Eritrea. This is important because this allows us to better assess how religious diversity and other factors affect the extent to which religious leaders and communities are supportive of freedom of religion or conscience. In countries where authoritarian regimes were hostile toward religion, such as in Eastern Europe and in Southeast Asia, it is difficult to know whether religious leaders supported liberal democracy simply because they sought to win freedoms for their own religious institutions at the expense of others, or whether they wanted to win religious liberty for all. In sub-Saharan Africa, most authoritarian regimes allowed a great deal of religious freedom, and so we can examine how Christian and Muslim leaders used such freedoms—whether they used such freedoms to promote exclusive privileges for the religious institutions they led, or religious freedom for all.

The book focuses in a special way on the case of Nigeria, one of the most religiously diverse and vibrant countries in the world, where the encounter between Christianity and Islam is thought to produce the kind of uncompromising religious extremism that makes liberal democracy impossible. By taking a close look at how Christianity and Islam affect political actions and attitudes in Nigeria, we can confirm or debunk the idea that Nigeria's religious diversity is a major obstacle to liberal democracy in the country. However, Nigeria not only provides an ideal setting to test hypotheses concerning the impact of religion on liberal democracy, but a close study of how Christianity and Islam affect political culture in the country promises important insights that will contribute to our understanding of how religion affects political culture more generally.

THE PLAN OF THE BOOK

In the next chapter, I critically review the conventional wisdom concerning the application of Christianity and Islam to politics and point to evidence to call it into question. That conventional wisdom focuses on differences between religious traditions themselves to explain the variation in political theologies that we find in the world. In other words, according to the conventional wisdom, whether and how religious leaders attempt to influence political actions and attitudes of those who belong to the religious institutions they lead depends on whether the religious community in question is Protestant or Catholic, Christian or Islamic. However, I go on to argue that the political theologies we find in the world have less to do with whether the religious community in question is Protestant or Catholic, Christian or Islamic, than the religious and political context in which the community is located. Much of the evidence points to the fact that something about time and place affects how religious leaders choose to apply their religious traditions to politics and the impact that religious observance has on political behaviors and attitudes. Further, I introduce a theory for why Christian and Muslim religious communities tend to be more conducive to a liberal democratic political culture in religiously diverse and integrated settings. That explanation focuses on how religious diversity and integration affect the strategies that Christian and Muslim leaders use to grow their religious institutions and maximize their influence over the wider society.

In Chapter 3, I test this theory on evidence from sub-Saharan Africa. I explore the variation in the extent to which sub-Saharan Africa's Christian and Muslim religious leaders have openly supported pro-democracy movements. I find that religious diversity and education matter. In the region's most religious diverse and better-educated countries, Christian and Muslim leaders tended to be openly supportive of pro-democracy movements. In the region's most religiously homogeneous and poorly educated countries, Christian and Muslim religious leaders were not as openly supportive of pro-democracy movements and in some cases were openly hostile to them. In Chapter 4, I point to evidence from cross-national survey research conducted by the Afrobarometer project that indicates that Christianity and Islam are more conducive to political participation and support for democracy in religiously diverse countries than in religiously homogeneous countries. Chapter 5 focuses on three country cases: Nigeria, Senegal, and Uganda. Based on a survey conducted in 2006 and 2007, I compare how religious observance affected political participation and religious tolerance in these three countries. Surprisingly, the results show that religious observance, among Christians and Muslims, had a more positive impact on religious tolerance in religiously diverse Nigeria than in predominantly Muslim Senegal and predominantly Christian Uganda.

In Chapter 6, I take an in-depth look at the case of Nigeria and the results of the survey I conducted there in 2006. I compare the impact of religious observance on political culture across four settings within the country that vary in terms of their religious diversity. These locations are Ibadan (highly diverse), Jos (moderately diverse), Kano (predominantly Muslim), and Enugu (predominantly Christian). I find that Christianity and Islam were more conducive to key liberal democratic values in Ibadan, the most diverse and integrated of the four settings. I point to statements made by Christian and Muslim religious leaders across these four settings that indicate that such leaders tended to be more encouraging of political participation and respect for the separation of religious and state authority in Ibadan, the most religiously diverse and integrated of the four settings precisely *because* it was (and remains, I might add) a religiously diverse and integrated environment. Although a snapshot in time (and this explains why I always use the past tense when presenting the results), the survey data from 2006 suggest that religious segregation, rather than religious diversity, has inhibited the religious tolerance that makes liberal democracy feasible in Nigeria and provides a baseline for assessing how changes across time in religious diversity and other sociopolitical conditions affect the likelihood that Christianity and Islam are applied in ways that promote or impede tolerance.

The final chapter is devoted to drawing important lessons and to raising new questions for further research. I present the key takeaway points and discuss what the results do and do not allow us to reasonably conclude. In the end, I propose how we might continue to take steps forward and develop a deeper understanding of how and why Christian and Islamic communities do or do not become harbingers of a political system that is characterized by civic engagement and social tolerance.

2

Time, Place, and the Application of Religion to Politics

For Christians, a classic question is not only "What would Jesus do?" but "What did Jesus mean?" A Christian may appeal to the Gospel of Mark (Chapter 12, verse 17), where Jesus says, "Render unto Caesar what is Caesar's and to God what is God's," to justify the separation of religious and state authority or to discourage Christians from questioning the policies of political leaders and participating in politics. Others may claim that Jesus in no way intended to justify the separation of religious and state authority when he made this statement. Rather, he was allowing for the possibility that one could be a good Jew and still pay taxes to the imperial state. One could also claim that Jesus was proclaiming that a good Jew was not necessarily guilty of idolatry or of worshiping false gods by dealing in coins that featured the image of a human being who claimed divinity (i.e., Caesar). In other words, one may argue that Jesus was warning his hearers not to be overly concerned with money, no matter the image that appeared on the coin. Another example from the sayings of Jesus concerns the "Kingdom of God." What did Jesus mean? What is the nature of the Kingdom of God? Is it in heaven or on earth? If on earth, is it to exist only in people's hearts, or is it to exist in the society and its laws? Some Christians may point to Jesus' proclamation of the Kingdom of God throughout the gospels to justify political activism devoted to the construction of an explicitly Christian social and political order. In a sense, this is how liberation theologians interpret scripture. While they do not promote theocracy, they argue that scripture, rightly interpreted, calls Christians to cooperate with God and participate in efforts to narrow the gap between the way the world is and the way God intends it to be. In other words, they believe that Jesus did not just come to tell people to tolerate injustice and wait for a better day in heaven. Instead, they believe that Jesus came to call people to take responsibility for the world and to address conditions, such as extreme poverty and political repression, that prevent people from making the most of their potential (Gutierrez 1988; Sobrino 1991). Other Christians may point to the Gospel of John (Chapter 18, verses 36 to 37), where Jesus tells the Roman Governor Pilate that his "Kingdom is not of this world," to discourage such political and social activism.

Conversations I have had with religious leaders in sub-Saharan Africa and experiences in churches there over the past decade illustrate the many different ways in which Christian leaders may apply their faith to politics. In Uganda, for example, the Roman Catholic bishops all agree that they have a responsibility to use their influence to promote justice and peace in their country. Nonetheless, they have not always agreed on the best way to promote justice and peace. John Waliggo, a Ugandan theologian-political scientist and close advisor to Uganda's Catholic bishops from the 1980s until his death in 2007, told me that some of the bishops believed in an "in your face" approach, while others believed in "quiet diplomacy" in their attempts to promote greater respect for democratic processes.[1] In my travels though Kenya, Nigeria, Uganda, and Zambia, I have visited many Catholic churches and have attended many liturgies. Although I never heard a Catholic priest call for authoritarian rule or the integration religious and state authority from the pulpit, in some settings I found priests more willing than in others to talk about politics and to appeal to scripture, as well as the Catholic Church's social teaching, to justify their openly pro-democratic political activism. In southwestern Uganda, a Catholic priest in the town of Mbarara told me that he thought people come to church to be fed spiritually and, therefore, he refuses to preach politics in church.[2] Another Catholic priest in Lagos, Nigeria, told me that he believes that he has a responsibility to address political problems in church since these problems are "real life" and because "a Christian voice that speaks of peace, tolerance, and justice needs to be heard to counter those voices that are combative and intolerant."[3] There is considerable variation in how Africa's Christian leaders think they should apply their religion to politics. If there is variation and debate within the Catholic Church, with its official teaching authority, the bishops and the pope, we can expect even more variation and debate within churches with less centralized authority structures.

Just as Christians often disagree over "what Jesus meant" and how to apply Christianity to politics, Muslims often debate the application of the Koran and the sayings of the Prophet Mohammed to social relations and politics. The *ulama,* those Muslims with special qualifications to interpret sources of God's revelation, have expressed opinions that vary in the extent to which they promote and support actions and attitudes conducive to liberal democracy. For example, some Muslim scholars would interpret *Surah* 2,256, "no compulsion in religion," to justify Islamic support for religious liberty, while others would regard such indifference in religious matters to be a rejection of the "submission" to God called for in the Koran. While religion should never be relegated to the purely private sphere, according to Muslims (and to many Christians, for that matter), not all Muslims believe that this means that Islam requires the integration of religious and state authority. Hefner (2005) points to Abdolkarim Soroush in Iran, Nurcholish Madjid in Indonesia, and Rachid Ghanouchi in Tunisia as examples of Muslim scholar-activists who have argued that Islam calls for a separation of religious and state authority (not to be confused with separation of religion and state, which they believe would be against the spirit of Islam). While they agree that religious and state authorities should cooperate and that religious teachings must always influence social and political life (there should be no separation of religious and public life), these scholar-activists claim that separation of religious and state authority is best for the faith and for the state. Religious leaders should not dictate public policy, nor should state agents enforce religious norms. They suggest that religion is more susceptible to corruption if political leaders capture the religion or if religious leaders capture the state, as has been the case in Iran. Muslim participants in Indonesia's pro-democracy movement of the 1990s appealed to religion to justify their support of democracy and human rights (Hefner 2005; Barton 2002). While Indian Muslim scholar Sayyid Abdu'l-Hasan 'Ali Nadwi argued that there was a need for Muslims to mobilize politically as a way of safeguarding their religious and cultural identity (Zaman 2002), Wahid al-din Khan taught that faithful Muslims should renounce political activism and focus instead on strengthening the Muslim community from within (Hefner 2005). Khan argues that the idea that state and religious authority should be integrated is the product of a historical and social context in which society was entirely made up of Muslims, which is now not even the case in Arab countries and the Middle East. In sum, members of the *ulama* have applied Islam to politics differently. As Hefner (ibid.) writes, "[There is]. . . a *contestive pluralization* centered on rival interpretations of Muslim politics, and rival efforts to organize in society and across the state-society divide."

In sub-Sahara Africa, too, I find Muslim religious leaders appeal to their faith to justify very different political positions. For example, in the northern Nigerian city of Kano, one imam openly encouraged people to make sure that everyone who visits Kano from the outside knows that "this city belongs to Allah" and that, while non-Muslims should always be welcomed in peace, they should know that "Islam will always be the religion of this city."[4] In Ibadan, a city in Nigeria's southwest, an imam stressed the importance of recognizing that "Nigeria belongs to Muslims and Christians." He went on to criticize the way the *Shari'ah* had been enshrined in the constitutions of twelve predominantly Islamic northern states of Nigeria. He said it made Christians feel like second-class citizens and provoked conflict between Christians and Muslims. The imam said, "Whether someone is a Christian or a Muslim, no one should be made to feel like a second-class citizen anywhere in this country."[5]

In short, there has been a great deal of variation in how leaders of the same religious faith tradition, whether Christians or Muslims, have applied their faith tradition to politics across time and across space at the same point in time. How do we explain these differences that exist even within the same religious tradition? We want to know why religious leaders choose to apply their faith traditions in ways that promote or impede political participation, support for democracy, and respect for freedom of religion, speech, and association. While religious leaders are confined to some extent by the scriptures and, especially in the case of some Christian churches, the boundaries that those responsible for official social teaching have erected, there remains a great deal of latitude to apply their religion, whether Christianity or Islam, in ways that may either promote or impede liberal democracy. If the Koran and the sayings of the prophet Mohammed can be used just as easily to promote actions and attitudes that are conducive to liberal democracy as the Bible and the sayings of Jesus, does it finally come down to the educational background, experiences, and personalities of the religious leaders? Should we say that some religious leaders are more conservative or liberal than others, and just leave it at that? I think we can do better than that by examining the various contexts and experiences that may shape the way religious leaders apply religion to politics.

Let us consider the example of Egyptian Muslim scholar-activist Sayyid Qutb. Qutb was an immensely influential thinker who wrote on, among other things, the political role of Islam. Qutb, who was executed by the Egyptian government in 1966, applied Islam to politics in a way that does not allow for the separation of religious and state authority thought essential to liberal democracy. His experiences in Egypt and in United States during the late 1940s and early 1950s help explain the Islamism that he promoted. In his article "The America I Have Seen" (1951), he made it clear that he wanted to prevent the Islamic world from becoming like the West, which he saw as faithless and increasingly materialistic. He thought that the one way to prevent that from happening was to enshrine Islamic religious law as the law of the land, establish strict limits on freedom of expression, and completely integrate religious and political authority. As interpreted by Qutb, Islam is neither conducive to nor compatible with liberal democracy. As noted above, there are members of the *ulama* who disagree with Qutb's application of Islam to politics. Although 'Ali Nadwi, Kahn, and Soroush certainly agree with Qutb that Islam condemns licentiousness and promiscuity, they argue, unlike Qutb, that Islam, correctly interpreted, is conducive to freedom and representative government.

Among the factors that distinguish Qutb from other Muslim scholar-activists is the society where his ideas were formed and the times in which he lived. Qutb grew up in predominantly Muslim Egypt during the early and mid-twentieth century. During the early part of this period, much of the Middle East was under colonial rule, and Islam was being pushed out of public life by Gamal Abdel Nasser, who ruled Egypt from 1956 until his death in 1970. It is not just Qutb's experience in the United States that is important for understanding why he promoted the integration of religious and state authority, but his experiences in his homeland, Egypt. There is good reason to doubt that Qutb would have applied religion to politics in exactly the same way had he been born at a different time or in a difference place. Sayyid Abdu'l-Hasan 'Ali Nadwi and Wahid al-din Kahn, both religious leaders who have claimed that Islam is conducive to liberal democracy, grew up in religiously diverse areas of India in the latter half of the twentieth century. Soroush did not grow up in a setting as religiously diverse as India, but grew up in Iran. However, Soroush lived under the post-1979 Islamic Republic in that country long enough to have serious concerns that the integration of religious and state authority was tarnishing Islam in the view of Iran's younger generation.

A comparison of Qutb and other Muslim scholar-activists suggests that whether Muslim religious leaders encourage or discourage political participation and respect for basic freedoms that enhance the prospects of liberal democracy depends on experiences that are contextualized by time and place. This does not mean that the environment in which a religious leader grows up or lives affects the way that the religious leader applies religion to politics in a mechanical and deterministic way. People may appropriate their experiences in various ways, and there are many factors that may affect how they apply their religious traditions to politics. The point I make here is that context matters, and it is impossible to understand the different political applications of a religion without some awareness of the different contexts in which religious leaders seek to preserve and promote the influence of that religion. Even within countries, there are different contexts that may affect how religion is applied to politics. For example, in predominantly Muslim countries like Turkey and Egypt, there is considerable disagreement about the application of Islam to social life and political life. There are those who believe in a socially and politically privileged place for Islam, and those who believe in allowing for more pluralism and in preserving the secular nature of the state. These different visions for society were made manifest in violent showdowns that took place in both countries during 2013. The task at hand is to explain these different ways of applying religion to politics—one that is conducive to liberal democracy and one that is not.

In their insightful book *God's Century: Resurgent Religion and Global Politics* (2011), Toft, Philpott, and Shah note that, when it comes to liberal-democratic movements, religious leaders may choose to be "free riders," "supporting actors," "leading actors," or "reactionary resisters." In other words, religious leaders may watch from the sidelines and enjoy new freedoms in the event that they are won by movements led and supported by others, they may actually lend support to such movements, or they may initiate pro-democracy movements themselves and openly take the lead in the struggle for greater political and civil freedoms. Of course, they may also choose to oppose movements for liberal democratic reform. The question is, what determines the choices they make?

THE CONVENTIONAL WISDOM

According to those who promote what I call the conventional wisdom, the religion itself, rather than time or place, is determinative. If there is room for choice at all on how to apply religion to politics, those who espouse the conventional wisdom propose that such choices are highly constrained by religious teachings and traditions. In other words, the conventional wisdom holds that how religion is applied to politics depends on whether the religious institution in question has the ideological resources in its scriptures and tradition to justify liberal democracy.[6] Western Christianity is thought to have the ideological resources to support liberal democracy, and Islam is either thought not to have them at all or to have fewer of them than Western Christianity. Therefore, Western Christian religious leaders, especially mainline Protestant leaders, are more likely to be supporting or leading actors in movements for liberal democracy, and Islamic religious leaders (as well as Orthodox religious leaders) are more likely to be active resisters and in certain circumstances free riders. Protestantism in particular is thought to be inherently more conducive to liberal democracy than other faith traditions because its organizational structures are democratic,[7] and/or its political theology (i.e., its ideas about what constitutes legitimate political authority, the proper relationship between sacred and secular authority and the responsibilities of the individual believer vis-à-vis government) encourages participation in public life and support for basic freedoms. If we were to rank Christianity and Islam according to their democracy-promoting potential, the conventional wisdom would lead us to rank mainline Protestantism first, Roman Catholicism and some strands of Evangelical Protestantism second, Pentecostal Christian churches third, and Islam last.

In other words, the conventional wisdom holds that religious ideas and sacred scriptures matter and that they confine the ways in which religious leaders can authentically apply religion to politics. If Muslim leaders are faithfully Islamic, so the thinking goes, they will necessarily be less encouraging of liberal democracy than Christian leaders who are being faithful to their Christian tradition. In fact, it is thought that those Muslim leaders who have been most faithful to their religious tradition have been blatantly hostile toward liberal democratic norms and values. Theorists dating at least as far back as Alexis de Tocqueville have suggested that Islam itself is an obstacle to democracy. In *Democracy in America,* Tocqueville argued that Islam was too detailed in its prescriptions and uncompromising when it comes to the relationship between religious and state authority to allow for democracy.[8] More recently, Huntington (1996: 70) argued that it is the refusal of Islam to legitimize any authority except for religious authority that makes Islam less compatible with and conducive to democracy than Western Christianity. "God and Caesar, church and state, spiritual and temporal authority, have been a prevailing dualism in Western culture. . . In Islam, God is Caesar; [in Confucianism,] Caesar is God; in orthodoxy, God is Caesar's junior partner," writes Huntington (ibid.). Several others have agreed with Huntington. "There is nothing in the political traditions of the Arab world—which are the political traditions of Islam—which might make familiar, or indeed intelligible, the organizing ideas of constitutional and representative government," writes Kedourie (1994: 5–6). According to Pipes (1983) and Lewis (2003), it is the privileging of divine law over legislated law that makes Islam essentially incompatible with liberal democracy.

There is plenty of evidence that appears to support the view that Western Christianity is more compatible with democracy than Islam.[9] In the 47 countries where Muslims make up a majority of the population, only one, Senegal, was ranked "free" and 10 were ranked partly free by Freedom House as of 2013 (Freedom House 2014).. By contrast, of the 60 countries in the world with populations over 3 million where Protestants and Roman Catholics make up 65 percent or more of the population, 53 were considered to be "free" or "partly free" as of 2013, according to Freedom House (Ibid). It is worth noting that those predominantly Christian countries that were "not free" as of 2013 are all found in one region of the world, sub-Saharan Africa, whereas Muslim countries that were "not free" are located in various regions of the world. The predominantly Muslim countries that were classified in the same way represent various regions of the world and appear to share little in common except Islam. They include Central Asian (e.g., Tajikistan and Turkmenistan), Middle Eastern (e.g., Saudi Arabia and the United Arab Emirates), and North and sub-Saharan African countries (e.g., Algeria and Guinea). The predominantly Christian countries that were "not free" are all found in sub-Saharan Africa and share similar cultural, historical, and economic characteristics apart from Christianity to which we might point to explain the deficit of democracy. The predominantly Muslim countries that were not democratic include countries that do not share similar geographic location, cultural, historical, or economic characteristics. They are countries that have one thing in common. They are all predominantly Islamic countries.

This may lead us to conclude that there is something about Islam that is impeding democracy. However, it would be premature to do so.

THE PROBLEM WITH THE
CONVENTIONAL WISDOM

Just because a religious faith tradition is discouraging participation in democratic institutions and support for basic freedoms in a certain place at a particular point in time, it does not necessarily follow that this religious faith tradition always has been and always will be an impediment to democracy. While religious ideas and sacred scriptures do guide religious leaders, they do not confine them. Religious leaders have applied religious ideas and sacred scriptures in various ways and have developed or amended social teachings in response to changing circumstances. There is plenty of evidence to suggest that the effects of a religious faith tradition on political culture depend on time and the place. The argument that Protestantism is more compatible with and conducive to democracy than Roman Catholicism is largely based on evidence from Western Europe of the nineteenth century, and there is good reason to think that this *was* at least partly true. In the same way, the argument that Western Christianity is more compatible with and conducive to liberal democracy than Islam is largely based on a comparison of North America and Western Europe with the Middle East that is largely confined to the late twentieth century. We simply should not generalize about the relationship between religious traditions and political culture based on such geographically and temporally limited comparisons. It is possible that Islam is impeding liberal democracy in the Middle East more so than in other regions of the world. However, it does not necessarily follow that it always has or that it always will.

Just as evidence since the mid- to late 1960s calls into question the assertion of the incompatibility of Roman Catholicism and democracy (Huntington 1991), evidence from before the late twentieth century and from beyond the Middle East calls into question the assertion of the incompatibility of Islam and liberal democracy. For example, the Islamic-led Ottoman Empire gave important self-governing roles to leaders of different groups, defined largely as religious communities: the Muslims, the Greeks, the Armenians, and the Jews. As Stepan (2001: 234) suggests, in some historical periods there was more respect for freedom of expression, especially religious expression, under Muslim rulers than in many Christian-dominated societies of the same historical period.[10] It may surprise many to learn that the position of Jews after the Islamic conquest of southern Spain was in every respect an improvement, as they went from persecuted to protected minority (Sen 2006: 64–66).[11] In her book *The Ornament of the World: How Muslims, Jews and Christians Created a Culture of Tolerance in Medieval Spain* (2002), Maria Rosa Munocal notes that "Muslim-ruled Spain was a contender with Baghdad for the title of the most civilized place on earth." It is not only striking that Muslim-ruled Spain was considered relatively tolerant compared to Christian-ruled Spain, but also that Islamic Baghdad was, at the time, considered a standard for tolerance and the advances in learning that go with it.

We need not search as far back in time as the Middle Ages or the Ottoman Empire to find evidence to indicate that Islam is not necessarily incompatible with democracy and freedom of expression. When we broaden our view of predominantly Islamic countries beyond the Arab world to countries like Indonesia, Bangladesh, Pakistan, India, and even Iran, we find reason to question the view that Islam is incompatible with democracy. In Africa and Asia, in particular, there is evidence to indicate that Islam has not been the obstacle to democracy that many theorists lead us to expect. We have already noted that Senegal has been relatively democratic in recent years (Gellar 2005) and, after a yearlong episode of political instability in Mali, free and fair elections resumed in 2013. Free and fair elections have taken place in Indonesia, Turkey, Bangladesh, and Malaysia since at least the mid-1990s. While it is possible that the democracy-impeding effect of Islam is overwhelmed by other democracy-inducing factors, such as economic development, advances in education, and a growing middle class, it is also possible that Islam is promoting democracy. We could also find that Islam is having no discernible impact on the democracy and freedom that prevails in these predominantly or significantly Islamic settings.

Even within the contemporary Arab world, the conventional wisdom that Islam is incompatible with democracy does not seem to be holding up so well. While it is possible that Muslims who took to the streets to demand an end to authoritarian regimes in Tunis, Cairo, and Benghazi in 2011 were less religiously observant than those who did not, there is good reason to doubt that this was the case since the regimes they sought to overthrow were not religiously based, and the rulers they intended to unseat were not known as great champions of Islam. For these very reasons, it is more likely that religious observance had a positive effect, if any effect at all, on whether Muslims in these North African cities chose to take to streets to call for change.

Toft, Philpott, and Shah (2011) find that no single religious tradition had a monopoly on pro-democratic activities between 1972 and 2009. They claim that Muslim actors played a democratizing role in twelve countries across Africa, Asia, and Europe during this period. These include Kenya, Mali, Nigeria, India, Indonesia, Iraq, Kuwait, Pakistan, Turkey, Bosnia-Herzegovina, Kosovo, and Serbia. By democratizing role, they mean that Muslim religious leaders did at least one of the following in a sustained way: (1) protested or organized opposition to an authoritarian government, (2) presided or participated in a religious ceremony or program that bears anti-authoritarian implications, (3) coordinated or cooperated with transnational actors to weaken an authoritarian regime or strengthen a new democratic system, (4) actively supported domestic opposition groups, and/or (5) mediated between political actors to facilitate the transition to a more democratic order. While one might take issue with the rather low threshold for the "democratizer" classification put forward by Toft, Philpott, and Shah, no one can take issue with the fact that at least some Muslim leaders in each of the countries they mention promoted democracy in one way or another at one time or another between 1972 and 2009. These findings are sufficient to call into question the conventional wisdom and invite us to take a closer look at events in some of these countries. As Toft, Philpott, and Shah (2011: 103) put it, ". . . it is clear that whatever characteristics helped make Catholic and Protestant pro-democratic actors so prevalent could not have been their exclusive franchise. There was political salvation—or at least democratization—outside the church."

Since the mid-1990s, democracy has faired well in Indonesia, the world's largest Muslim majority country (i.e., approximately 190 million of 216 million people in Indonesia are Muslim). During Suharto's thirty-two-year 1965–1998) dictatorship, most analysts who wrote about politics did not list Islam as a major obstacle to democratization (Hefner 2000; Liddle 1992: 60–74). Islam was never a major part of Suharto's power base. In fact, participants in the pro-democracy campaign dedicated themselves to developing religious arguments in support of their efforts to promote freedom (Barton 2002; Hefner 2000). Stepan (2001: 238) notes that the two largest and most influential Islamic organizations at the start of the transition from the Suharto dictatorship, *Nahdatul Ulama* [NU] and *Muhammediyah*, both had over 25 million members. They were led by Abdurrahaman Wahid and Amien Rais, respectively, two outspoken supporters of religious tolerance and democracy. Rais played a crucial role in helping to keep student protests peaceful and focused on democracy, while Wahid argued against an Islamic state and in support of respect for religious pluralism (Liddle 1999: 94–116). Hefner (2000) refers to "civil Islam" that has developed over time in Indonesia. Unfortunately, after the fall of Suharto, there occurred a great deal of ethno-religious violence. As I note below, this unfortunate development is not all that surprising, given Indonesia's religious landscape and the way that ethnicity overlaps with religious identity in some areas. However, the point here is that Indonesians applied Islam to politics in a way that justified political pluralism, and Islam was applied so as to mobilize people in support of a movement that eventually pushed a dictator from power.

Although Bangladesh and Pakistan, the world's second and third largest Islamic countries, have had military regimes of late, and Pakistan in particular has had struggles with religious extremism in relation to the U.S.-led war to topple the Taliban in Afghanistan, in recent times both Bangladesh and Pakistan have been above the threshold for democracy. The 1996 election in Bangladesh satisfied all of Dahl's (1971) eight institutional guarantees (Stepan 2001: 241). On the Freedom House scale of 1 to 7, in which 1 = most free and 7 = least free, Bangladesh received a score of 2 for political rights in 1996, the same as Taiwan and South Korea. Until the military coup of 1999, there had been five consecutive free and fair elections in Pakistan since 1988 (Rose and Evans 1997: 83–96).

Evidence from Iran also calls into question the view that Islam is incompatible with democracy.[12] Iran is considered an Islamic theocracy, rather than a democracy. Looking at Iran from the outside, most analysts attribute the lack of democracy to Islam. However, when we look inside Iran, we note that Islam is not always and everywhere impeding democracy. While some Iranians have appealed to Islam to support the veto power held by religious authorities, others are appealing to Islam in their struggle to diminish the powers of the clerical establishment so as to give elected representatives real policymaking authority (Filali-Ansary 2001). The 2009 presidential election and its aftermath reveal the complexity of the relationship between Islam and support for a liberal democracy. Although the incumbent Mahmoud Ahmadenijad was supported by the clerical establishment and Iran's Council of Guardians, opposition candidate Mir-Hossein Mousavi was supported by many other Iranians who argued that Mousavi's vision for Iran, including greater respect for civil liberties and less clerical control over government, represents a more authentically Islamic political system. Iranians who applied Islam to politics in a more moderate way would eventually succeed in electing Hassan Rouhani to the presidency in 2013.

The cases of Indonesia, Bangladesh, Pakistan, and Iran all seem to support Norris and Inglehart's (2004) claim that Islam is not an obstacle to democracy but may be an obstacle to individual freedoms. Norris and Inglehart find that Muslims are as supportive of democracy as other people in the world.[13] However, they find that Muslims are much less supportive of liberal values associated with the "sexual revolution" and freedom of expression (ibid.: 154). In other words, they claim that most Muslims want democracy, but many are not prepared to accept the legal protection for those who would engage in or promote lifestyles they consider to be contrary to the teachings of Islam. This suggests that many Muslims support what Zakaria (2003) calls "illiberal democracy."

Although many Muslims may be more conservative than many Christians when it comes to individual freedoms and the right to self-expression in several societies, there is a great deal of variation in support for liberal values within the wider Islamic community across the world, and even within regions. For example, according to the Pew Research Center (2013), a higher percentage of Muslims in Iraq (91 percent), the Palestinian territories (89 percent), and Jordan (71percent) believe that the Islamic religious law, the *Shari'ah*, should be "the law of the land" than in Lebanon (29 percent) and Tunisia (56 percent).[14] Further, within all four of these countries, we can expect to find differences between Muslims, with some more supportive of freedom of expression and a separation of religious and state authority than others (Hefner 2005; Brown 2000; Roy 1994; Zubaida 1993). As Sen (2006: 65) argues, "This is not only because of the idea of *ijetehad* or religious interpretation, but also because an individual Muslim can choose to decide what other values and priorities he or she [deems important] without compromising a basic Islamic faith." Further, there is no way of knowing from this country-level data whether and to what extent liberal values are affected by religious observance. Are Muslims who are more religiously observant more or less supportive of basic freedoms than those are less religiously observant? It is more difficult to predict the impact of religious observance than one might think. For example, the results of survey research conducted in Nigeria during the late 1990s indicate that the most religiously devout Muslims were more likely to favor separation of religious and state authority than those who were the least religiously observant (Bratton, Mattes, and Gyimah-Boadi 2005: 175). Just because some Muslims are more religiously observant than others does not necessarily mean that they are more politically conservative, and less supportive of democracy or the individual freedoms associated with liberal democracy. In sum, all Muslims do not think alike when it comes to political matters, and the different perspectives within Islam are not easily explained by differences in the degree of religious devotion.

We have focused a great deal on differences within Islam, but it is also important to recognize that there are significant differences within Western Christianity and that these differences, too, call into question the conventional wisdom. The differences within Christianity that have been receiving the most attention of late concern those between Pentecostal churches and the older, more mainline churches, meaning the Roman Catholic, Anglican, Lutheran, and Presbyterian churches. Pentecostal churches have been growing dramatically in many parts of the developing world since at least the 1980s (Jenkins 2006; Pew Research Center 2006). For example, the Pew Research Center (2006) estimates that nearly 50 percent of Brazil's population is Pentecostal.[15] In sub-Saharan Africa the percentage of Christians who are Pentecostal has grown by 20 percent between 1980 and 2009 (see Yong 2010). This growth typically occurs at the expense of the mainline churches, such as the Anglican, Lutheran, Presbyterian, and Roman Catholic churches (see Pew Research Center 2006). Some Pentecostals are known for their poor opinion of the mainline Christian churches, which they believe have wandered from the Bible, tolerate too much sinful behavior, and are not open to the healing power of the Holy Spirit of Christ (Anderson 2013).[16] While it is not the purpose of this book to explain why people leave mainline Christian churches for Pentecostal churches, it is important to recognize that Pentecostal churches are thought by some theorists to be less conducive to liberal democracy than the mainline Christian churches. This is because they are thought to discourage participation in public life (Walker 1983) or, when they encourage political activism, they tend to promote religious intolerance (Marshall 2009). Some theorists have argued that Pentecostalism encourages people to spiritualize social and political problems and to blame them on personal sin rather than political institutions or bad governance. Corruption may be seen as a problem, but, according to some Pentecostals, it is not a problem that can be tackled by political activism. Pentecostals are thought to believe that society's problems are due to personal immorality and evil that can only be addressed spiritually. Energy focused on politics is misplaced. "Born-Again" Christians, as Pentecostals often call themselves, simply focus on living out their Christian lives according to biblical directives until Christ comes again and brings an end to the evil in the world as only He can do (Yong 2010).

As in the case with Islam, there is evidence to support the assertion that Pentecostal Christianity is less conducive to liberal democracy than mainline Christianity. There are as yet no predominantly Pentecostal countries to compare with predominantly Catholic, mainline Protestant or Islamic countries [Although there soon may be! The growth of Pentecostal Christianity in Africa, Southeast Asia and Latin America is dramatic.]. Yet, when we look within countries we do find evidence to suggest that Pentecostal Christianity has not been as encouraging of liberal democratic values as mainline Christianity. For example, a study in Guatemala found a negative correlation between Pentecostal involvement and voting, community volunteerism, and social activism (Steigenga 2001). Marshall (2009) and Imo (2008) note that, in Nigeria, leaders of Pentecostal Christian and evangelical churches largely refrained from political activities during the 1970s and 1980s. However, these authors join others in claiming that this political quietism has given way to political activism and very strident Pentecostal political theologies that seek to Christianize or Pentecostalize societies, regardless of the socio-religious composition of the environments in which they find themselves.

While mainline Protestant and Roman Catholic leaders played leading or supportive roles in pro-democracy movements of the 1990s in many sub-Saharan African countries, Evangelical and Pentecostal leaders in these same countries were less than supportive of pro-democracy movements, and often threw their support behind autocrats or would-be autocrats who attempted to scrap new democratic institutions. Gifford (1998) notes that Pentecostal leaders supported autocrats like Rawlings in Ghana and Moi in Kenya, and would-be autocrat Chiluba in Zambia, who attempted to do away with presidential term limits. These three presidents were particularly good at cultivating and making the most of the support offered by Pentecostal religious leaders. Chiluba, for example, declared Zambia to be a "Christian nation" and dedicated it to Jesus Christ (Phiri 2008). Some Pentecostal preachers, even those visiting from the United States and Europe, heaped praise on leaders like Chiluba and Moi, practically anointing them as God's favorites. However, some Pentecostals thought leaders like Moi and Chiluba did not go far enough to politically enshrine Christianity. For example, Zambian televangelist Nevers Numba criticized Chiluba for not completing the Christianization project. Numba founded the National Christian Coalition in 1997 in order to complete the task (Yong 2010).

In Nigeria, Pentecostal political mobilization is at least partly a response to perceived efforts by Muslims to make Nigeria an Islamic state. Marshall (2009) makes reference to a "Born-Again political theology" that calls for enough individuals to be converted (i.e., become Born-Again Christians) so that society will be ordered as God wishes. This political theology calls for a Born-Again Christian to lead the country as president—not a nominal or mainline Christian, and certainly not a Muslim. Marshall (2009) refers to the Born-Again project as a totalizing one that seeks to win people for Christ and to turn nations into Christian nations. Yong (2010) observes that Pentecostal political theology is anti-Islamic wherever there is a significant Muslim presence, as in Nigeria and other African countries, and anti-Catholic wherever there is a significant Catholic presence, as in many countries of Central and South America. Such a totalizing Pentecostal project does not sit well with many mainline Christians, not to mention Muslims, and is on a direct collision course with the religious totalitarianism promoted by many Islamists. Marshall (2009: 219) writes, "Islam, as a competing theocratic project violently excludes the possibility of national conversion [to Christianity]." The Pentecostal or Born-Again project has many points in common with radical reformist Islam, according to Marshall (ibid.). Their political theologies are mutually exclusive.

However, there is evidence to indicate that the relationship between Pentecostalism and politics is more complex than some have suggested. First of all, there has been variation across time, and it begs an explanation. If Pentecostals have gone from encouraging political quietism to promoting political activism over the past thirty years, this in itself indicates that there is not a single or unchanging way to apply Pentecostalism to politics. Second, as in the case of Islam and mainline Christianity, there is a great deal of variation in the political actions and attitudes encouraged by Pentecostal religious leaders from place to place at the same point in time (Yong 2010). Perhaps no other version of Christianity, if we can even properly refer to it as a single version, can be applied to politics in as many different ways as Pentecostal Christianity. This is partly due to the fact that it focuses on the individual's relationship with God, is rooted in an unmediated reading of the Bible, and does not have a tradition of officially approved social teaching to provide some kind of precedent or boundaries to the ways religion is to be applied to politics. "For Pentecostals, political structures in and of themselves are neither more nor less legitimate; the decisive factor appears to be the extent to which they permit or prevent the spread of the gospel and the exercise of faith," writes Marshall (2009: 215).

We find Pentecostals in various parts of the world applying their faith to politics in different ways, not all of which call literally for the total conversion of the nation. Pentecostals are not always and everywhere clamoring for the state to privilege Christianity of the Born-Again variety over other faiths, or promoting a totalizing project that does not end until everyone is a Born-Again Christian. Some actively promote religious liberty for all. In Chile, Pentecostal theologian Juan Sepulveda (1988) of the *Mision Iglesia Pentecostal* has argued that Pentecostalism calls for liberation of the poor and freedom for all. According to Sepulveda, a proper reading of scripture would lead the Christian to reject religious discrimination of any kind. In their book *Global Pentecostalism: The New Face of Christian Social Engagement* (2007), Miller and Yamamori find a great deal of evidence to suggest that Pentecostal involvement is actually encouraging civic engagement *and* support for democracy. They suggest, "Pentecostal churches potentially function as schools for democracy, especially if they stay true to the idea of priesthood of all believers and the equality of all persons before God" (2007: 153). In his study of Evangelicals (including Pentecostals) in the United States, Smith (2000) notes that many Pentecostals are respectful and tolerant of different faiths and are not comfortable with a totalizing project that seeks conversion of the nation or a privileged place for Christianity vis-à-vis the state.

In its 2006 survey, *Spirit and Power: A 10-Country Study of Pentecostals,* the Pew Research Center found that a slightly smaller percentage of Pentecostal respondents than other Christian respondents supported freedom of speech in the United States and Latin America, but that a slightly larger percentage of Pentecostals supported freedom of speech to a greater degree than other Christians in the three African countries and three Asian countries included in the survey. The Pew study also found that there was virtually no difference between Pentecostals and other Christians in terms of their support for freedom of religion for religions other than their own across all 10 countries (Pew Research Center 2006). While the Pew report's data does not allow us to go so far as to claim that Pentecostalism is promoting tolerance and respect for religious freedom in these countries, it does show that Pentecostal Christians are not necessarily less religiously tolerant than members of other Christian churches. In sum, there is evidence to suggest that Pentecostalism does not always and everywhere encourage or discourage actions and attitudes conducive to liberal democracy.

We cannot easily predict the impact of religious institutions on political culture simply by knowing whether the institution is Protestant or Catholic, Evangelical,

Pentecostal, or mainline Protestant, Christian or Muslim, *Sunni* or *Shia*. We must also know something of the social, economic, political, and religious context in which religious institutions exist. When we look back in time and across the contemporary world, we find that neither Christianity nor Islam always and everywhere impedes or promotes attitudes and actions that are conducive to liberal democracy. While the personalities of religious leaders, as well as their courage and commitment to live out their faith, are bound to affect how they apply their religious traditions to politics, an explanation for the variation in political theologies promoted across the world that is based on the personality profiles of religious leaders is ultimately unsatisfying and unhelpful from a policy perspective. I agree with Philpott (2007) that ideas or political theologies matter and with Stepan (2001) that the world's oldest and most transnational religious traditions include ideas that may be used to support or impede a liberal democratic political culture.

WHAT IS POLITICAL THEOLOGY?

Following Philpott (2007: 7–10), I define political theology as "the set of ideas that a religious body holds about legitimate political authority. . . a set of propositions about politics that people hold in their minds, share and develop through language and discourse, and use to persuade and motivate." Based on the sacred texts and traditions of Christianity and Islam, there are many different political theologies possible and many dimensions to each political theology. However, the dimensions in which we are most interested include ideas about the appropriate relationship between sacred and secular authority and the characteristics of a good or faithful citizen. Does a religious tradition or community teach that the state should endorse or support a particular religious institution, all religious institutions, some religious institutions, or none? Does the religious faith tradition or community teach that the faithful citizen should concern herself with political matters, vote in elections, participate in demonstrations, support freedom of religion, speech, and association, or that she should concentrate on religious matters strictly defined and leave politics to the politicians (or to God)? Does a political theology encourage the faithful to adopt the posture of subjects who obey their rulers or that of active citizens to whom their government should be responsible?

There are two major dimensions to political theologies. One dimension concerns basic freedoms and the other concerns political activism. These dimensions are illustrated in Figure 2.1. When it comes to the freedom dimension, religious leaders may promote political theologies that fall anywhere along the spectrum between complete rejection of basic freedoms and support for basic freedoms. Among these basic freedoms is the freedom of religion, which may permit religion and state partnerships but forbids the integration of religious and state authority. The anti-freedom extreme includes religious leaders who call for the integration of religious and state authority or, for the most politically ambitious of religious leaders, the superiority of religious authority over state authority. Iran's religious establishment would fall closer to this end of the spectrum as would leaders of Afghanistan's Taliban. Qutb would fall towards this end of the spectrum as well. Looking back in time, Catholic leaders in

Figure 2.1 Dimensions of Political Theologies

medieval Spain and other parts of the world before the Second Vatican Council would be placed closer to this end of the spectrum. At the other end of the spectrum are religious leaders who call for respect for basic freedoms and the separation of religious and state authority. Christian and Muslim religious leaders have rarely called for radical or complete separation of religion and state. However, Protestant leaders and many Catholic leaders, at least since the Second Vatican Council, have openly promoted religious liberty and come out against state-sponsored religious persecution. They would fall on the pro-freedom end of the spectrum as would Muslim leaders like Soroush, Nadwi, and Kahn mentioned earlier in this chapter. When it comes to the political activism dimension, religious leaders may promote a political theology that falls anywhere between intense political activism and complete political quietism. In Figure 2.1, these two dimensions intersect each other, creating four basic types of political theologies: (1) anti-freedom-quietistic, (2) anti-freedom-activistic, (3) pro-freedom-quietistic, and (4) pro-freedom-activistic. The pro-freedom-activist political theology is that which is most conducive to liberal democracy. The anti-freedom-activistic political theology would be the least conducive to liberal democracy since it promotes political mobilization for an avowedly illiberal and undemocratic purpose, the integration of religious and political authority that allows for no freedom of religion.

As I have already indicated, there is evidence that a religious institution can become more or less supportive of pro-freedom political activism across time. The Catholic Church is a good example. Before the Second Vatican Council (1962–1966), the Catholic Church was not a great champion of democracy and religious freedom. It officially condemned democracy and religious liberty. In some predominantly Catholic countries, the Catholic Church collaborated with authoritarian regimes that granted the church special privileges and restricted the rights of new religious movements. After Vatican II, the Catholic Church officially changed its tune, endorsed democracy, and supported religious liberty. By the early 1970s, the church disassociated itself with autocrats and authoritarian regimes in several countries (beginning in Spain and Portugal and continuing in Latin American countries such as Chile and Brazil). Thus, there is a significant difference in the official political theology promoted by the Catholic Church before Vatican II and after Vatican II. This is illustrated in Figure 2.2.

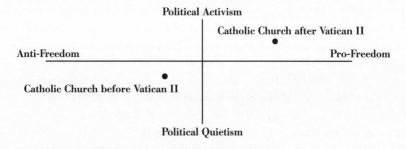

Figure 2.2 Catholic Church's Political Theologies before and after Vatican II

Figure 2.3 Catholic Church's Political Theologies in Chile and Argentina, 1970s

Although the Catholic leaders officially changed Church teaching with respect to religious liberty and democracy at Vatican II, not all Catholic leaders were supportive of such changes. Although it was an extremely important event in the life of the Catholic Church and provided the theological justification for pro-freedom political activism, the Second Vatican Council did not produce immediate change in the political theologies promoted by church leaders. Even after Vatican II, the Catholic Church was not always and everywhere a great champion of democracy and religious liberty. In some countries, church leaders were much slower to accept the church's official teaching on democracy and religious liberty than in others. For example, the Catholic Church in Chile was much more supportive of pro-freedom political activism than the Catholic Church in Argentina during the 1970s and early 1980s (Gill 1998; Pierson 1974; Mecham 1966; Aliaga 1989). This is illustrated in Figure 2.3.

Given the four basic types of political theologies that religious leaders may promote, we would like to know what explains why religious leaders choose to promote one type of political theology over the other three. Since there is variation from one setting to the next in the type of political theologies promoted by leaders of the same religious institution, we would like to know what it is about setting that makes religious leaders representing the same religious tradition more likely to promote a pro-freedom-activist political theology in one setting than in another. Since there is good reason to believe that the political theologies promoted by Christian and Muslim leaders are fluid and subject to change, even in one setting, we would like to know why religious leaders change the type of political theology they promote over time. Something about time and place affects how religious leaders choose to apply their religious traditions to politics and the impact that these great transnational religious traditions have on political actions and attitudes. Ideas about the will of God do matter, and so do traditions of social teaching that develop over time. Theology, not only social and political conditions, matters. There are boundaries to political theologies or parameters to how religion might be applied to politics. However, in religions as old and global as Christianity and Islam, such parameters are very broad, and we have seen a wide range of behaviors inspired or justified by sacred scriptures and traditions. The parameters may be broader in Islam than in Western Christianity or in Pentecostal and mainline Protestant churches than in the Roman Catholic Church with its centralized official teaching authority. However, even in relatively hierarchical religious institutions with a tradition of social teaching that includes how religious principles are to be applied to politics, like the Roman Catholic Church, there is room for leaders to maneuver, and evidence indicates that maneuver they have. Both Christianity and Islam include ideas or theologies that may be used to justify and to condemn liberal democracy, and Christian and Muslim leaders have used them to do both. When we look back across time and across space today, we are prompted to conclude that something about time and place make it more likely that both Christian and Muslim leaders choose to emphasize certain ideas about God and God's will for the political order rather than others.

THE IMPORTANCE OF TIME AND PLACE

It is clear that religious systems, especially Western Christianity and Islam, have been applied to politics in various ways across time and place (Minkenberg 2007). Just as there is no such thing as a "Christian blueprint" for government, there is essentially no such thing as a detailed "Islamic blueprint" for government, argues Ehteshami (2006: 93):

> There does not in fact exist a specific form of Islamic state and the *Quran* and the *Sunnah* (the customs and practice of the Prophet as enshrined in the *Hadith*) are inevitably open to interpretation. Nor does the *Sharia* prescribe any definite pattern to which an Islamic state should conform or carry with it a constitutional theory for such a state. Islamic practices may be driven by the canons and scriptures but they are dictated by cultural values and practices, and historical experiences prevalent in different Muslim countries.

One aspect of time and place that is thought to affect the type of political theology promoted by religious leaders is the degree to which the state is hostile toward religion. Where political regimes are authoritarian in nature and hostile toward a religious institution or religion itself, we may assume that religious institutions are bound to be more supportive of liberal democratic values or pro-freedom political activism.[17] There is plenty of evidence from the late twentieth century to support this assertion. In Poland the Roman Catholic Church was famously at the forefront of the pro-democracy movement and promoted freedom of religion, social justice, and freedom of expression (Anderson 2003). In countries like Lithuania and Latvia, the Roman Catholic Church called for greater freedoms not only for itself, but also for other Christian churches, including Pentecostals (ibid.). In Iran, Muslim leaders were calling for greater freedom of religious expression during the secular authoritarian regimes of Reza Shah Pahlavi (1921–1941) and Muhammad Reza Shah (1944–1979) (Siavoshi 2002). Even in Afghanistan during the 1980s, the leaders of the Taliban were fighting for freedom to express their Islamic faith against an atheistic Soviet occupation.

However, time would tell that, in each of these cases and most infamously in Afghanistan, many of these religious leaders were only seeking freedom and privileges for their own religious institutions. They were not seeking freedom for any religion, and they were not seeking the total separation of religious and state authority.[18] In these religiously homogeneous countries where there was repression of religion, leaders of once-dominant majorities were seeking to restore their religious pre-eminence. They actively sought to privilege their own religious institutions with the state and devoted themselves to doing all that they could to use the state to curtail the freedom of religious rivals or potential rivals.

In countries transitioning from anti-religious authoritarian regimes, we find that leaders of some historically dominant religious institutions went from promoting religious liberty to favoring restrictions on religious liberty and a privileged place for their particular religious community. They went from endorsing pro-freedom political activism to promoting anti-freedom political activism. For example, after the fall of communism, some Roman Catholic leaders in Poland were interested in establishing a new political status quo that would constitutionally enshrine the status and influence of the church. According to Anderson (2007), "Many [Polish] church leaders believed that their role in opposing the old communist system gave them the right to restore their religious guardianship over the future development of the nation." Rather than attempt to restrict the rights of religious minorities, Catholic leaders in Poland sought special constitutional recognition. Similar developments occurred in Lithuania and Latvia, where the Roman Catholic Church and the Lutheran churches, respectively, sought privileges and pushed for limits on the freedom of other religious institutions to enter and operate in these countries (Flis 2000; Anderson 2003). Leaders of these churches in Lithuania and Latvia were less successful than Catholic leaders in Poland in achieving such privileges, in part because they were less active in promoting freedoms during communist rule, and could not claim the legitimacy that the Catholic Church in Poland could claim.

A good example from the Islamic world is Iran. The Iranian revolution of 1979 made Iran more democratic than it was under the rule of Muhammad Reza Shah, but it certainly did not make Iran more liberal. After the struggle for freedom of religious expression, Iran's religious revolutionaries sought to severely restrict religious freedom and the right to form political organizations to those who pledge their loyalty to the theocratic system of governance, a system that gives unelected religious leaders ultimate authority over the country's policies (Siavoshi 2002).

One might argue that religious liberty is but one freedom among many, and that it is wrong to suggest that the Roman Catholic and Lutheran churches in countries like Poland, Lithuania, and Latvia were discouraging a liberal democratic political culture just because they were promoting a special place for their churches in society. I argue that it is difficult, if not impossible, to promote a special place for one's religious institution without also encouraging discrimination against other religious institutions at some level. Such religious discrimination has negative consequences on freedom of speech and association. In the same way, I argue that it is impossible to promote religious liberty without also encouraging other basic freedoms. Religious freedom is often referred to as "the first freedom" and the precondition for all modern freedoms because, at its core, religious liberty is freedom of conscience and concerns the "right to privacy." However, freedom of religion is not only the right to believe in God or not (which, by the way, one can do even under an anti-religious regime), but also the right to associate peacefully and to openly profess what one believes, as long as one is not seeking to impose one's beliefs on others. As such, religious liberty is a foundational freedom. Although freedom of religion may exist where other basic freedoms do not (as has been the case in many sub-Saharan African countries, as I discuss in the next chapter), freedom of speech and association are impossible to achieve without freedom of religion. Freedom of religion is a necessary but insufficient condition for the expansion of liberty more generally, and freedom of religion cannot be encouraged or discouraged without also encouraging or discouraging freedom of speech and association. The question then remains, when and where are religious leaders likely to promote pro-freedom political activism, civic engagement, and respect for religious liberty?

A THEORY OF RELIGIOUS-BASED SUPPORT FOR PRO-FREEDOM POLITICAL ACTIVISM

The theory I propose in this book points to religious diversity as a crucially important factor for explaining the variation in religious-based support for civic engagement and respect for religious liberty. Religious diversity affects how religious leaders decide to achieve their goals. What are their goals? I assume that Christian and Muslim religious leaders have essentially the same goals wherever they are: (1) grow their religious communities as large as they can, and (2) influence the norms and values of the wider society.

In religiously homogenous societies, leaders of dominant religious institutions typically do not need to achieve these goals through political activism. Of course, exceptions include leaders of dominant religious institutions where there are anti-religious authoritarian regimes. The Catholic Church in Poland under communism and the *Shia* community in Iran under the Shah are cases in point. Leaders of dominant religious institutions in religiously homogeneous societies are less likely to promote religious freedom, unless it is freedom for their own institutions from state control or repression. In societies that have recently become religiously diverse, I propose that leaders of long-dominant religious majorities do everything in their power to realize these goals (i.e., growth and influence) by promoting relatively demanding forms of political activism but not necessarily tolerance or respect for religious liberty. They promote activism in the hope of maintaining or retrieving cultural or political dominance. This is often the case where religious demography has recently changed or is very fluid and political institutions are in flux, such has been the case recently in Lebanon, Nigeria, and Bosnia. Leaders of long-dominant religious majorities, as well as politicians in these societies, often appeal to the fears that members of the long-dominant religious majority have about being dominated by members of smaller but growing religious communities. In societies that have recently become religiously diverse, leaders of long-dominant religious majorities seek to maintain their dominance over religion and their privileged relationship with the state, in the likely event that they have such a privileged relationship. In societies that have been religiously diverse for a long period of time, we are likely to find religious leaders who recognize, or have learned from their predecessors, that the best way to achieve their goals of expansion and influence is to eschew attempts to become the dominant religious community and to instead work to ensure that no religious community becomes dominant. In religiously diverse societies, religious leaders learn to "live and to let live" and to promote the same "live and let live" ethic among the members of the religious institutions they lead. This was the case in several religiously diverse societies of northern Europe. After many decades of civil war following the Reformation, religious and political leaders decided it would be in their best interest to respect religious liberty and the separation of religious and state authority (Gill 2008).[19]

THE GOALS OF CHRISTIAN AND MUSLIM RELIGIOUS LEADERS

Christianity and Islam are transnational and expansion-oriented religions. Jesus sent his followers out to "make disciples of all nations, baptizing them in the name of the Father and of the Son and of the Holy Spirit" (Matthew 28:19) and the Koran instructs ". . . fight them until there is no more *fitnah* (disbelief) and all believe in Allah alone throughout the world" (Koran 8:39). Christianity and Islam seek to influence culture, the norms and values that guide behavior and determine the boundaries between acceptable and unacceptable conduct. While there are certainly some Christian communities that do not actively seek converts or seek to shape the public realm, the vast majority of Christian churches, like Islamic communities, desire to grow and to shape the world around them according to their understanding of God's will. Although there have been and continue to be Christian and Muslim leaders who seek to grow their religious communities because of the influence and material wealth that such growth promises to give them personally, many sincere Christian and Muslim leaders seek growth and influence in order to narrow the gap between the way the world is and the way they believe God wants it to be (i.e., more equal, more free, more just, more humane). Therefore, there are two premises or axioms upon which I build the theory put forward in this book: the religious growth axiom and religious influence axiom.

The Religious Growth Axiom

Christian and Muslim religious leaders will do all they can to maintain and increase membership in their religious communities.

In her book *Political Spiritualities* (2009: 202), Ruth Marshall quotes the overseer of Redeemed Christian Church of God in Nigeria, Pastor A. E. Adeboye:

> "The plan of God is not limited to Nigeria alone. Very soon, there will be an extension when the Pentecostal Fellowship of Nigeria will become the Pentecostal Fellowship of Africa. And that is not the end of the whole vision. . . . Brethren, may I tell you that the strategy that we are going to use to win Nigeria has to be the strategy of an invading army. . . . If you want to take over Nigeria, you better win the students, win the market women, the media, the broadcasters, the rich, the poor, and the press. Glory be to God, I am sure they are here today. By the time they leave, they will be born again."

Omar, an imam in the southwestern part of Nigeria near Ibadan, noted that the very word "Islam" means to submit, and he argued that all Muslims should be inviting all people to submit to God's will:

> "Allah calls us to do all that we can to attract people to the way. He wishes us to worship Him. I will do all I can to get more people to become good Muslims. That's my job. We do not force people to become Muslims, but we invite people."[20]

Although Christian and Muslim religious leaders may vary in their methods and approaches, the vast majority of them seek to retain their members and grow their religious communities. Thus, the first basic building block of the theory I put forward in this book is the assumption that Christian and Muslim religious leaders want to maximize membership of the religious communities they lead. The goal of ever-expanding membership may be motivated primarily by spiritual concerns. Taking him at his word, Pastor Adeboye, quoted above, desires that people be born again and saved by Jesus. Taking Imam Omar at his word, he desires that God be worshiped correctly as Muslims and that this be reflected in their everyday behaviors. For both Christians and Muslims, sacred scriptures urge believers to spread the truth about God, as revealed in Jesus and by the Prophet Mohammed, respectively. If religious leaders believe that they have the "best way to God," they will seek to attract more people to their religions. Christian and Muslim religious leaders want the freedom to serve their membership effectively so as to strengthen them in their faith and to recruit new members to the religious communities they lead. Among other things, serving their members effectively means providing religious education and meaningful religious experiences or inspiring messages. Recruitment techniques may vary from place to place and may include the use of print, audio, and visual media, or preaching in streets and public squares (Hackett 1998).

Religious leaders will oppose any attempts to limit their freedom to provide religious education to their members and to advertise or market their religions to those considered potential members. Who do Christian and Muslim religious leaders consider "potential members?" Leaders of different religious communities may agree not to recruit from each other's communities, as some Christian and Muslim leaders have done in parts of the world where Muslims form the majority of the population or where both Christians and Muslims exist in large numbers. For example, while there may be no formal agreement, Roman Catholic leaders in many parts of Nigeria and Senegal typically do not promote attempts to convert Muslims, and Muslims do not seek to convert Roman Catholics. In fact, in parts of both countries, many Muslims send their children to Catholic schools, confident that their Islamic faith will be respected (Paden 2005; Stepan 2013). While there is variation in the extent to which Catholics and Muslims have competed for adherents across time, we know that today there are certain Christian communities, particularly Pentecostal groups, that take a much more aggressive approach to Islam than Roman Catholics typically do. Nonetheless, in many societies there is often greater competition among Christians of different denominations and sects than between Christians and Muslims or people of other religious traditions. In predominantly Christian countries where there is a great deal of intra-Christian religious diversity, there is a high degree of fluidity, with people leaving Catholicism for Protestant churches and vice versa. In countries like Kenya, Brazil, and the United States, many Christians are searching with their minds, hearts, and feet, leaving one church to join another (Jenkins 2002b). Within Protestantism, the fluidity is greatest, with people moving from one Protestant church to another (Pew Research Center 2006). Christian churches often seek to attract new members from other Christian churches, and they do so with some success in parts of the world where there is a great deal of intra-Christian religious diversity.

Though there is evidence to suggest that active and explicit recruitment of new members, or the "missionary impulse," in its most direct form is less vigorous among some mainline Christian churches today than it has been previously, many Evangelical and Pentecostal Christians overtly seek converts. In many parts of sub-Saharan Africa and Latin America, there has been significant growth in Evangelical and Pentecostal Christianity, and this growth has taken place largely at the expense of mainline churches, such as the Roman Catholic, Anglican, Lutheran, Methodist, and Presbyterian churches (Micklethwait and Wooldridge 2009; Pew Research Center 2006, *Spirit and Power: A 10-Country Survey of Pentecostals*).[21] Pentecostal Christians are also less likely to shy away from trying to convert Muslims than are Roman Catholics and mainline Christians (Marshall 2009: 202).

The motivations driving religious leaders to expand the religious communities are likely to be very complex. While we cannot and should not dismiss the possibility that there are spiritual reasons that motivate religious leaders to increase the membership of their religious communities, such as having more people "saved," it is also important to recognize that there are this-worldly reasons. Religious leaders may seek to expand membership because they desire to increase the financial intake of the religious institutions they lead. More members may mean more people donating financially to the religious community. In religious communities where tithing is mandatory, this would certainly be the case. When and where religious leaders are actually supported financially by the contributions offered by members of their local religious communities rather than by the state or an international religious institution, they have an especially strong incentive to increase membership and/or to seek to recruit members from among the wealthiest segments of society. In sum, there are a variety of reasons that most Christian and Muslim religious leaders seek to expand membership.

The Religious Influence Axiom

Christian and Muslim religious leaders will do all that they can to influence the public realm according to the norms and values of their religious faith traditions.

Worldly or material motivations, on the one hand, and spiritual motivations, on the other, are not always easily separated or distinguished when considering reasons that religious leaders seek to expand their religious communities and influence the wider society. As noted, if religious leaders believe that they are called to spread the faith they represent, they will do all that they can to influence the society around them according to that faith. In other words, religious leaders may be motivated to increase membership in their religious communities by their desire to influence the society around them according to the norms, beliefs, and values of these religious communities. Typically, there is strength in numbers. Though religious minorities may be very influential if their membership includes a disproportionate number of people who are exceptionally wealthy, highly educated, and/or highly placed in government or public life, generally the size of a religious community is both a cause and a consequence of social and political influence. All else being equal, we can expect that a religious community with more members will get more attention from politicians than a religious community with fewer members. Therefore, a larger religious community is expected to have greater political influence. The problem is that large religious communities are often divided along class lines or other social cleavages. In sub-Saharan Africa, politically relevant ethnic divisions often cut through large religious communities like the Catholic Church.[22] Thus, it is not only size that matters. The ability to act as a block is what ultimately makes some religious communities more politically influential than others. The larger the block, the greater the political influence. Political influence allows religious leaders to defend and promote the freedom and/or state-sanctioned privileges enjoyed by their religious communities.

Religious leaders seek to influence social and political life according to the norms and values of the religious communities they lead or, at the very least, religious leaders will do all that they can to ensure that the state does not discriminate against the religious communities they lead. As noted above, the desire for social influence may explain why maintaining or expanding membership matters to religious leaders. All else being equal, a large and growing religious community is more likely to influence the norms and values society than a small or shrinking religious community.

This does not mean that all Christian and Muslim religious leaders devote themselves to growth and influence, especially if it means a majority of nominal members who are not true believers. As already noted, there are Christian leaders who are less concerned about influencing society than about ensuring that their religious communities remain faithful and pure. They would rather have a small, observant, and devout religious community than a large one with a significant number of unobservant or nominal members. The Amish, Mennonites, and Quakers represent Christian communities that emphasize the faithfulness of those who belong over the number of those who belong. During his papacy (2005–2013), Pope Benedict XVI hinted that he would prefer to have a smaller and more devout church than a big church that demands or inspires very little of people (Seewald 2010). One may find such a message surprising coming from the leader of the largest Christian church in the world—a church that has devoted itself so vigorously to growth and worldly influence throughout most of its two thousand year history.

However, in an ideal world, I assume that most Christian and Muslim religious leaders, including Pope Benedict XVI, would like both large *and* observant religious communities. Further, there is evidence to suggest that many religious leaders consider nominal membership preferable to no or low membership. Despite the reference to Pope Benedict XVI in the above paragraph, Roman Catholicism is the Christian tradition with the longest history of stressing the importance of membership in the Church even if religious belief and practice are not totally in line with Catholic teaching. As one Nigerian Catholic priest said,

> "We do not expect everyone to be perfect. This is a big Church. We accept people where they are. We consider non-practicing Catholics to be Catholics and we hope that they will become more active. We do not give up on them."[23]

I assume that big is beautiful for most Christian and Muslim religious leaders and, if many of them had their way, they would enjoy a monopoly over religion. This does not mean that all Christian and Muslim religious leaders would condone achieving such a monopoly by law or force. For example, many Christian religious leaders dream out loud about and pray for Christian unity. However, typically the unity they dream of and pray for would be in the church they lead, rather than in "other churches" or in a newly created universal church. While again recognizing that religious leaders may be sincere, motivated by a deep spiritual calling, in their attempts to get everyone to join the religious communities they lead, let us consider the more temporal and perhaps less edifying motivations. Where religious leaders enjoy a monopoly, there would be no religious competition. Without competing religious communities, religious leaders would need to exert less effort to influence society. In other words, running a religious institution would be less costly. There would be no need for as much marketing. There may even be less of a need to provide as much service. Without competing religious communities, it might even be possible to receive subsidies from the state. With a monopoly over religion, religious leaders could rest assured that no other religious community would gain greater influence over society than their own religious community. The greater the religious competition for influence in a society, the more time and resources religious leaders must devote to maintaining or gaining social influence.

Further, the assumption is that a religious monopoly means religious harmony, and religious competition means religious conflict.

Is it true that religiously homogeneous or monopolistic settings are more truly peaceful than religiously diverse and competitive settings? I propose that religiously monopolistic settings may be more peaceful, but generally the peace that exists in such societies is not the result of religious tolerance. Typically, the peace is rather superficial and is the result of fear of social or legal sanctions that tend to exist where there is a religious monopoly. While competition between religious groups for influence over society can lead to religious conflict, I propose that religious competition does not always result in such conflict. If sustained over a sufficiently long period of time and followed by religious integration, religious diversity can prompt religious leaders to encourage accommodation, compromise, and religious tolerance. With time, religious leaders in religiously diverse settings learn that the best way to promote the growth and the influence of their religious communities is to encourage civic engagement as well as respect for religious liberty. I explain the evolution of religious-based support for civic engagement and religious freedom in the following three propositions.

Proposition 1

Religious leaders will tend to be more encouraging of political activism in religiously diverse settings than in religiously homogeneous settings.

This proposition assumes that where there is religious diversity, religious communities compete for adherents and/or influence over the wider society. Religious leaders are likely to be more encouraging of political engagement where there is such competition than where there is little or no competition. This is because religious leaders in religiously diverse societies must compete with leaders of other religious communities to ensure that the voice of their religious community is not drowned out by the voices of rival religious communities. In religiously diverse societies, religious leaders must work hard to ensure that other religious communities do not gain greater influence over the state and win unfair advantages in the struggle to maintain and grow membership. In religiously homogenous societies, where religious competition is largely absent, religious leaders need not work as hard at retaining or expanding membership and influencing the wider society.[24] This is why, all else being equal, we can expect religious leaders in religiously homogeneous societies to be less encouraging of political activism than religious leaders in religiously diverse societies. Religiously homogeneous societies where the state is anti-religious, as was the case in Poland under Communist rule, would be an exception. There, the state declared war on the dominant Catholic Church and the Catholic Church encouraged political activism to change the political status quo.

Proposition 2

As societies become more religiously diverse, leaders of growing religious minorities promote political activism to reduce the privileges of long-dominant religious majorities, and leaders of long-dominant religious majorities encourage political activism in an attempt to preserve cultural and religious hegemony.

In religiously homogeneous settings where religious minorities manage to grow, leaders of these growing religious minorities promote political activism in an attempt to decrease the privileges of long-dominant religious majorities. This in turn prompts leaders of long-dominant religious majorities to become more politically active in an attempt to preserve such privileges (Gill 1998).[25] As religious minorities grow, politicians see the value in appealing to the interests of religious minorities in an attempt to gain or retain political power. As the influence of the growing religious minorities approximates that of the long-dominant religious majorities, religiously inspired political activism becomes intense and possibly violent.

Proposition 3

Where there is sustained religiously diversity, leaders of all or most religious communities encourage political activism to promote religious liberty and the separation of religious and state authority.

Frustration with the lack of progress in the struggle to gain or maintain cultural and political hegemony prompts religious leaders to change tactics. They go from encouraging political activism to achieve cultural and political hegemony for their religious communities to promoting political activism to ensure that no religious community achieves cultural and political hegemony at the expense of others. In societies that have for long been religiously diverse, there is greater likelihood that the relationship between religion and state is settled so that there is religious liberty and separation of religious and state authority.

The logic that undergirds this proposition is similar to that of Mancur Olson (2000), who argues that when and where those interested in power consider complete social dominance too costly to achieve, they will put their energy into ensuring that others are never able to achieve it. In the same way, when religious leaders decide that it is too costly to achieve special advantages vis-à-vis the state that help them to grow their religious communities and influence the wider society, they will work toward ensuring that no religious leader will ever achieve such special advantages. In religiously diverse settings, religious leaders are likely to find the costs of achieving their goals by securing special privileges for their religious communities too high. They are likely to decide that it is less costly to work hard to ensure that no religious community ever enjoys such special advantages vis-à-vis the state. The preferred course of action for religious leaders in religiously diverse settings is to promote state neutrality in religious affairs and respect for religious liberty.

My reasoning builds on the work of Anthony Gill (2002, 2008), who proposes that in the most religiously diverse settings, every religious institution behaves like a minority institution. Where all religious institutions are minority institutions, "all religious firms [institutions] will prefer a minimum level of religious liberty that allows all existing faiths to practice freely within reason. [This is because] imposing restrictions on one faith could potentially lead to religious conflict wherein one's own religious institution finds itself under repressive legislation" (Gill 2002: 10). Gill (2008) goes on to argue that religious liberty or freedom of conscience is likely to emerge in a religiously diverse society where there is also political competition. He argues that, in such a society, politicians will try not to offend any one of the competitive religious groups, and religious leaders will try to use their influence to prevent any one religious group from becoming more politically influential than any other.

I propose that religious leaders first choose to promote separation of religious and state authority, religious liberty, and other freedoms in religiously diverse settings not so much because they are committed to these freedoms in principle, but because they see it as the best way to protect and promote the religious faith tradition that they represent and the religious community that they lead. In other words, the decision that religious leaders make to promote freedom of religion is, at least initially, a strategic choice based on the religious context. If support for religious liberty were a principled choice from the beginning, we would find leaders of dominant religious communities in religiously homogeneous settings just as likely to promote religious liberty as leaders of religious communities in religiously diverse settings. This has not been the case. Religious leaders in religiously homogeneous settings have always been slow to support religious liberty and, all else being equal, generally have not supported freedom of religion until settings become religiously diverse enough so that the benefits of accepting religious liberty outweigh the costs of resisting it.[26]

This does not mean that religious support for separation of religious and state authority and religious liberty may not become a matter of principle over time, especially where there has been a significant degree of religious integration. Religious-based respect for religious liberty and separation of religious and state authority has become a matter of principle in societies that have been religiously diverse for the longest periods of time. However, I propose that religious support for separation of religious and state authority and religious liberty begins initially as a defense mechanism used by religious leaders who would prefer to enjoy a monopoly over religion. Under the conditions of sustained religious diversity, religious leaders support religious liberty as the best way to prevent other faith traditions from establishing dominance over society and the faith traditions that they represent. In other words, religious leaders begin to think, "if we cannot enjoy a monopoly over religion, we will at least make certain that no religious group enjoys a monopoly."

A kind of *détente* emerges between different religious communities in religiously diverse societies. It does not emerge magically, and it may not emerge at all if certain religious groups are driven from the society or a geographic area is cleansed of certain religious groups. Where the *détente* does emerge, it often does so only after the costs of seeking dominance become painfully apparent. These costs may be financial, as religious institutions spend resources on the struggle for dominance rather than on other needs, or the costs may be human because the struggle for dominance has included deadly inter-religious conflict. Further, the *détente* between religious groups can be short-lived unless it is followed by religious integration. Where there is religious integration we find multi-religious ethnic groups, educational institutions, workplaces, and neighborhoods. Where there is multi-religious mixing, it is more difficult for religious leaders who might still be interested in cultural or political hegemony to promote such hegemony. We find that religious communities are more conducive to liberal democratic ideals or are, at the very least, not the obstacles to liberal democracy that they can be in religiously homogeneous societies or religiously diverse and segregated societies.

To sum, the theoretical framework I propose above is captured in Figure 2.4. I propose that the relationship between religious diversity and the probability that religious leaders promote actions and attitudes that are conducive to liberal democracy tends to be curvilinear. As a society becomes more religious diverse, we can expect leaders of long-dominant religious majorities to promote political activism, but not tolerance. In other words, leaders of religious majorities are likely to encourage anti-freedom political activism (Proposition #1 and Proposition #2 above, combined). This is illustrated in Figure 2.4 by the downward dip in the dashed curve as we move, left to right, from little or no religious diversity to some religious diversity. However, as the society becomes more religiously diverse to the point when religious groups are almost equal in terms of the percentages of the population they represent, religious leaders (i.e., leaders of the former majority and the former minority) are more likely to promote not only peaceful political participation or civic engagement but tolerance as well. This is illustrated in Figure 2.4 by the upward trend in the curve as we move, left to right, from less religious diversity to more religious diversity (Proposition #3 above). I assume that, at a certain point, religious leaders are as supportive of civic engagement and tolerance as they can possibly be and, therefore, the curve flattens out as we move left to right. This assumes that the society remains religiously diverse and that the society becomes religiously integrated as well.

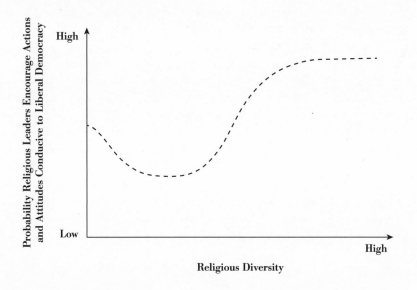

Figure 2.4 Religious Diversity Probability That Religious Leaders Encourage Actions and Attitudes Conducive to Liberal Democracy

SUMMARY

Christian and Muslim leaders have been leading actors, supporting actors, free riders, and reactive resisters with regard to pro-democracy movements at various times and places. In this chapter, I have shown that the conventional wisdom cannot stand up to empirical scrutiny. Christianity is not always and everywhere more conducive to political rights and civil liberties than Islam. Some Christian religious leaders have promoted anti-freedom political theologies, and some Muslim religious leaders have promoted pro-freedom political theologies. Evidence suggests that differences in time and place shape the variation in the political theologies we observe in the world. The question remains, what is it about a particular social, economic, political, and religious context that explains this variation?

In this chapter I have proposed a theory that points to religious diversity to explain the variation in religious-based support for pro-freedom political theologies. In short, I argue Christian and Muslim religious leaders are more likely to promote liberal democratic ideals in religiously diverse settings than in religiously homogeneous settings. In religiously diverse settings, religious leaders learn over time that the best way for them to further the interests of their religious institutions is to promote civic engagement and respect for religious liberty. Religious leaders realize that it is much less costly for them to use their influence to ensure that no religious group gains special state-granted privileges over the others than to attempt to gain those privileges for the religious institutions they lead. The question remains, is there evidence to support this theory? Do we find that Christian and Muslim religious leaders are in fact more openly supportive of liberal democracy in religiously diverse societies than in religiously homogeneous societies?

In order to answer this question, I propose that we consider evidence from sub-Saharan Africa. Why sub-Saharan Africa? In authoritarian regimes that repressed organized religion, such as those in communist Europe and Asia, all major religious institutions promoted pro-freedom political activism. This means there is no variation in the key dependent variable: religious-based support for pro-freedom political activism. We could stop there and simply say that we now know under what conditions religious leaders promote religious liberty: where there is none. However, this is not a very interesting or helpful conclusion. We want to know how religious leaders exercise choice where the options are not constrained by anti-religious regimes. Most of Sub-Saharan Africa's post-independence authoritarian regimes have allowed a high degree of religious freedom, and there has been variation in religious-based support for pro-freedom political activism. There has also been significant variation in Christian-Muslim religious diversity across countries and across time within countries in sub-Saharan Africa. Variation in the key dependent and independent variables means that sub-Saharan Africa is a particularly good testing ground for my theory and other plausible explanations for why religious actors do or do not play leading or supporting roles in pro-democracy movements.

3

The Role of Religious Leaders

"The church has done good things for us, but many missionaries sided with the colonialists when we fought for independence," said Maina, a Kenyan man old enough to remember what life was like in his country during the 1950s. Maina went on to add, "But things changed over the years. The church spoke out and helped us to end the Moi dictatorship and to get our second independence."[1] Maina's observations are telling. He notes that the mainline Christian churches in Kenya went from supporting to opposing a political status quo that was undemocratic and disrespectful of freedom of speech and association for Africans. Many Christian leaders went from promoting a political theology that was largely unsupportive of basic freedoms and encouraged political quietism to one that supported basic freedoms and promoted political engagement.

Christian religious leaders in several sub-Saharan African countries have been credited with playing an important and decisive role in bringing about democratic political change that has taken place since the late 1980s and early 1990s, but Christian religious leaders have not always and everywhere been supportive of pro-freedom political activism (Bratton and Van deWalle 1997; Gifford 1998). There have been changes across time, and there is also variation across countries at the same point in time, in just how openly Roman Catholic and mainline Protestant churches have supported pro-democracy movements. While it is true that leaders representing these religious traditions have participated in or hosted pro-democracy rallies and have issued public statements in print or from the pulpit that emboldened and galvanized disparate groups that called for an end to authoritarian rule, it is also true that they remained silent in the face of political repression, or even openly defended dictators or would-be dictators for many years (Gifford 1998). While they have sponsored civic education programs to make people aware of their rights and have attempted to mobilize them to exercise such rights (Gifford 1998, 2009; Cullen 1994), they have also discouraged respect for basic freedoms at certain times and in certain places (Quinn and Quinn 2003; Falola 1998). Though some observers lead us to expect Christian religious leaders to support liberal democracy to a greater degree than Muslim religious leaders (Huntington 1991; Kedourie 1994), the political positions that sub-Saharan Africa's religious leaders have taken do not break down neatly according to religious tradition. As Maina's experience in Kenya illustrates, Christian religious leaders in sub-Saharan Africa have not always and everywhere been supportive of pro-democracy movements.

In the same way, the region's Muslim religious leaders have not always and everywhere opposed such movements or remained on the sidelines watching other religious leaders promote democracy. At certain times and in certain countries, Muslim religious leaders have been openly supportive of pro-democracy movements.

In sub-Saharan Africa, as elsewhere in the world, it is clear that whether Islam and Christianity impede or promote liberal democracy depends less on something inherent or unchanging about the religions themselves than on how religious leaders and ordinary people of faith apply their religious traditions to politics. As we have established, explicit support for liberal democracy cannot be found in the Bible or the Koran, and both Christianity and Islam include ideas that may be interpreted so as to encourage or discourage actions and attitudes conducive to liberal democracy. The Bible and the Koran can be used to justify political theologies that fall anywhere along the spectrum between quietism and activism and anywhere between support for basic freedoms and opposition to such freedoms. Social and political changes that promise greater freedom to individuals and communities have been inspired, supported, or discouraged by both Christian and Muslim religious leaders. While the debate about the integration of religious and state authority is especially intense among Muslims today, such debates are not absent in Christian circles. For example, some Nigerian Christians believe that their religion prohibits them from voting for candidates for public office who are not observant Christians (Marshall 2009). Others reject this application of Christianity to politics and believe that one can be a good Christian and also vote for candidates of different faith backgrounds (Pew Research Center 2006). During the early days of the Pentecostal revival in many parts of the world, Pentecostal preachers often discouraged political engagement (Marshall 2009). However, that has largely changed. In many parts of the world, Pentecostal preachers are encouraging their members to become involved in politics and to do all that they can to promote Christian values in the wider society (Miller and Yamamori 2007; Marshall 2009). As I suggested in the previous chapter, there must be conditions that vary across time and place that affect whether Christian and Muslim religious leaders choose to openly promote, oppose, or neither openly promote nor oppose pro-democracy movements. Further, I propose that religious diversity, which varies across time and place, promises to explain how Christian and Muslim leaders choose.

In this chapter, I present evidence from sub-Saharan Africa that reveals a correlation between two factors—religious diversity and educational attainment—and the extent to which Christian and Muslim religious leaders promoted pro-freedom political activism during the 1980s and 1990s. Sub-Saharan African countries where Catholic, Protestant, and Muslim religious leaders played leading or supporting roles in pro-democracy movements tend to be the region's most religiously diverse and better- educated countries. They are countries where there are significant Christian and Muslim populations, or countries that are predominantly Christian or Islamic but where there is a great deal of diversity within these faith traditions. They are also countries where children spend more years in school. Christian and Muslim leaders tended to be least openly supportive of pro-democracy movements in countries that are predominantly Christian or Islamic *and* where there is little diversity within these two faith communities. These are also countries where children spend fewer years in school. Before discussing these findings, I set the scene by describing the religious and political context in sub-Saharan Africa.

CHRISTIANITY AND ISLAM IN SUB-SAHARAN AFRICA

Islam and Christianity have grown dramatically in sub-Saharan Africa over the past century. *The World Christian Encyclopedia* (Barrett et al. 2001) estimates that less than 25 percent of sub-Saharan Africa was Christian in 1900. By the year 2010, it was estimated that 57 percent of the region's population was Christian (World Religion Data Base; Pew Research Center 2010). Approximately 30 percent of sub-Saharan Africa's population was made up of Muslims in 2010, as compared to 14 percent in 1900.

Christianity came to most parts of sub-Saharan Africa together with European colonialism during the mid- to late nineteenth century. Those responsible for establishing colonial rule usually expected and received the support of Christian missionaries in their attempt to pacify local populations and to win popular approval for their colonizing efforts back home in Europe (Hastings 1996; Haynes 1996; Isichei 1995). Missionaries tended to live among local people, learn local languages, and address the material needs of local populations through Western medicine and education. To many Europeans back home, Christian missionaries represented the kinder, gentler, and nobler face of the colonial enterprise (Hoschild 1998). And in the newly democratizing states of nineteenth- and early twentieth-century Europe, a certain degree of popular support was important if the colonial enterprise was to win the financial backing of governments.

On the ground in Africa, colonial administrators expected the charitable efforts of Christian missionaries to decrease the need to physically force local populations into labor in extractive industries. While some missionaries were perceived by colonial authorities as good partners in this regard and helped bring Africans to profitable labor, not all of the missionaries proved as cooperative as colonial administrators had hoped. Many missionaries, even those who shared the national identity of the colonial administrators and European settlers, denounced the brutality of colonial policies that forced people off land or pressed them into labor under harsh conditions (Roberts 2008). Missionaries either took it upon themselves to defend African interests or were appointed to represent Africans in territories where legislative councils were established.

Because the introduction of Christianity accompanied colonial rule, many observers thought that independence would mark the beginning of the end for Christianity in sub-Saharan Africa. The assumption was that Christianity was a foreign religion, valued by Africans only as a means of economic survival and advancement during foreign rule. The expectation was that Christianity would cease being such an important means of advancement when colonial rule would come to an end. However, Christianity continued to grow in the run-up to independence and in the years that followed (Johnson and Grim 2008). The possible causes of this continued growth in

Christianity are multiple. Christian churches continued to be among the most important providers of education and healthcare in societies where the stresses that accompanied population growth and urbanization were particularly acute. Many Africans may have become Christians to secure material benefits under conditions of severe scarcity and economic change. Growth in Christianity also may have been the result of inculturation. During the 1950s and 1960s, mainline churches began to Africanize worship services and religious art. Christian leaders began to discard some of the European customs thought to be necessary for authentic Christian worship (e.g., the use of the Latin language) and to embrace African customs that were thought to make Christian worship more locally authentic and attractive (e.g., the use of drums and other local instruments).[2] There is good reason to believe that many Africans became Christians between the 1950s and 1970s not just because of the material benefits offered by the churches, but because they found the Christian message more intelligible and meaningful than during previous decades.

Islam predates Christianity in West Africa, having been introduced between the eleventh and twelfth centuries. Muslim traders introduced Islam, and large Muslim populations have existed in what is today Senegal, Mali, Niger, and northern Nigeria for several centuries. Along the East African coast, Islam was introduced as early as the eighth century. While Islam predates the introduction of Christianity in most parts of eastern and southern Africa, it remained largely confined to coastal areas until the introduction of European colonial rule (Isichei 1995). The completion of railways that linked the coastal areas with inland locales promoted the spread of Islam. The railway allowed Muslim traders, as well as Christian missionaries, to travel into the interior of Africa with greater ease. Disease, animal wildlife, and other challenges no longer presented insurmountable obstacles.

Where those responsible for establishing European colonial rule found well-organized Islamic communities, as in northern Nigeria, much of Senegal, Mali, northern Sudan, and Niger, they usually discouraged or prohibited Christian missionaries from trying to establish missions. Generally, European colonial administrators were more interested in establishing or maintaining good order than they were in promoting Christianity. If they thought that Christianity would help establish a good working order that would allow greater productivity, they promoted Christian missions. If they thought that Islam was already serving that purpose quite well, they did not support Christian missions. For most colonial administrators, religion was a means to an end, and they preferred to maintain the religious status quo, regardless of the faith tradition or denomination, where they found religious leaders ready to cooperate with them in their efforts to achieve productive and self-sustaining colonies (Quinn and Quinn 2003; Falola 1998).

With the exception of areas where European colonial administrators found well-ordered Muslim communities or where they sensed that the rivalry between Protestant and Catholic missionaries would be destabilizing, those seeking to expand both Christianity and Islam could work freely in sub-Saharan Africa during the colonial era. This was the case both by design, as decided by European powers in 1890 with the Brussels Declaration,[3] and by default, since there were not enough colonial administrators on the ground to effectively police, regulate, and confine missionary activity in many areas, even if they wanted to do so. Second, both colonial administrators and missionaries, whether Protestant or Catholic, shared some sense of purpose. Colonial administrators in most parts of sub-Saharan Africa welcomed Christian missionaries without significant discrimination between Catholics and Protestants. While predominantly Catholic colonial powers, particularly Belgium and, to a lesser extent, France, favored Catholic missionaries, they did not completely prohibit Protestant missionaries from operating in the territories they claimed (Hastings 1979). The British colonial administrators did not prohibit Catholic missionaries from operating in the territories they claimed, and generally allowed the Catholic Church to flourish; British colonial territories would become some of the most religiously diverse societies in sub-Saharan Africa.[4]

RELIGIOUS DIVERSITY

As I proposed in the previous chapter, there are good theoretical reasons to think that differences in religious diversity may help explain the variation in the extent to which Christian and Muslim religious leaders encourage behaviors and attitudes conducive to liberal democracy. However, we need to test this proposition. In order to test the proposition that religious leaders are more openly supportive of liberal democracy in religiously diverse settings, we need to develop a good measure of religious diversity. This is not such an easy task. There are different types of religious diversity. There is intra-Christian diversity and intra-Islamic diversity. If we fail to consider a society's religious landscape very carefully or only observe that landscape from far away, we may not notice such diversity. When we enter a country and examine it close up, we may find a surprising degree of diversity in what, from afar, appears to be religiously homogeneous country. A predominantly Christian country may include many different sizable Christian churches and sects. Even a predominantly Catholic country can have a surprising degree of diversity. Some Catholic movements and associations emphasize certain aspects of Catholic doctrine over others, such as social justice, charitable works, particular forms of piety, or the prohibition of abortion. Particularly where the Catholic community is quite large, there is often a surprising degree of competition between Catholic groups for the hearts and minds of Catholics. At the risk of oversimplifying the differences, some of these groups are called more theologically or ritually conservative, and others more liberal. Similarly, we may find a high degree of intra-Islamic diversity in predominantly Muslim societies. In a few Muslim countries, the *Sunni–Shia* divide may be significant. Iraq and Lebanon are examples of such countries. And although the overwhelming majority of predominantly Muslim countries are predominantly *Sunni*, there can be a remarkable diversity among Sunnis. As discussed in the previous chapters, we find different schools of thought and interpretations or applications of the Koran on matters of morals, faith, and the conduct befitting a good Muslim. In some countries, we find different Sufi orders or brotherhoods. In parts of North Africa and sub-Saharan Africa, Sufi brotherhoods or orders have been especially strong. There are also movements or organizations that seek to reform and/or rid their countries of such brotherhoods because they consider them not only insufficiently orthodox but also accommodating to pre-Islamic or un-Islamic cultural influences and social forces. In Nigeria, these "anti-innovation legalist movements," as Paden (2005) refers to them, have become increasingly active in recent decades. There is considerable diversity within Islam and Christianity that often goes unrecognized. Intra-religious diversity, and competition within Christianity and Islam—not just inter-religious diversity or the competition between Christians and Muslims—may have a significant impact on the type of political theologies that religious leaders promote.

We must decide on a measure that captures the dimensions of religious diversity that are most likely to affect the type of political theologies that religious leaders promote and, in turn, the way ordinary Christians and Muslims apply their religious traditions to politics. This is a rather difficult task because it means that we really cannot count those religious movements within world religions (such as Christianity and Islam) or within large denominations (such as Roman Catholicism) that have political agendas already. We cannot count Islamist movements that promote the integration of religious and state authority as a distinct religious movement in our measure of diversity because it is precisely that distinction that we are trying to explain. We are interested in explaining why some Muslims are Islamists or even *Salafis*, while others are not. We cannot count Christian movements founded to enshrine the Bible as the law of the land as a distinct religious group. This is because in doing so, we would be confusing that which we are trying to explain, the political application of religion, and that which may explain it, religious diversity. Therefore, the type of diversity in which we are interested in measuring is a diversity that exists independently of and prior to religious-based political movements.

The diversity in which we are interested concerns theological/religious differences (i.e., differences concerning what one must believe about God and how God should be worshiped) that exist between Christianity and Islam, as well as within Christianity and Islam. Between Christianity and Islam, these religious differences are obvious. Although both world religions share certain beliefs and moral codes in common, a Christian must believe that God came to earth in the person of Jesus Christ. Further, the Christian must believe that Christ was crucified to death and raised from the dead. To be a Muslim, one cannot believe this about Christ. To be a Muslim, one must, among other things, believe that God is one and that Mohammed is God's Prophet. For Christians, Mohammed is not considered a prophet, and the Koran, God's word dictated to Mohammed, is not authoritative.

Whether and the extent to which differences within Islam and Christianity are primarily or mostly theological, rather than political, is less obvious. Many of the religious differences and the diversity within Christianity and Islam have their origin in political differences. Political differences can lead to true theological differences and can give rise to diversity of religious belief and practice. This has been the case with respect to the differences between Catholics and many Protestant groups in Europe and the differences between many Protestant groups themselves. Perhaps the formation of the Church of England is the most obvious example. The Church of England was largely founded for political reasons. Over time, theological justification for the break with the Roman Catholic Church followed. Real differences in doctrine and belief emerged between Catholics and Anglicans. Although it remains difficult to know whether pre-exisiting political orientations are driving theological positions, there is reason to believe that many differences between Christians are genuinely religious in nature. These differences may include disagreements over whether the Bible is to be taken literally, whether it is acceptable to drink alcohol, and whether openly gay men and women should be ordained priests, bishops, or ministers. Christians may refer to these religious differences to justify switching from one church or sect to another, whether in Africa or other parts of the world.

Just as in the case of Christianity, the major religious differences within Islam, such as the distinction between *Sunni* and *Shia*, can be traced to political conflict rather than theological debate. However, such religious differences have become real religious or theological distinctions in their own right. Whether a Muslim believes in independent reasoning and the ongoing interpretation of the Koran, or believes that the gates of independent reasoning and interpretation, or *ijitihad*, have been closed, is one example of an important religious difference that may not necessarily be driven by pre-existing political orientations. Whether one believes that God continues to reveal Himself by using human reason, or one believes that God has revealed Godself once and for all and that a good Muslim must simply apply the Koran and the *Hadith* without contextualization, is an important theological difference of opinion. These intra-Islamic differences, like the intra-Christian differences, may have political origins and political consequences, but they are essentially religious differences—differences concerning what one believes about God and how God is to be worshiped.

Social scientists have developed measures of religious diversity that do capture important dimensions of such diversity, such as the number of distinct groups in a society and their relative size. For example, one such measure is the religious fractionalization index (RFI), developed by economist Alberto Alesina and his colleagues (2002).[5] This measure of religious diversity is defined as follows:

$$\mathrm{RFI}_j = 1 - \sum_{i=1}^{n_j} p_{ij}^2$$

With regard to the RFI formula, let j index country and i index religious groups. Let p_{ij} be the share of people in the country who self-identify with religion i and suppose that in country j there are n_j different world religions. The authors of this measure demonstrate that the RFI is an estimate of the probability that two randomly selected individuals within a society would be of different religious groups. This measure is bounded at zero if there is one religion and approaches 1 with many equally sized religions, so increasing values mean more religious diversity.

Another estimate of religious diversity, developed by Jose Montalvo and Marta Reynal-Querol (2003), is the religious polarization index (RPI).[6] Montalvo and Reynal-Querol hypothesize that religious communities that are nearly equal in terms of size are more likely to view each other as competitors for adherents and social influence than religious communities that are very different from each other in terms of size. Intense religious competition can mean growth-inhibiting and democracy-impeding religious conflict. These characteristics are present in the index that is defined as follows:

$$\mathrm{RPI}_j = 1 - \sum_{i=j}^{n} \left(\frac{0.5 - p_{ij}}{0.5} \right)^2 p_{ij}$$

Again, let j index country and i index religious groups. Let p_{ij} be the share of people in the country who self-identify with religion i and suppose that in country j there are n_j different world religions. In essence, the RPI considers the deviation of the proportion of each religion from the maximum, 0.5. Therefore, in order to weight equally positive and negative differences from 0.5, the measure takes the square of the difference. Like the RFI, higher values mean more religious diversity. The RPI reaches a maximum of 1 where there are two religious groups that are of equal size and a minimum of zero when there is one religion.

The RFI and RPI will produce identical values when there are equally sized religions in a country. The two indexes do, however, produce different values when the relative sizes of religions differ. Consider two countries with four religions. In Country B, there are four equally sized religions, while in Country A there is a dominant religion with 80 percent of the population and four smaller religions with 5 percent of the population each. The RPI will produce values of 0.35 and 0.75 in Countries A and B, respectively, while the same values for the RFI are 0.59 and 0.75. Notice that RPI increases considerably moving from Country A to B, indicating that there has been a rapid increase in religious diversity as group size becomes equalized. In contrast, in the case of the RFI, the movement from a dominant religion to equally sized religions does not produce nearly the same change.

While both the RFI and the RPI capture the number and the relative size of different religious groups, neither one considers the nature of the differences between religious groups. If we assume that the impact of religious communities on the political actions and attitudes of those who belong to them depends on the extent to which religious communities see themselves as competitors for adherents and influence, the nature of the differences between religious groups in a society matters. Competition between denominations within broad faith traditions, such as the competition for adherents between Catholics and Protestants or among the many Protestant groups themselves, may be more intense than the competition between broad faith traditions, such as Christianity and Islam. In settings where Christians and Muslims have long existed side by side, there is often little or no effort to draw converts from one faith to the other. In these settings, Christian and Muslim religious leaders have come to agree that they will not seek converts from each other. In a survey of more than 25,000 respondents across nineteen sub-Saharan African countries conducted in 2008 and 2009, the Pew Center's Forum on Religion and Public Life found little evidence of religious switching, of Christians becoming Muslims or Muslims becoming Christians.[7] In most societies where the vast majority of the population is already made up of sizable Christian and Islamic communities, the competition between Christians and Muslims often has more to do with influence over the wider society and state than with attempts to win converts from each other. This suggests that the nature of the differences between religious groups is likely to affect the intensity of the competition between them. In turn, the intensity of the competition between religious groups is likely to affect the extent to which such religious groups promote the political participation, religious liberty, and separation of religious and state authority that are characteristic of liberal democracy. We must therefore develop a measure of religious diversity that incorporates both intra-religious diversity (i.e., the diversity *within* a broad faith tradition like Christianity or Islam) and inter-religious diversity (i.e., the diversity of broad faith traditions) without weighting the number of religious groups over their relative size.

Adopting the same formula that political scientists Laakso and Taagepera (1979) used to measure the effective number of political parties in a country, I develop measures of religious diversity that account for the nature of the differences between religious groups. One is an estimate of the effective number of world religions (i.e., inter-religious diversity) in a society, and the other is an estimate of the effective number of denominations within world religions (i.e., intra-religious diversity) in a society. In sub-Saharan Africa, inter-religious diversity is essentially the balance between Christianity, Islam, and African traditional religions. Intra-religious diversity is denominational diversity, or the balance between religious groups within broad religious traditions like Christianity and Islam. I call the estimates of inter-religious diversity the INTER-RD scores and of intra-religious diversity the INTRA-RD scores.

The effective number of religions (INTER-RD score) for each country is calculated as follows: Let j index country and i index religious groups. Let p_{ij} be the share of people in the country who self-identify with religion i and suppose that in country j there are n_j different world religions (i.e., Islam, Christianity, African traditional religions). The effective number of totally different religions or INTER-RD score is then defined as follows:

$$ER_j = \frac{1}{\sum_{j=1}^{n_j} p_j^2}$$

The effective number of sub-religious groups (INTRA-RD score) for each country is calculated in the same way, substituting denominations within religions (e.g., Roman Catholic, Anglican, Presbyterian, and Pentecostal) for totally different religions (e.g., Christianity, Islam, and African traditional religions). Note that if all religious groups are of equal size, then $p_{ij}=1/n_j$ and hence, the number of effective religious groups equals n_j which is the number of religious groups. If one religious group represents a large majority, the number of effective religious groups is only slightly larger than 1.

Besides the fact that the measures I propose capture the nature of religious differences and not just the differences themselves, the other major distinction between the measures I propose and the others is that the measures I propose are continuous and are not bounded by 1. This is because the measures I propose, the INTER-RD and INTRA-RD estimates, do not represent probabilities of selecting members of different religions, as the RFI and RPI do. Instead, the INTER-RD and INTRA-RD scores represent the effective number of totally different religious traditions and the effective number of denominations within these religious traditions, respectively. This is important because these measures are not subject to the weighting problems of an index.

Measures of religious diversity, including INTER-RD and INTRA-RD, will only be as good as the raw data used to calculate them. By raw data, I mean the percentages of Christians, as well as Christian denominations, and Muslims, as well as subgroupings of Muslims, that make up a country's population. While there is no such thing as a perfect source of data, there are sources of data that are better than others because of the methodology employed. Unfortunately, national censuses in many countries of sub-Saharan Africa are notorious for having been poorly conducted because of a lack of capacity, political biases, or sensitivity with regard to ethnicity or religion and, therefore, are not consistently reliable. In countries like Nigeria, the government's official census does not even include a question on religious affiliation because of fears that official government counts would be hotly contested and would aggravate tensions between Christians and Muslims.

The source of religious-demographic data that we use for calculating INTER-RD and INTRA-RD scores are taken from the *World Religions Database* (WRD) (Johnson and Grim 2008) and the WRD's print predecessor, the *World Christian Encyclopedia* (WCE) (Barrett, Kurian, and Johnson 2001). Because we need to account for differences within as well as between different world religions, we need data that count denominations very carefully and thoroughly. No other source disaggregates religious demographic data along denominational lines to the extent that the WRD/WCE does. Further, no other source goes as far back in time as the WRD/WCE. The WRD/WCE uses a combination of government censuses, commissioned surveys, and censuses conducted by religious groups themselves to arrive at estimates. The WRD/WCE data have been criticized, especially for using estimates provided by religious groups themselves. There is concern the WRD/WCE is systematically over-counting members of groups whose self-reports are included in estimates (McClymond 2002; Jenkins 2002b; Anderson 2002). Nonetheless, the WRD/WCE data are highly correlated with other sources, such as the CIA World Factbook, the World Values Survey, the Pew Global Assessment Project, and the US Department of State (Hsu, Reynolds, Hackett, and Gibbon 2008). Although the WRD/WCE data are not beyond criticism, for our purpose, which requires accounting for religious subgroups that often go uncounted in other sources, we consider the WRD/WCE to be the best source of religious-demographic data available.

In Table 3.1, I have arranged sub-Saharan African countries so that we may compare their INTER-RD and INTRA-RD scores with their RFI and RPI scores. The table reveals how we lose an appreciation of inter-religious diversity that exists in a society if we choose to use either the fractionalization or polarization indexes. For example, Zimbabwe is considered the most religiously diverse country in sub-Saharan Africa according to the polarization ranking. Along with several other predominantly Christian countries, Zimbabwe is considered more religiously polarized than Nigeria, despite the fact that Nigeria includes almost the same percentage of Muslims as Christians. It is clear that the polarization index weights intra-religious

Table 3.1 A Comparison of Religious Diversity Measures and Rankings

Inter-Religious Diversity Ranking		Intra-Religious Diversity Ranking		Religious-Fractionalization Ranking		Religious-Polarization Ranking	
Cote d'Ivoire	2.99	Malawi	5.87	Cameroon	0.88	Zimbabwe	0.96
Togo	2.77	CAR	5.83	Malawi	0.82	Burundi	0.95
Liberia	2.73	Ghana	5.76	Ghana	0.80	Angola	0.91
Tanzania	2.67	Kenya	5.76	Benin	0.79	Guinea	0.91
Cameroon	2.56	Cameroon	4.64	CAR	0.79	Ethiopia	0.91
Sierra Leone	2.55	Tanzania	4.41	Kenya	0.78	CAR	0.90
Ghana	2.47	Togo	3.96	Cote d'Ivoire	0.76	Chad	0.90
Benin	2.45	Zambia	3.95	Nigeria	0.74	Togo	0.90
Nigeria	2.43	Ethiopia	3.76	Zambia	0.74	Cote d'Ivoire	0.89
Mozambique	2.42	Cote d'Ivoire	3.73	Zimbabwe	0.74	Liberia	0.89
Chad	2.33	Liberia	3.60	Cameroon	0.73	Cameroon	0.89
Ethiopia	2.29	Zimbabwe	3.58	Lesotho	0.72	Zambia	0.89
Burundi	1.90	Namibia	3.40	DRC	0.70	Ghana	0.88
Guinea	1.86	Congo-B	3.29	Mozambique	0.68	Tanzania	0.88
Kenya	1.76	Mozambique	3.24	Congo Rep.	0.66	Uganda	0.85
Malawi	1.65	Rwanda	3.09	Togo	0.66	Guinea	0.84
South Africa	1.45	Uganda	2.99	Gabon	0.66	Nigeria	0.84
Zambia	1.44	South Africa	2.98	Namibia	0.66	DRC	0.84
Mali	1.44	Nigeria	2.87	Chad	0.64	Mozambique	0.83
Rwanda	1.44	DRC	2.81	Tanzania	0.63	Kenya	0.83
CAR	1.99	Sierra Leone	2.62	Angola	0.63	Benin	0.82
Sudan	1.88	Chad	2.54	Uganda	0.63	Malawi	0.82
Zimbabwe	1.84	Angola	2.39	Ethiopia	0.62	E. Guinea	0.81
Gambia	1.32	Benin	2.31	Guinea	0.61	South Africa	0.79
Senegal	1.28	Gabon	2.28	Rwanda	0.51	Sudan	0.71
E. Guinea	1.27	Burundi	1.90	Burundi	0.51	Rwanda	0.71
Uganda	1.23	Sudan	1.88	Liberia	0.49	Congo Rep.	0.66
Gabon	1.21	Guinea	1.87	Sudan	0.43	Lesotho	0.64
Niger	1.21	Mali	1.44	E. Guinea	0.26	Mali	0.62
Congo-B	1.19	E. Guinea	1.32	Niger	0.20	Gabon	0.53
Namibia	1.16	Gambia	1.32	Mali	0.18	Gambia	0.48
Angola	1.13	Senegal	1.28	Senegal	0.15	Niger	0.42
DRC	1.10	Niger	1.21	Gambia	0.09	Senegal	0.32
Mauritania	1.01	Mauritania	1.01	Mauritania	0.01	Mauritania	0.02

(i.e., intra-Christian in the case of Zimbabwe) diversity over inter-religious diversity. When considering the balance between Christians and Muslims, Nigeria is certainly more polarized than Zimbabwe. The religious fractionalization index also emphasizes intra-religious diversity over inter-religious diversity. Once again, take Zimbabwe as an example. While Zimbabwe is ranked as the third most religiously fractionalized country in sub-Saharan Africa according to the religious fractionalization index, it is ranked in the bottom third in terms of inter-religious (i.e., Christian-Muslim) diversity. Like the RPI, the RFI is weighting intra-Christian diversity over inter-religious diversity. Therefore, I propose that we use the indicators that I develop in this book to measure religious diversity. These are the effective number of religious groups (INTER-RD) and effective number of sub-religious groups (INTRA-RD).

According to the measures I develop in this book, how do sub-Saharan African countries rank in terms of religious diversity? As Table 3.1 shows, the country that has the most inter-religious diversity is Cote d'Ivoire with close to 3 effective religions, followed by Liberia, Tanzania, and Cameroon, with 2.7, 2.7, and 2.6 effective religions, respectively. Because the two largest religions in most countries are Christianity and Islam, the third religion typically represents a summation of those who follow African ethno-traditional religions. For example, 38 percent of Ivorians professed these traditional religions as of 1990, and that percentage dropped to only 37 percent by 2000 (Barrett et al. 2001). The remainder of the Ivorian population was split between Christians and Muslims. As of 1990, 44 percent of the Liberian population followed ethno-traditional religions, while the remainder largely professed Christianity, and a smaller but significant percentage of the population professed Islam. There are countries where very few people identify with ethno-traditional religions, so that the overwhelming majority in the country practices either Christianity or Islam. Nigeria is one such country. Nigeria is almost evenly split between Christians and Muslims, and its INTER-RD score is 2.42. While other countries that have large percentages of their populations adhering to ethno-traditional religions have a higher number of effective religions, in few countries has the contest between Christians and Muslims for influence over the state been greater than in Nigeria. The sub-Saharan African countries with the least inter-religious diversity include Mauritania, in which Islam is the one effective religion, and the Democratic Republic of Congo, Angola, Congo Republic, and Namibia, where Christianity is the one effective religion.

The sub-Saharan African countries that have the most intra-religious diversity include Malawi and the Central African Republic, with almost 6 effective sub-religious groups or denominations, followed by Ghana and Kenya, with over 5 effective sub-religious groups. Predominantly Muslim countries are over-represented among countries with the least intra-religious diversity. For example, Mauritania, Niger, Senegal, Mali, and Gambia have essentially no effective sub-religious groups. Although there are different Sufi brotherhoods in some of these countries, especially in Senegal and Niger, these brotherhoods do not represent distinct religious sub-traditions, such as the *Sunni* and *Shia*. The vast majority of Muslims in sub-Saharan Africa are Sunni, and we do not find significant sub-religious diversity in the region. While most of the countries with the highest number of effective sub-religious groups are predominantly Christian countries, there are predominantly Christian countries with little intra-religious diversity. As we might expect, these tend to be countries where colonial powers did favor the Roman Catholic Church and, therefore, the Roman Catholic Church still dominates. Equatorial Guinea, which is almost entirely Roman Catholic, is the predominantly Christian country with the least intra-religious diversity. There are countries with both a relatively high degree of inter- and intra-religious diversity. They have a high number of effective religions and a high number of religious subgroups. These countries include sizable Christian and Islamic populations and there are many large Christian denominations and, to a lesser extent, Islamic groups. They include Ghana, Nigeria, and Cameroon.

ETHNIC DIVERSITY IN SUB-SAHARAN AFRICA

Any study of the impact of religious diversity on the kinds of actions and attitudes encouraged by religious communities should also consider ethnic diversity and, more specifically, the degree to which ethnic and religious identities overlap with each other. The political and economic impact of ethnic diversity in Africa has been the subject of much more research than the political impact of religious diversity (Horowtiz 1985; Bates 1981; Fearon and Laitin 2003; Posner 2005). Colonial rule essentially imposed states on African societies and changed or created new political boundaries. Through no choice of their own, many different ethno-linguistic groups found themselves within the same European-created states. Essentially, Africa included states of nations rather than nation-states. At independence, many politicians appealed to sub-national identities and ethnic group loyalty to gain or retain power over the state. They preyed on the fears of political domination that members of their ethnic groups had of other ethnic groups. Political scientists and economists have studied the degree to which ethnic diversity affects economic performance, political stability, and the prospects for democratic institutions since the end of the colonial era. Not surprisingly, many of them have found that Africa's ethnic diversity has impeded economic growth and has made the region's politics violent (Easterly and Levine 1997; Collier and Hoeffler 2004).

Since ethnic identities have been politically important and may affect the political importance of religious identities, ethnic diversity should be included in attempts to explain the variation in religious-based support for pro-freedom political activism. The measure of ethnic diversity that I use is the Politically Relevant Ethnic Group index (PREG) developed by Posner (2004). Based on extensive literature reviews about politics in African countries since independence, Posner determined which ethnic groups have been mobilized for political purposes.[8] The PREG index may be interpreted as the probability of selecting members of two different *ethnic groups that have been mobilized for political purposes* (i.e., politically relevant ethnic groups) when randomly selecting two individuals. Table 3.2 includes the average religious diversity rankings alongside ethnic diversity rankings for select African countries.

It is important to note that in some countries ethno-linguistic identities and religious affiliation overlap, while in others they cut across each other. Where

Table 3.2 Religious Diversity and Ethnic Diversity (Effective Number of Religions 1990 and 2000 and Politically Relevant Ethnic Group [PREG] Index 1990)

Inter-Religious Diversity Ranking		Intra-Religious Diversity Ranking		Ethnic Diversity PREG	
Cote d'Ivoire	2.99	Malawi	5.87	DRC	0.80
Togo	2.77	CAR	5.83	Cameroon	0.71
Liberia	2.73	Ghana	5.76	Zambia	0.71
Tanzania	2.67	Kenya	5.76	Chad	0.66
Cameroon	2.56	Cameroon	4.64	Nigeria	0.66
Sierra Leone	2.55	Tanzania	4.41	Angola	0.65
Ghana	2.47	Togo	3.96	Uganda	0.63
Benin	2.45	Zambia	3.95	South Africa	0.64
Nigeria	2.43	Ethiopia	3.76	Liberia	0.62
Mozambique	2.42	Cote d'Ivoire	3.73	Sierra Leone	0.60
Chad	2.33	Liberia	3.60	Tanzania	0.59
Ethiopia	2.29	Zimbabwe	3.58	Kenya	0.57
Burundi	1.90	Namibia	3.40	Malawi	0.55
Guinea	1.86	Congo-B	3.29	Namibia	0.55
Kenya	1.76	Mozambique	3.24	Ethiopia	0.54
Malawi	1.65	Rwanda	3.09	Niger	0.51
South Africa	1.45	Uganda	2.99	Cote d'Ivoire	0.49
Zambia	1.44	South Africa	2.98	Togo	0.49
Mali	1.44	Nigeria	2.87	Gambia	0.48
Rwanda	1.44	DRC	2.81	Ghana	0.44
CAR	1.99	Sierra Leone	2.62	Sudan	0.41
Sudan	1.88	Chad	2.54	Zimbabwe	0.41
Zimbabwe	1.84	Angola	2.39	Mozambique	0.36
Gambia	1.32	Benin	2.31	Senegal	0.33
Senegal	1.28	Gabon	2.28	Benin	0.30
E. Guinea	1.27	Burundi	1.90	Burundi	0.26
Uganda	1.23	Sudan	1.88	Rwanda	0.26
Gabon	1.21	Guinea	1.87	CAR	0.23
Niger	1.21	Mali	1.44	Gabon	0.21
Congo-B	1.19	E. Guinea	1.32	Congo	0.19
Namibia	1.16	Gambia	1.32	E. Guinea	0.19
Angola	1.13	Senegal	1.28	Mali	0.13
DRC	1.10	Niger	1.21	Botswana	0.00
Mauritania	1.01	Mauritania	1.01	Lesotho	0.00

religious identities cut across ethnic identities, we find people of different religions or religious denominations within one ethnic group and it would be difficult to predict the religious identity of a person just by knowing his or her ethnic identity. Where religious identities overlap with ethnic identities we find people who share religious identity also share ethnic identity and it would be rather easy to predict a person's religious identity based on his or her ethnic identity. Such overlapping indicates a high degree of religious and ethnic segregation. Such segregation may be intentional or an accident of history. Such segregation is intentional wherever ethnic and/or religious leaders discourage mixing with members of the other group(s). It is largely an accident of history wherever such overlapping differences are the result of how a religion originated and spread in a particular society. For example, most members of the Igbo ethnic group are Christians and a very high percentage are Roman Catholics, in large part because Christian missionaries, particularly Catholic missionaries, concentrated their efforts at spreading their Christian/Catholic faith in southeastern Nigeria. The Igbo have formed the vast majority of the population in southeastern Nigeria for hundreds of years. A very high percentage of the Hausa-Fulani ethnic group in Nigeria are Muslims, in large part because the Hausa were mostly Muslims when the British claimed Nigeria and colonial authorities did their best to prevent Christian missionaries from operating in the area.[9]

Regardless of how overlapping identities have come to exist and are sustained, we can expect that religious communities will be less conducive to religious tolerance where religious and ethnic identities overlap with each other. There is ample anecdotal evidence that there is more inter-group tension and even deadly violence where religious and ethnic identities overlap than where we find members of different ethnic groups within most major religious groupings. Where there is violence, it is difficult to determine how much of such violence is due to inter-ethnic tensions and how much is due to inter-religious differences. This is the case in Nigeria, where members of the Hausa-Fulani and most ethnic groups that have for long called the far north of the country their homeland are Muslims, while the Igbo and ethnic groups that have for long called the southeastern part of Nigeria home are mostly Christians. There has been a great deal of violence in some parts of Nigeria where these two overlapping groups are present. However, there is variation in the extent to which there are overlapping identities, even within countries like Nigeria. For example, about half of Nigerians who are of Yoruba ethnic background identify as Christians and half identify as Muslims (Laitin 1986; Paden 2005; Falola 1998). Religious identity not only cuts across the ethnic group, it cuts across biological families among many Yoruba. Similarly, in Kenya we find that the Kikuyu, Luo, Luhya, and Kamba ethnic groups include Catholics, Protestants of various denominations, and, to a lesser extent, Muslims. Among the Baganda in Uganda, we find Catholics, Anglicans, Protestants of other types, and Muslims.

EXPLAINING VARIATION IN RELIGIOUS-BASED SUPPORT FOR LIBERAL DEMOCRACY IN SUB-SAHARAN AFRICA

Now that we have set the scene in sub-Saharan Africa, we can test the theory that I put forward in the previous chapter versus other plausible explanations for the variation in the extent to which sub-Saharan Africa's Christian and Muslim religious leaders have promoted political theologies that are conducive to liberal democracy, or what I call pro-freedom political activism. Let us begin with other plausible explanations. The first hypothesis (H1) that we examine is that implied by the conventional wisdom, which focuses on the inherent nature of religious institutions and leads us to expect a clear and consistent difference between Christian and Muslim religious leaders.

> *H1*: Christian religious leaders are more supportive of pro-democratic movements than Muslim religious leaders, and mainline Protestant and Roman Catholic religious leaders are more supportive of such movements than Evangelical and Pentecostal religious leaders.

At first glance, there seems to be plenty of anecdotal evidence from sub-Saharan Africa to support this hypothesis. Since the 1980s, many leaders of Western Christian religious institutions, especially the Roman Catholic and mainline Protestant churches, have played either leading or supporting roles in pro-democracy movements. They have been famously vocal in their criticism of authoritarian regimes and in their support for democratization. Most Muslim and Pentecostal Christian religious leaders have not appeared to play such roles.

For example, in Ghana, the leaders of mainline Protestant churches and the Catholic bishops issued joint communiqués calling for an end to the excesses of the government under Jerry Rawlings and for more political openness during the 1980s and 1990s (Dickson 1995). In Liberia, Roman Catholic Archbishop Michael Francis was actively engaged in the pro-democracy movement. Archbishop Francis criticized the abuses of which Samuel Doe and Charles Taylor were guilty and brought international attention to gross human rights violations (Toft, Philpott, and Shah 2011). During the same years, the mainline Protestant churches that formed the National Council of Churches of Kenya (NCCK) and the Catholic Bishops Conference of Kenya were very vocal in their criticism of President Daniel arap Moi and the abuses of power that prolonged his rule through the 1990s (Gifford 1998; Throup and Hornsby 1998). When the Catholic bishops of Malawi issued their 1992 Lenten pastoral letter that denounced the dictatorship of President Hastings Banda, the pro-democracy movement in Malawi gained worldwide attention, legitimacy, and momentum (Freston 2001; Nzunda and Ross 1995; Cullen 1994). In Madagascar, the mainline Christian Council of Churches played a central role in the *forces Vives* that brought an end to the autocratic reign of President Ratsiraka in 1992 (Raison-Jourde 1995). Mainline and Evangelical Christian churches in Zambia helped bring an end to one-party rule under President Kenneth Kaunda in 1991 and blocked his successor, Frederick Chiluba, from changing the Zambian constitution to allow himself unlimited terms (Phiri 2001; Gifford 1998).

Compared to mainline Christian religious leaders, Muslim religious leaders in sub-Saharan Africa have not been very vocal when it comes to political matters, and some of those who have been most outspoken often discouraged the religious tolerance necessary for liberal democracy. Haynes (1998) notes that there is ambivalence in the way that many African Muslims view liberal democracy. Although sub-Saharan Africa's Muslims have long had a reputation for moderation, Quinn and Quinn (2003) argue that the majority of African Muslims have become "conservative-traditionalists," or even "Islamist-Fundamentalists," who reject the secular state and therefore liberal democracy. During the 1980s and 1990s, Muslim leaders in Nigeria, such as Malam Ibrahim al-Zakzaky and Yakubu Yahaya, gained thousands of followers and called for a more aggressive brand of Islam—for an Iranian-like revolution that would privilege Islam in the constitutions of northern states (Falola 1998: 195–196). They preached that Islam and the state should be fully integrated. In March 1991, Yahaya led thousands of followers to the offices of the *Daily Times* newspaper in Katsina and burned the offices because of articles that included remarks that they believed dishonored the Prophet Mohammed (Falola 1998: 196). Islamists have managed to enshrine the *Shari'ah* in the constitutions of twelve of Nigeria's thirty-six states. In Sudan, the government in Khartoum privileged Islam throughout the territory and made life extremely difficult for Christians in the south. Of course, this contributed to a civil war that culminated in a peace treaty and the separation of the south from the north and the establishment of a newly independent and predominantly Christian country in 2011, South Sudan.

However, if we take a more historical view, evidence suggests that the leaders of Christian churches have not always and everywhere been great champions of liberal democracy, and Muslim religious leaders have not always been free riders or reactionary resisters to liberal democratic movements. When we look to the immediate pre-independence era in sub-Saharan Africa, we find that many leaders of the mainline Christian churches (i.e., including the Roman Catholic, Anglican, Lutheran, and Presbyterian churches) were not supportive of democratic reforms called for by nationalist leaders (Haynes 1995).[10] During the time of Africa's independence movements of the 1950s and the immediate post-independence period, many leaders of mainline Christian churches were the reactionary resisters. For example, the Catholic bishops of Malawi have not always been the great champions of democracy that they were during the 1990s. Gifford (1998: 27) notes that their "silent complicity" during previous decades begs explanation. Interestingly enough, those religious leaders that are thought to have been least supportive of democratic political change during the 1990s, namely the leaders of independent Christian churches and Muslim religious leaders, were generally more supportive of Africa's independence movements than leaders of mainline Christian churches.

In order to understand why mainline Christian leaders in sub-Saharan Africa tended to be "reactionary resisters" in the face of independence movements in the region, we must consider how mainline Christian leaders expected independence to affect the mission of the religious institutions they were leading. During the colonial era, main-line churches largely enjoyed a monopoly over the provision of education and health services, and their leaders had reason to think that governments in independent Africa would nationalize schools and hospitals. They also had reason to believe that such a move would be endorsed by former colonial powers and the international community, either because of colonial-era guilt or optimism about the capacity and commitment of post-independence governments to deliver these public goods (Gifford 1995; Njoroge 1999).

Leaders of independent Christian churches and many Muslim religious leaders were more supportive of political independence than mainline Christian leaders because their institutions were less intimately connected to colonial administrations, and they had much less to lose in the post-independence era since they tended not to sponsor major educational institutions and health facilities. In fact, leaders of independent churches and Muslim leaders in several countries had reason to believe they had something to gain. If the mainline religious bodies were stripped of direct control of their schools, clinics, and hospitals, leaders of independent Christian churches and Muslim religious leaders could expect to compete more effectively for adherents and influence over the wider society.[11]

During the immediate post-independence period (i.e., the 1960s and 1970s in most sub-Saharan African countries), Christian and Muslim religious leaders largely refrained from criticizing African heads of state who consolidated their rule by introducing single-party regimes and/or personal dictatorships. Religious leaders in sub-Saharan Africa were mostly silent as politicians who assumed power through competitive elections at independence sought to end such elections and to curtail the freedom to criticize their policies. There is evidence to indicate that the silence represented consent to some degree. Religious leaders were persuaded by Africa's new autocratically minded presidents, prime ministers, and generals that broad freedoms and competitive political processes would lead to ethnic conflict and would hinder the economic development that Africa so sorely needed. There is also evidence to indicate that mainline Christian religious leaders remained largely silent not because they condoned single-party, personal, and military regimes, but because they wanted to ensure that they enjoyed a good working relationship with African governments so as to preserve the monopoly over the provision of education and healthcare that they enjoyed (Haynes 1996; Gifford 1998). It is also important to note that many African political leaders at the time, having been leaders of independence movements, still enjoyed popular legitimacy. In the most agriculturally advanced or strategically important countries, they also enjoyed access to resources because of the commodity boom of the 1960s and 1970s (Bates 1981) and, at the height of the Cold War, generous foreign aid from Western countries and/or the Soviet Union. It is understandable that most religious leaders refrained from openly criticizing political leaders who could use the considerable resources at their disposal to impede the mission of their religious institutions.

By the end of the 1980s and the early 1990s, the economic and political climate had changed dramatically. The commodity boom came to an end. The collapse of the

Soviet Union meant the end of the Cold War. The United States and Western countries no longer found it expedient to support authoritarian regimes. Most African governments were thoroughly discredited, state coffers were empty, and poverty worsened.[12] Under these conditions, many leaders of mainline Christian churches broke their silence and began to criticize authoritarian rule and to call for democratic reforms. They often cited scripture and the official teachings of their churches in order to justify their positions (Gifford 1995; Haynes 1996; Cullen 1994).

While mainline Protestant and Roman Catholic leaders played leading or supporting roles in the pro-democracy movements of the 1990s in many countries, Evangelical and Pentecostal leaders in these same countries were less than supportive of such movements. In fact, in some cases they were reactive resisters. Gifford (1998) notes that some Pentecostal leaders threw their support behind the autocratic efforts of Rawlings in Ghana, Moi in Kenya, and Chiluba in Zambia. These three African presidents were particularly good at cultivating and making the most of the support offered by such religious leaders. Chiluba, for example, declared Zambia to be a Christian nation and dedicated it to Jesus Christ (Phiri 2001). Moi and Chiluba, in particular, became the darlings of some Evangelical and Pentecostal churches—examples of the kind of God-fearing leaders Africa needed. Some Pentecostal preachers, even those visiting from the United States and Europe, heaped praise on leaders like Chiluba and Moi and practically anointed them as God's favorites (Gifford 1995; Haynes 1996). Such visiting preachers criticized mainline Christian leaders for meddling in political affairs. They accused Catholic and mainline Protestant leaders of being involved in politics because they were interested in attaining political power themselves. More recently, President Museveni in Uganda and President Kagame in Rwanda have established especially close relationships with fast-growing Pentecostal churches, many of which have American ties, in the hope that such churches might check the influence of more resourceful and potentially critical mainline churches, particularly the Anglican and Roman Catholic churches.

Whether Evangelical and Pentecostal religious leaders encouraged or discouraged support for pro-democracy movements seems to have had more to do with the extent to which religious leaders received or expected to receive special support from those in power than with ideology. Leaders of some Evangelical and Pentecostal Christian churches both needed and received financial support and privileges from President Chiluba in Zambia and President Moi in Kenya.[13] The leader of the Deliverance Church (DC) in Kenya put it quite plainly when he said in 2001, "[The DC] cannot afford to be seen on a constant warpath with the government as it does not have the resources and does not have the international contacts to fall back on for support in case of deregistration" (Karanja 2008). Leaders of internationally connected mainline churches did not need financial support from these African presidents since they received significant financial backing from associated churches and organizations abroad. Having a widespread presence in the provision of educational and health in both countries, the Roman Catholic and Protestant churches had less of a need for state-conferred privileges. These churches already enjoyed a privileged social position and widespread popular legitimacy due to the services they provided. The government might credibly threaten to deregister independent churches like the DC, but it could not credibly threaten to deregister the Roman Catholic, Anglican, and other mainline churches. The favors granted or promised to the independent and Pentecostal churches by Chiluba and Moi probably made it more likely that the leaders of the Roman Catholic and mainline Protestant churches would use their rather significant popular influence among the poor (and among the relatively wealthy, for that matter) to promote liberal democracy in Zambia and Kenya. Rulers who sought to prolong their rule in Zambia and Kenya had come to depend (even if reluctantly) on these internationally connected mainline churches to provide basic services in their countries. This meant that the leaders of these churches were relatively free to criticize attempts by rulers to halt the democratization process and to consolidate their own hold on power.

In sum, the anecdotal evidence described above does not conform to the expectations of the conventional wisdom. We find that many leaders of mainline Christian churches have gone from being reactive resisters or free riders during the late colonial period to being leading and supporting actors during the late 1980s and early 1990s. We find that many leaders of Pentecostal and independent churches went from being supportive actors during the late colonial period to being reactive resisters in the late 1980s and early 1990s. Who is to say that Pentecostal Christian leaders will not become supporting actors again? In fact, some observers have pointed to evidence that leaders of Pentecostal churches in some countries have become supporting actors of democratization movements (Miller and Yamamuri 2008). Muslim religious leaders went from being supportive actors in the late colonial period to being free riders during the 1960s and 1970s and then to being supportive actors again during the late 1980s and early 1990s. In several countries, including Kenya and Zambia during the 1990s, Muslim religious leaders teamed up with mainline Christian religious leaders to call for greater respect for civil liberties and for multiparty democracy (Throup and Hornsby 1998).

While this narrative account of events is revealing, we want to do more than examine anecdotal evidence. In order to more thoroughly test the plausibility of the conventional wisdom, I seek to identify whether there is a systematic and predictable relationship between the role that religious leaders played with regard to pro-democracy movements and their religious faith traditions. I use the categorization used by Toft, Philpott, and Shah (2011) as the dependent variable of interest. They use descriptive accounts of events that took place in countries between 1972 and 2009 to distinguish between those where religious leaders were "leading actors," "supporting actors," "free riders," and "reactionary resisters" in relation to pro-democracy movements.[14] Religious leaders who are leading actors help shape some of the pro-democracy movement's defining dynamic. They "typically appear onstage early, frequently, and volubly" (Toft, Philpott, and Shah 2011: 97). Religious actors who play supporting roles do not appear as early or often as leading actors, yet they lend their voices in support of pro-democracy movements at critical junctures. Free riders are religious actors who simply do not take a position one way or another with regard to pro-democracy movements. Reactive resisters are religious actors who openly oppose pro-democracy movements.

Although we do find that most of sub-Saharan Africa's religious leaders who played leading or supporting roles in pro-democracy movements were mainline Christians, there is reason to question the assertion that these leaders were more supportive of pro-democracy movements *because* they were mainline Christians. If Christianity itself were determinative, we would expect all mainline Christian religious leaders to have been openly supportive of pro-democracy movements and we would not expect to find other religious leaders among the democratizers. As Table 3.3 shows, not all mainline Christian leaders played leading or supportive roles. In fact, there are more than twice as many countries where mainline Christian religious leaders did not play leading or supporting roles (i.e., 21) than countries where they did (i.e., 9). Further, not all religious leaders who played democratizing roles were mainline Christians. We find that Muslim religious actors played supporting roles in the pro-democracy movements of three countries: Kenya, Nigeria, and Mali. This suggests that an explanation for the variation in religiously based support for liberal democracy that focuses on something inherent about faith traditions and particular denominations is not very satisfying.

Another plausible explanation for the variation in religious-based support for pro-freedom political activism is human development. Where people are better off and more highly educated, we might expect Christian and Muslim religious leaders to feel greater popular pressure to speak out in support of freedom. We test a second hypothesis (H2) below:

H2: Christian and Muslim leaders are more likely to openly support pro-democracy movements in countries where human development indicators, particularly educational attainment, are the greatest.

Advances in human development and education are thought to make religion less important in people's lives or, at the very least, to decrease the extent to which people are willing to take orders from religious leaders who appeal to spiritual authority rather than reason. The argument goes something like this: religious leaders, especially those who appeal to religion to encourage intolerance and promote authoritarian rule (e.g., presumably authoritarian rule that privileges the religious institution they lead), get less of a hearing in societies where people are more highly educated and generally better off. We assume that people who are highly educated and who have lived near and/or studied with people of different religious backgrounds for some time are less likely to approve of religious leaders who encourage anti-freedom political activism. In societies where people enjoy relatively high levels of human development, religious leaders know that they will get less of a hearing and will discredit their religious institutions if they try to discourage religious tolerance and promote authoritarian rule. Therefore, it is thought that most religious leaders in such societies refrain from doing so.

Table 3.3 Role in Pro-Democracy Movements, 1972–2009

Role of Religious Leaders in Pro-Democracy Movements	Catholic Leaders	Protestant Leaders	Muslim Leaders
Leading Actors	Benin	Ghana	
	Ghana	Kenya	
	Kenya	Malawi	
	Liberia	Namibia	
	Malawi	South Africa	
	Mozambique	Zambia	
	South Africa		
	Zambia		
Supporting Actors	Burundi	Congo-B	Kenya
	Congo-B	Liberia	Nigeria
	Namibia	Mozambique	Mali
	Nigeria	Nigeria	
Neither Leading Nor Supporting Actors	Angola	Angola	Angola
	Cameroon	Cameroon	Cameroon
	CAR	CAR	CAR
	Chad	Chad	Chad
	DRCongo	DRCongo	DRCongo
	Ethiopia	Ethiopia	Ethiopia
	E. Guinea	E. Guinea	E. Guinea
	Gabon	Gabon	Gabon
	The Gambia	The Gambia	The Gambia
	Guinea	Guinea	Guinea
	Cote d'Ivoire	Cote d'Ivoire	Cote d'Ivoire
	Mauritania	Mauritania	Mauritania
	Niger	Niger	Niger
	Rwanda	Rwanda	Rwanda
	Senegal	Senegal	Senegal
	Sierra Leone	Sierra Leone	Sierra Leone
	Sudan	Sudan	Sudan
	Togo	Togo	Togo
	Tanzania	Tanzania	Tanzania
	Uganda	Uganda	Uganda
	Zimbabwe	Zimbabwe	Zimbabwe

Source: Toft, Philpott, and Shah (2011)

There is evidence to suggest that the educational attainment of their religious communities does affect the way in which religious leaders choose to apply religion to politics. For example, I spoke to one Muslim religious leader in the city of Ibadan who noted that Muslims in his relatively upscale and religiously diverse neighborhood would not accept an interpretation of their religion that tells them they should not have the right to vote or that they should not be free to meet to discuss politics or even religion:

> These people are not stupid. They would laugh at me if I told them that Islam says that they should obey their political leaders without question. They would laugh at me and stop attending prayers at [my] mosque. I would never do that because I myself do not believe that is what Islam demands.[15]

There is also evidence that people who enjoy higher levels of human development not only reject an application of faith that discourages political activism, but also demand pro-freedom political activism of their religious leaders. A Catholic priest in the Buru Buru estate of Nairobi, a predominantly Christian upper middle-class neighborhood, indicated that Christians in his parish expect the leaders of the church to speak out and promote more accountable and responsive government in Kenya:

> Our people expect the church to promote good government. They do not expect us to preach politics all the time. They do expect their bishops and priests to condemn corruption and injustice. If we do not do it, they wonder if we really believe in the gospel we preach.[16]

Of course, in societies where people are better educated we can expect religious leaders to be better educated as well. Better-educated religious leaders may find it more difficult to use religion to justify religious intolerance and authoritarian rule. The assumption here is that advances in education make it increasingly difficult for religious leaders to justify in their own minds restrictions on religious liberty. In part, this is may be due to the interaction they have had with people of different religious backgrounds while studying at the higher levels of the educational system. Highly educated religious leaders are less likely to think that it is acceptable to impede freedom of religion, speech, and association in the name of religion, even if a significant number of their adherents who are not as well educated might be easily persuaded that this would be acceptable. According to this line of thought, we can expect religious leaders in relatively developed and educated societies to be more supportive of actions and attitudes conducive to liberal democracy, especially religious liberty.

As shown in Table 3.4, there is evidence to suggest that sub-Saharan Africa's religious leaders have tended to be more openly supportive of pro-democracy movements between 1972 and 2009 where the Human Development Index (HDI)[17] was the highest and, in particular, where educational attainment was the greatest. There are three variables upon which I focus. One is the average HDI for each country for the years 1980, 1990, 2000, and 2005. The second is the average combined school-age

Table 3.4 Human Development Indicators and Religious Support for Democracy

Role of Religious Actors vis-à-vis Democracy	Country	HDI Average/ Median	Average/ Median Combined School Enrollment	Average/ Median Years of Schooling
Religious Leaders Are Leading Actors 1972–2009	Benin Ghana Kenya Liberia Malawi Mozambique South Africa Zambia	0.371/ 0.364	49.3/ 50.7	3.83/ 3.35
Religious Leaders Are Supporting Actors 1972–2009	Burundi Congo-B Mali Namibia Nigeria	0.357/ 0.344	44.0/ 46.4	3.23/ 2.4
Religious Leaders Are Neither Leading Nor Supporting Actors 1972–2009	Angola Cameroon CAR Chad Congo-K Ethiopia E. Guinea Gabon The Gambia Guinea Ivory Coast Mauritania Niger Rwanda Senegal Sierra Leone Sudan Tanzania Togo Uganda Zimbabwe	0.332/ 0.326	39.9/ 37.1	2.69/ 2.35

enrollment for each of the same years. The third variable of interest is the average number of years of formal schooling for each country for each of those years. The average HDI for sub-Saharan Africa overall during these years was 0.343. In sub-Saharan African countries where religious leaders played a leading role in pro-democracy movements, the average HDI was slightly higher than the average, at 0.371. In countries where religious leaders played neither leading nor supporting roles, the HDI was just below the average, at 0.332. We also find that HDI was on average 0.014 greater in countries where religious leaders were leading actors in pro-democracy movements than in countries where they were supporting actors, and 0.039 greater in countries where religious leaders played leading roles in pro-democracy movements than in countries where religious leaders were neither leading nor supporting actors. The average combined (boys and girls) school enrollment rate was almost 10 percentage points greater in countries where religious leaders were leading actors than in countries where they were neither leading nor supporting actors. In sum, while the evidence is rather weak when it comes to a relationship between human development and the extent to which sub-Saharan Africa's religious leaders were openly supportive of pro-democracy movements, the evidence for a positive relationship between education and such support is stronger.

Another plausible explanation concerns the level of political repression. Therefore, we test the following hypothesis:

H3: Religious actors are more openly supportive of pro-democracy movements where the level of political repression is most severe.

We would like to think that Christian and Muslim religious leaders have become religious leaders precisely because they want to serve God by serving others and that their public pronouncements on political matters are not necessarily a cold calculation of what is in their own political or material best interest or that of the religious institutions they lead. Therefore, this hypothesis (H3) assumes that religious leaders sincerely care about the well-being of the people in their societies and, therefore, they are more likely to speak out in defense of citizens the worse things become for them. It also assumes that religious leaders are reluctant to become openly involved in politics and that they speak out on political matters only as a last resort (e.g., where repression is intolerable and few if any organizations exist to effectively check an authoritarian regime and defend the population from excessive brutality). In other words, religious leaders would prefer to avoid becoming embroiled directly in politics and leave it to other leaders in society if they can. However, as political repression under authoritarian regimes becomes especially severe and there is little reason to expect that working behind the scenes will be an effective way to promote human rights and basic freedoms, or that other organizations, if they exist at all, will be effective at promoting respect for human rights and basic freedoms, religious leaders decide to speak out and openly promote the end of repressive authoritarian rule. Religious leaders may be concerned about basic rights even in societies where such political repression is relatively mild. However, the assumption is that, in relatively open societies, people have recourse to other organizations (e.g., political parties and secular political action groups) or the media in order to defend their rights. Therefore, religious leaders perceive less of a need to speak out and become directly embroiled in political issues where governments are less repressive.

As Table 3.5 shows, there is no correlation between level of political repression and religious-based support for pro-democracy movements in sub-Saharan Africa between 1972 and 2009.[18] The same goes for the average level of democracy, as measured by Polity IV (the higher the value, the greater the level of freedom/democracy).[19] In fact, the Freedom House data indicates that religious leaders were more openly supportive of pro-democracy movements in countries that were relatively free. We may be concerned that we are confusing cause and effect—that in fact freedom is greater in some countries precisely because religious leaders openly supported pro-democracy movements. Therefore, I drop data for years 2000 and 2005. By dropping data from these years, we eliminate the years by which time most sub-Saharan Africa countries had already introduced democratic reforms (that may have been introduced precisely because of the pro-freedom political activism of religious leaders during the 1980s and 1990s). I restrict analysis to Polity IV measures from 1980 and 1990, the years before the breakdown of many authoritarian regimes in the region. I list the average and median Polity IV scores pertaining to these two years for countries in each of the three categories (in bold and italics). There is still no evidence to suggest a systematic relationship between level of political repression and religious-based support for pro-democracy movements. In fact, we find that the level of political repression was on average just as severe in countries where religious leaders did not play leading or supporting roles in pro-democracy movements (i.e., −5.54 average and −7 median) as in countries where religious leaders did play leading roles in such movements (i.e., −5.18 average and −7 median). The difference in political repression seems not to be a very satisfying explanation for the variation in religious-based support for pro-freedom political activism.[20]

Another plausible explanation concerns ethnic diversity. It is quite possible that the degree of ethnic diversity affects whether and the extent to which religious leaders openly support liberal democracy. Exactly how ethnic diversity may be expected to affect religious-based support for pro-democracy activism is a matter of debate. Ethnic diversity may reasonably be expected to increase or decrease the likelihood that religious leaders lead or board the pro-democracy bandwagon. However, for the sake of argument, let me propose the following:

H4: Religious leaders are more supportive of liberal democracy in ethnically homogeneous countries than in ethnically diverse countries.

The assumption that underlies H4 is that religious leaders want to promote the unity of their religious institutions. They may be less likely to promote democracy in ethnically diverse societies because they are afraid that political competition in such societies will be ethnically based and will lead to ethnic conflict. Assuming that religious communities in ethnically diverse societies are also ethnically diverse, religious

Table 3.5 Religious-Based Support for Democracy

Role of Religious Actors vis-à-vis Democracy	Country	Political Repression Average/ Median Freedom House	Political Freedom Average/ Median Polity IV	Inter-Religious Diversity Average/ Median	Intra-Religious Diversity Average/ Median	PREG Average /Median
Religious Leaders Are Leading Actors 1972–2009	Benin		.10/			
	Ghana	9.09/	2.00	2.01/	4.18/	0.54/
	Kenya	9.00		1.98	3.70	0.57
	Liberia		**−5.18/**			
	Malawi		**−7.0**			
	Mozambique					
	South Africa					
	Zambia					
Religious Leaders Are Supporting Actors 1972–2009	Burundi	9.10/	−0.42/	1.62/	2.48/	0.36/
	Congo-B	10.0	−1.0	1.31	2.58	0.26
	Mali					
	Namibia		**−4.0/**			
	Nigeria		**−7.0**			
Religious Leaders Are Neither Leading Nor Supporting Actors 1972–2009	Angola					
	Cameroon					
	CAR					
	Chad					
	Congo-K		−3.36/			
	Ethiopia		−4.5			
	E. Guinea	10.80/		1.69/	2.72/	0.47/
	Gabon	11.0		1.30	2.57	0.49
	The Gambia					
	Guinea		**−5.54/**			
	Ivory Coast		**−7.0**			
	Mauritania					
	Niger					
	Rwanda					
	Senegal					
	Sierra Leone					
	Tanzania					
	Togo					
	Uganda					
	Zimbabwe					

leaders are concerned that ethnic conflict will severely fracture the religious communities that they lead. In the most religiously homogeneous societies, we can expect religious leaders to be especially concerned of how ethnically based political competition will affect their religious communities. Therefore, while they may not be openly opposed to pro-democracy movements, especially if such movements are multi-ethnic in composition, religious leaders are unlikely to be at the forefront of such movements because they are concerned that political pluralism in the context of ethnic diversity will damage the unity of their religious communities.[21]

Before we look for evidence of a correlation between ethnic diversity and religious-based pro-freedom political activism, let me present a fifth hypothesis concerning religious diversity that is implied by my theory:

> H5: Religious leaders will tend to be more openly supportive of liberal democracy in religiously diverse countries than in religiously homogeneous countries.

The logic underlying H5 was presented back in Chapter 2. To summarize, religious leaders are more likely to support movements that promote basic freedoms where such freedoms do not threaten and even promise to enhance their attempts to attract converts and influence the wider society. In religiously homogeneous countries, leaders of the dominant religious communities are likely to see pro-democracy movements as threatening to a political status quo in which they have enjoyed a privileged place. The exceptions to this would be those religiously homogeneous countries where the state is hostile toward organized religion (e.g., Poland under Communist rule). In religiously diverse countries, religious leaders are less threatened by changes to the authoritarian political status quo and see greater freedoms as an opportunity to increase their influence over the wider society (through the democratic process) and to ensure that no religious institution enjoys a privileged position at the expense of the others.

While there is no correlation between ethnic diversity and religious-based pro-freedom activism, there is a correlation between religious diversity and such support. As can be seen in Table 3.5, the countries where religious leaders were leading actors in pro-democracy movements were on average more religiously diverse than countries where religious leaders were neither leading nor supporting actors. Using the measure of effective number of religions (INTER-RD) that I displayed for each country earlier in this chapter (in Table 3.1), I find that countries where religious leaders played leading roles in pro-democracy movements had on average 2.01 effective religions, as compared to 1.62 in countries where religious leaders played supporting roles and 1.69 where they did not play leading or supporting roles. There is a more substantial difference when it comes to effective number of religious subgroups (INTRA-RD). There were on average over 4 distinct religious subgroups (e.g., Christian denominations) in countries where religious leaders were leading actors, as compared to 2.48 where religious leaders played supporting roles and 2.72 where they played no role at all. I list the median effective number of religious groups for each category of countries to ensure that there are not one or two countries that drive the difference in means that we see. There is no evidence to suggest that religious leaders are more openly supportive of pro-democracy movements in religiously homogeneous countries that are ethnically diverse.

In order to more thoroughly test the plausibility of any of the explanations for why religious leaders have been more openly supportive for democracy in some countries of sub-Saharan Africa than in others, we need to take a closer look at the data. Therefore, I run logistical regression analysis on national-level data. Logistical regression analysis allows us to determine whether a change in the variables of interest (i.e., HDI, education, political repression, ethnic diversity, or religious diversity) is in any way associated with the probability that religious leaders openly led or supported efforts to bring about democratic change. Sub-Saharan African countries that were categorized by Toft, Philpott, and Shah (2011) as countries where religious leaders played either a leading or supporting role were assigned a score of 1, and all other sub-Saharan African countries were assigned a score of 0. This is the dependent variable.

Although Toft, Philpott, and Shah categorize countries according to the role that religious leaders played in pro-democracy movements between 1972 and 2009, it is important to note that there were few if any significant pro-democracy movements in sub-Saharan Africa before the late 1980s. In fact, until the late 1980s and early 1990s, we find few sizable and effective pro-democracy movements emerging in the region beyond South Africa. With a few exceptions, sub-Saharan Africa's religious leaders did not feature all that prominently in pro-democracy movements anywhere until the late 1980s (Gifford 1995; Haynes 1996).[22] For this reason, the explanatory variables used in the analysis are taken from 1980 and years that follow. Rather than countries (which total 48 in sub-Saharan Africa), we use country years as the units of analysis. These years are 1980, 1990, 2000, and 2005. The explanatory variables include the Human Development Index for each of these years, the average number of years of schooling for school-aged boys and girls for these years, the POLITY IV democracy score for these years, and the combined average IRD score for every sub-Saharan African country for each of these years. Remember that the combined average IRD score is the average of the effective number of world religions, such as Christianity and Islam (a measure of INTER-religious diversity), and the effective number of sub-religions or denominations within these world religions (a measure of INTRA-religious diversity).[23] In other words, the INTER-RD score and the INTRA-RD score are summed and divided by two for each country.

The results indicate that only three of the explanatory variables described above have a substantively and statistically significant association with the religiously led or supported pro-democracy movements between 1988 and 2009: two in a positive way and one in a negative way. The complete results are displayed in Table 3.6. The two variables that are positively associated with the probability that religious leaders would have initiated or supported pro-democracy movements are combined effective number of religious groups (the IRD score) and average years spent in school. The one variable with the negative association with the probability that religious leaders would have initiated or supported pro-democracy movements is the number of politically relevant ethnic groups. Of these three variables, the results suggest that the effective number of religious groups has the most consistently positive relationship with religiously led or supported pro-democracy movements.

Table 3.6 Covariates of Religious-Based Support for
Pro-Democracy Movements in Sub-Saharan Africa,
1989–2000

	Logistic Regression Coefficients (Standard Errors)		
	Model 1	Model 2	Model 3
Intercept	−2.10	−1.86	−2.503
	(1.494)	(1.201)	(1.389)
Democracy	0.12*	0.99	0.124*
(Polity IV)	(0.067)	(0.116)	(0.061)
Ethnic Diversity	−2.91	−3.92	−2.42
(PREG)	(0.119)	(2.006)	(0.197)
H. Development	2.98	___	___
(HDI)	(0.268)		
Education 1	___	0.40*	___
(Years in School)		(0.184)	
Education 2	___	___	.0.028
(Enrollment)			(0.018)
R. Diversity	1.01*	0.92*	0.94*
(Avg. Inter/Intra)	(0.44)	(0.43)	(0.41)
N	49	52	58
Percent Correct	69.4	67.3	55.2

*P-value<0.10

We are interested in to what extent differences in religious diversity have an effect on the probability that religious leaders played a leading or supporting role in pro-democracy movements, while controlling for human development, average years of formal schooling, level of democracy, and number of politically relevant ethnic groups in a country.[24] Therefore, I use the results of logistic regression analysis reported in Table 3.6 to calculate marginal effects. The marginal effect essentially tells us how a change in the number of religious groups affects the percentage-point change in the probability that religious leaders were at the forefront (i.e., openly initiators or supporters) of pro-democracy movements. We find that, on average, the probability that religious leaders in a country with 1 clearly dominant religion initiated or led a pro-democracy movement in sub-Saharan Africa is 30 percent. That is actually pretty high. However, the probability that religious leaders would have done the same increases by nearly 60 percentage points (to 90 percent) in countries with 2 effective religious groups. Further, the probability that religious leaders either initiated or openly supported pro-democracy movements reached 100 percent where there were 3 effective religious groups. Thus, each additional religious group has a very positive effect on the probability that sub-Saharan Africa's Christian and Muslim religious leaders supported the pro-democracy movements of the 1980s and 1990s.

We are also interested in whether differences in educational achievement in a country have any effect on the probability that religious leaders played a leading or supporting role in pro-democracy movements. In our analysis, we control for the level of democracy, the number of politically relevant ethnic groups, and the religious diversity (i.e., effective number of religions). So, we essentially do the same thing we did with the effective number of religious groups. I use the logistical coefficients to calculate the marginal effects of each additional year of schooling on the probability that religious leaders supported pro-democracy movements, while controlling for human development, level of democracy, effective number of religious groups, and number of politically relevant ethnic groups. The marginal effect of the average number of years spent in school on the probability that religious leaders supported pro-democracy movements is not nearly as profound as the association we find between effective number of religions and religiously led or supported pro-democracy movements. In countries where the average number of years spent in school was 5, the probability that religious leaders would have played a leading or supporting role in pro-democracy movements was below 5 percent. In countries where the average number of years spent in school was 7, the probability that religious leaders would have done the same is 12 percent. The change in the probability that religious leaders played leading or supporting roles in pro-democracy movements increases at a greater rate with higher levels of schooling. For example, the change in the probability that religious leaders would have played a leading or supporting role in pro-democracy movements increases by just 2 percent between 2 and 4 years of formal schooling. However, the probability increases by 6 percent between 5 and 7 years of formal schooling.

SUMMARY

This chapter has been focused on explaining the variation in the extent to which sub-Saharan Africa's Christian and Muslim religious leaders have openly supported pro-democracy movements. While there are various plausible explanations for such variation, I point to evidence that shows that such religious leaders have tended to be more supportive of pro-freedom political activism in countries that are religiously diverse than in countries that are religiously homogeneous. The level of education in a society also seems to increase the chances that religious leaders openly promote liberal democracy, though to a lesser degree than religious diversity.

While the national-level data from sub-Saharan Africa suggest that Christian and Muslim religious leaders tend to be more supportive of democracy in more highly educated and religiously diverse settings than religiously homogeneous settings, we must now analyze individual-level data. The question remains, is religious observance more encouraging of liberal democratic values in religiously diverse settings than in religiously homogeneous settings? In the next chapter, I address this question by examining the impact of religious involvement on political actions and attitudes.

4

The Impact of Religious Communities

"When our religious leaders speak, we listen," said Abdu, a devout Muslim who resides in Jos, a religiously diverse city in Nigeria's Middle Belt. He added, "When they encourage [us] to get involved in politics to defend our rights, we do it."[1] In Kampala, the capital city of Uganda, another observant Muslim, named Hassan, stated, "We respect our religious leaders. That does not mean we do everything they say." Hassan concluded, "They know our religion, but they do not know politics."[2] It is one thing for religious leaders to encourage the members of their religious institutions to participate in politics and to be respectful of different faiths or people with different points of view, and it is quite another for members to follow the instructions of their religious leaders.

When we think about why Abdu is ready to take orders from religious leaders on political matters and why Hassan is not, several factors come to mind. First, Muslim religious leaders in Jos may be better communicators or may enjoy greater credibility than Muslim religious leaders in Kampala. Another plausible explanation is education. Hassan may be more educated than Abdu, and there is good reason to think that this is why Hassan is less likely than Abdu to take orders from religious leaders on political matters. It is possible that age or generational differences matter. Hassan may be younger and more urbane than Abdu. Finally, as I proposed in the previous chapter, difference in religio-political environment may be important. Abdu is in a religiously diverse country, Nigeria, where the place of Islam and Christianity in society is a major political issue, while Hassan is in a predominantly Christian country, Uganda, where there is currently little debate about the relationship between religion and the state.

While the conventional wisdom is that Muslims are in general more likely to take orders on political matters from their religious leaders than are Christians, there is little in the way of hard evidence to support this assertion. In fact, there is evidence to indicate that Muslims are generally no more likely to take advice dispensed by religious leaders on political matters than are Christians (Fish 2011). It would seem that many Muslims recognize that religious leaders are experts on religious matters, but not necessarily experts on public affairs. As the contrast between Hassan and Abdu illustrates, there is variation in the extent to which people who share the same religious affiliation are open to taking advice from religious leaders on matters of politics.

In the previous chapter, we found that Christian and Muslim religious leaders are more likely to have openly promoted pro-freedom political activism in sub-Saharan Africa's more religiously diverse settings than in the region's religiously homogeneous settings—at least since the late 1980s. In this chapter, we seek to determine whether there is any relationship between involvement in religious communities and components of a liberal democratic political culture, such as political engagement, support for democracy, and respect for basic freedoms, such as freedom of speech and association. I analyze Afrobarometer survey data, collected from eighteen countries in 2008, with the intention of discerning the effects of religious observance on the political actions and attitudes of individual Christians and Muslims in sub-Saharan Africa.

While the results reported here are based on data collected at one particular point in time, they do provide cross-national evidence that, at that point in time, religious-group activity and frequency of contact with religious leaders were having a more positive impact on voting and support for democracy among Christians and Muslims in sub-Saharan Africa's religiously diverse countries than in the region's religiously homogeneous countries. However, they also show that religious group activity and frequency of contact with religious leaders were having no discernible impact on respect for freedom of speech in either religiously homogeneous or diverse sub-Saharan African countries. The results indicate that Christian and Islamic religious communities in religiously diverse societies were more encouraging of voting in elections and support for democracy, but were neither encouraging nor discouraging of the tolerance that characterizes a liberal democratic political culture. Before discussing these findings, I will describe what I mean by political culture conducive to liberal democracy and will explain why the combination of political participation, support for democracy, and ideological and social tolerance are especially important for the emergence of liberal democracy where it does not yet exist and its consolidation where it is new.

A POLITICAL CULTURE CONDUCIVE TO LIBERAL DEMOCRACY

As of this writing, democratic political systems are widely accepted as the systems of choice. Even if not called "democracy," a political system with regular competitive elections and basic freedoms that allow people in a country to hold their governments accountable is preferred to a system where there are no elections or elections are not competitive, and where people are not free to hold their governments accountable. Although there may be concern that there has been a decline in the number of democracies over the last decade and that the democratic transitions in some countries seem to be stalled, halted, or reversed, popular support for democracy remains quite strong. People want a voice in how they are governed, and they want to be able to get rid of governments that are ineffective. World Values Survey data suggest that this has been the case since at least the mid- and late 1990s and that it is as true in predominantly Muslim countries as in those that are predominantly Christian.[3] Almost every leader in the world, in sub-Saharan Africa and beyond, recognizes that he or she must compete in elections that at least appear to be free and fair in order to enjoy the kind of legitimacy needed to govern effectively. There is reason to believe that a political culture that is supportive of democracy, defined strictly as a system of government with regular elections that allows citizens to decide by whom and how they are governed, is widespread across the world and, as indicated in the previous chapter, that Christian and Islamic religious institutions have played a positive role in promoting support for democracy in several countries (Toft, Philpott, and Shah 2011).

However, a political culture may be supportive of democracy without being supportive of basic individual freedoms, such as freedom of speech, association, and religion. A politically active majority may also seek to ensure that there will be majority rule with strict limits on the rights of religious, racial, and ethnic minority groups, and on individual freedoms such as those of speech and association. While democracy, strictly defined, is about rule of, by, and for the people, liberal democracy is about rule of, by, and for the people that respects the right of people to say, associate, and believe as they desire. In this way, there are at least two dimensions of a liberal democratic political culture, and they correspond to the two dimensions of a political theology introduced in Chapter 2. One dimension has to do with political participation as well as support for democracy—which, we assume, typically go together—and the other has to do with support for basic freedoms, including political rights and civil liberties for all, regardless of their social or economic characteristics and identities.

Political participation is extremely important, though insufficient, if democracy itself is to emerge and survive its infancy years. Some may point to low levels of voting and political engagement in established democracies, such as the United States and those of Western Europe, to argue that high levels of participation are not necessary to sustain democracy. Although there are liberal democracies where rates of voting and other forms of political participation are quite low, it is difficult to imagine how democratic institutions can be built where they do not yet exist or sustained where they are new and fragile without a relatively high degree of political participation and support for basic freedoms among the population.

A high degree of political participation *and* support for democracy, as well as respect for basic freedoms, sets a political culture that is conducive to liberal democracy apart from a political culture that is not.[4] In a society with a liberal democratic political culture, citizens are politically active *and* socially tolerant. Political activism is moderated by the idea that there are basic freedoms that all people should enjoy, regardless of their class, race, ethnicity, or religious affiliation. While citizens seek to promote their individual and group interests, in a liberal democracy most people do not seek to curtail the rights of minorities, limit freedom of speech, or restrict religious liberty.

LOOKING AT THE DATA

In order to assess the impact of religious involvement on participation in democratic institutions, support for democracy, and respect for basic freedoms, I analyze the fourth round of Afrobarometer survey data collected in 2008. The Afrobarometer is a comparative series of national mass attitudes surveys. The data are gathered through face-to-face interviews by teams of trained interviewers in the language of the respondent's choice. The fourth round includes eighteen sub-Saharan African countries and at least 1,200 respondents in each country. The Afrobarometer data are especially dedicated to gathering information regarding political and economic behaviors and attitudes. While not specifically designed to achieve a better understanding of how religious involvement is related to such actions and attitudes, the instrument does include questions about religious affiliation and religious involvement that allow us to work toward exposing such a relationship.

Although the Afrobarometer survey has been conducted four times between 1999 and 2008, I confine my analysis to the data collected in the fourth round of the survey because the questions used to measure religious involvement in the fourth round are more suitable for both Christians and Muslims than those used in previous rounds. For example, previous surveys asked about religious attendance, which is not a good measure of religious involvement for Muslims since attendance at Friday Mosque prayers is not an expectation of Muslims, especially Muslim women, in the same way that church attendance is for Christians. There is also variation across Christian churches as to the importance of weekly attendance at worship services. Rather than asking about religious attendance, the fourth-round questionnaire asked if respondents are members of a religious community and, if so, how active they are in that community. Respondents were asked if they are leaders, active participants, or inactive participants. While not perfect, the question is likely to provide a more inclusive measure of communal religious engagement that is appropriate for Muslims as well as Christians. Additionally, respondents were asked how often they contact religious leaders when in need (of advice or material support) or in order to offer their views. This is a good measure of the extent to which Christians and Muslims depend on the leaders of their religious communities and the frequency of their interaction with them. These interactions provide religious leaders with opportunities to influence the political actions and attitudes of those who belong to their faith communities. The questions pertaining to these key independent variables of interest are listed in Table 4.1. We are most interested in any evidence that the degree to which Christians and Muslims are active in religious groups and the frequency with which they contact their religious leaders are related in any way to their participation in democratic institutions, support for democracy, and respect for basic freedoms. The Afrobarometer survey questions pertaining to the key dependent variables of interest are also listed in Table 4.1.

Besides providing a more inclusive measure of communal religious engagement, the questionnaire used in the fourth round of the Afrobarometer does a better job of capturing distinct religious identities in each country than the questionnaire used in previous rounds. Respondents were allowed to freely identify with a religious group or none at all. In previous rounds the respondents were asked their religious identity, but the interviewers were forced by the survey instrument itself to categorize people very broadly as Christians, Muslims, or neither.[5] This meant that there was no way to assess the impact of the significant sub-religious or denominational differences that exist, and there was no way to compare Catholics, mainline Protestants, and Pentecostals. Interviewers were confined to predetermined and very broad religious categories. More than twenty religious subgroups within Christianity and Islam were available to interviewers in the fourth round of the survey, and this means that in most cases interviewers could record the actual responses of the respondents when asked about their religious identities. It also means that the data better reflect the diversity within Islam

Table 4.1 Indicators of Liberal Democratic Values, Afrobarometer Round 4 (2008)

Variable	Survey Question and Possible Responses
Key Independent	
Religious Group Activity	Are you an (3 =) official leader, (2 =) active member, (1 =) inactive member, or (0 =) not a member of a religious group (e.g., church or mosque)?
Contact Religious Leaders	During the past year, how often have you contacted religious leaders about some important problem or to given them your views? (3 = often, 2 = once or twice, 1 = only once, 0 = never)
Key Dependent	
Voting	In the most recent election, did you vote? (1 = yes, 0 = no)
Support for Democracy	Which of the following statements is closest to your opinion? (3 = Democracy is preferable to any other form of govt., 2 = In some circumstances, non-democratic govt. can be preferable, 1 = For someone like me, it does not matter what kind of govt. we have)
Respect Freedom of Speech	Do you agree or disagree? (1) People should be able to speak their minds about politics free of govt. influence, no matter how unpopular their views may be. (or) (2) Govt. should not allow the expression of political views that are fundamentally different from views of the majority. (4 = agree very strongly with first statement, 3 = agree with first statement, 2 = agree with second statement, 1 = agree very strongly with second statement)

and Christianity. This allows us to more precisely control for religious affiliation when we assess the impact of religious involvement on political actions and attitudes. The largest religious groups represented in the survey are Roman Catholics (22.9 percent of all respondents), Muslims (22.9 percent of all respondents), non-denominational Christians (13.5 percent of all respondents), Anglicans (5.6 percent), Pentecostals (5.2 percent), Evangelicals (3.4 percent), and Lutherans (2.9 percent).

Table 4.2 lists the countries included in the fourth round of the Afrobarometer survey with the total number of respondents and the combined effective number of religious groups or integrated religious diversity (IRD) scores for every country included in the survey. Remember that the IRD score represents an attempt to capture the type of religious diversity that exists in a society. I use a measure of sub-religious diversity (INTRA-RD) to capture the effective number of sub-religious groups within major world religions, and a measure of inter-religious diversity (INTER-RD) to capture the effective number of totally different world religions. The IRD score is the average of the effective number of world religions (INTRA-RD) and the effective number of sub-groups or denominations within these world religions (INTRA-RD). Among the countries with the highest IRD scores are Ghana, Malawi, Kenya, and Tanzania. They include not only a significant percentage of both Christians and Muslims, but a great deal of

Table 4.2 Religious Diversity (2000) in Countries Included in
Afrobarometer Survey Round 4 (2008)

County	Observations	Integrated Religious Diversity
Benin	1,192	2.73
Botswana	1,196	2.78
Burkina Faso	1,147	2.68
Cape Verde	1,264	1.07
Ghana	1,183	4.00
Kenya	1,100	3.53
Lesotho	1,184	3.10
Liberia	1,197	3.18
Madagascar	1,339	2.45
Malawi	1,141	3.72
Mali	1,217	1.43
Mozambique	1,147	2.84
Namibia	1,200	2.29
Nigeria	2,316	2.65
Senegal	1,186	2.29
South Africa	2,375	2.16
Tanzania	1,193	3.53
Uganda	2,421	2.11
Total	24,998	2.71

Note: Integrated religious diversity is the average of the effective number of religions [inter-religious diversity] and the effective number or religious subgroups [intra-religious diversity or denominational diversity within major religions]. Countries in the high religious diversity category are countries with a combined/integrated religious diversity [IRD] score greater than 3.5. Countries in the medium religious diversity category are countries with an IRD between 2.2 and 3.2. Countries in the low religious diversity category are countries with an IRD of less than 2.0.

intra-Christian and, in some cases, intra-Islamic diversity. These countries are followed by Benin, Botswana, Burkina Faso, Madagascar, Mozambique, Namibia, Lesotho, and Liberia. The countries with the lowest IRD scores are Cape Verde, Mali, Senegal, South Africa, and Uganda. Each of these countries is predominantly Christian or Muslim and, compared to other sub-Saharan African counties included in the fourth round of the Afrobarometer survey, they do not include a high degree of sub-religious diversity.

To analyze the data, I use logistical regression analysis. This method allows us to generate statements concerning the impact of changes in religious involvement on the probability that an individual voted, voiced support for democracy, and expressed respect for freedom of speech. The key independent variables, religious group activity and the frequency with which individuals contact religious leaders, are qualitative variables that range from 1 to 4, with 4 representing the highest level of religious activity (i.e., that one serves as an official leader in a religious group) or highest frequency of contact (i.e., that one contacted a religious leader often in the last year). I transform the key dependent variables into dichotomous variables that range from 0 to 1. When it comes to voting, only respondents who said they voted in the most recent election in their country received a score of 1. As regards support for democracy, respondents who said that *democracy is preferable to any other form of government* received a score of 1, and all others received a score of 0. Only those who said they agree very strongly with the statement "everyone should be able to speak their minds about politics free of government influence no matter how unpopular their views" received a score of 1.

A word of caution is in order before launching into analysis. There are hazards to coming to hard and fast conclusions based on survey research. This is especially true of survey research on support for democracy, respect for basic freedoms, and religious activity. It is worth recognizing that survey questions on support for democracy and basic freedoms may not capture very well the extent to which respondents do and do not support democracy and basic freedoms. For example, the question that asks whether one considers democracy to be preferable to any other form of government may not be the best question to ask if we are interested in measuring the extent to which people support democracy. There is reason to believe that the word "democracy" is a loaded term that is often associated with the West and therefore is viewed negatively by many Muslims (Shadid 2002). It is quite possible that we find people, especially Muslims, expressing dislike for democracy largely because of the word "democracy," rather than because they dislike a political system that promotes accountable and responsive government through regularly occurring multiparty elections.

It is also difficult to tap the extent to which people support freedom of speech. In the fourth round of the Afrobarometer, the question on freedom of speech is worded in such a way that respondents who do support freedom of speech and association may actually answer in a way that indicates that they do not support such freedom. Respondents were asked whether and how strongly they agree with one of two statements. They could not agree with both. One statement is "people should be able to speak their minds about politics free of governmental influence, no matter how unpopular their views." The other statement is "government should not allow the expression of political views that are fundamentally different from views of the majority." In several African countries, where laws are poorly enforced and there are groups that commit violent acts to achieve political ends, people may interpret "unpopular views" to be views that justify violence or extremism to achieve a political or social goal. In other words, when answering this question in the negative, people may be saying, "no, groups that promote violence as a way to achieve political ends should not be allowed by government to express their views." For example, many Nigerian respondents may have groups like *Boko Haram* in mind when they think of groups that hold "unpopular views." Many Kenyans may have groups like *Al Shabab* in mind when they think of groups that espouse "unpopular views." If so, such respondents are likely to be lumped with those who oppose freedom of speech. Yet, they may be quite supportive of freedom of speech for groups that use peaceful means to achieve political ends. Rather than being opposed to freedom speech, they may instead be opposed to freedom of speech for groups that commit acts of violence to further their social, religious, or political agendas. So much depends on how the respondents interpret "unpopular views," and we simply do not know how they do so.

As Steven Fish (2011) notes, it is important to keep in mind that we have no way of knowing for certain what individual respondents have in mind when answering survey questions and, therefore, we need to be cautious when inferring their attitudes based on their answers to such questions. Survey instruments are usually tested on samples of the populations for which they are intended in order to be sure that the questions people understand themselves being asked are the questions that we researchers intend to ask. However, in the absence of follow-up interviews with respondents, there is no way to know for certain whether we are rightly interpreting their responses. This is not to argue that all survey data, including the Afrobarometer data, are useless. We would not be analyzing such data if we thought that this were the case. Instead, I am arguing that we should interpret the results of public opinion research cautiously, with the awareness that we cannot be certain about what respondents were thinking when they answered questions that attempt to capture their points of view, particularly on issues such as democracy and basic freedoms.

Besides not knowing what respondents were thinking when they answered questions intended to tap their attitudes concerning democracy and basic freedoms, we do not know whether respondents told us the truth when asked about their voting behavior and religious engagement. In sub-Saharan Africa, democratic institutions are new. In many countries, there was a long struggle for multiparty elections. There is good reason to think that citizens are embarrassed to admit that they have not voted in recent elections (Holbrook and Krosnick 2010; Bratton, Mattes, and Gyimah-Boadi 2005). Therefore, citizens are likely to say that they voted in the last election when in fact they did not. In sub-Saharan Africa, there is reason to believe that religious engagement is even more socially desirable than voting. In other words, Christians and Muslims are likely to inflate the degree to which they are active in their religious communities and are embarrassed to admit little or no religious activity. Again, this does not mean that the Afrobarometer data that we are using are invalid. Rather, this means that we should use caution when assessing the impact of religious engagement, a socially desirable behavior, on voting, another socially desirable behavior. If we decide to wait for perfect survey data before addressing important questions, such as the relationship between religious engagement and actions and attitudes conducive to liberal democracy, we will be waiting a very long time (i.e., forever!) and learning nothing in the process.

With the above caveats in mind, let us analyze the Afrobarometer data and test the theory that I have outlined in Chapter 2. That theory suggests that religious engagement will have a more positive impact on actions and attitudes conducive to liberal democracy in countries with a higher effective number of religious groups.[6] In other words, as the effective number of religious groups increases, the theory predicts that religious observance will have an increasingly positive effect on voting, support for democracy, and respect for basic freedoms. We have two measures of religious engagement that are qualitatively different, and it is quite possible that religious group activity and frequency of contact with religious leaders have qualitatively different impacts on voting, support for democracy, and respect for basic freedoms. Therefore, we examine the effects of these two measures of religious engagement separately in each country, while we control for religious diversity and other factors (i.e., gender, age, years of schooling, urban or rural, dwelling, and religious affiliation), which may have an impact on voting, support for democracy, and respect for basic freedoms.

In Table 4.3, I display marginal effects. The marginal effects represent the change in the probability that a respondent answered yes to the question about a given action (i.e., voted) or attitude (i.e., support democracy or support freedom of speech) per a change in the independent variable (i.e., male, age, education, religious activity, effective number of religious groups, Catholic, Mainline Protestant, and Muslim). Under each dependent variable of interest there are two models. In each case, Model 1 is simply the marginal effect of the given independent variable for each dependent variable. For example, in Model 1, we see that men were 3.4 percentage points more likely to vote than women, and each additional year of age increased the probability that one voted by 1.1 percentage points. Further, each additional religious group decreased the probability that one voted by 0.5 percentage points. Model 2 inserts the two measures of religious engagement into the picture and represents the impact of religious engagement (i.e., how active one is in one's religious group and how frequently one contacts religious leaders) on voting, support for democracy, and support for freedom of association per the effective number of religious groups in a society.

Focusing on Model 2 of Table 4.3, we find that religious activity and frequency of contact with religious leaders had a more positive effect on the probability of voting where there was more than one effective religion than where there was only one effective religious group. At one effective religious group (in a religiously homogeneous society), each unit increase in religious activity actually decreased the probability that a person voted by 1.0 percentage point. However, at more than one effective religious group, religious group activity increased the probability that one voted. For each unit increase in religious group activity, the probability that one voted increased by 1.8 percentage points.[7] When we drop down to Model 2 and take a look at contact with religious leaders as our measure of religious engagement, we find that contact with religious leaders had no effect on voting where there was one effective religion (i.e., a religiously homogeneous society) but a positive effect on voting where there was more than one effective religion. However, the effect was rather slight. For every one-unit increase in frequency of contact with religious leaders, the probability of voting increased by 0.4 percentage points.

Table 4.3 Covariates of Voting, Support for Democracy, and Support for Free Speech, Afrobarometer Data Marginal Effects (Standard Errors)

Independent Variable	Mean of Independent Variable	Discrete Outcome: Yes = 1 and No = 0					
		Voted in Last Election (Mean = 0.71)		Support Democracy (Mean = 0.69)		Support Free Speech (Mean = 0.74)	
		Model 1	Model 2	Model 1	Model 2	Model 1	Model 2
Male	0.50	0.034	0.034	0.071	0.071	0.029	0.029
		(0.006)	(0.006)	(0.006)	(0.006)	(0.006)	(0.006)
Age	36.4	0.011	0.011	0.0001	0.0001	−0.0004	−0.0004
		(0.0002)	(0.0002)	(0.0002)	(0.0002)	(0.0002)	(0.0002)
Effective no. of religions	2.71	−0.005	−0.028	−0.010	−0.034	−0.013	−0.015
		(0.003)	(0.005)	(0.004)	(0.006)	(0.004)	(0.005)
How active in religion (1–4 scale)	1.21	0.030	−0.019	0.030	−0.012	0.009	0.007
		(0.003)	(0.004)	(0.004)	(0.011)	(0.003)	(0.010)
No. of religions x How active in religion			0.018		0.015		0.0007
			(0.004)		(0.004)		(0.004)
How often contact religions leaders (1–4 scale)	0.79	0.017	0.006	0.022	−0.0004	0.007	0.004
		(0.003)	(0.010)	(0.003)	(0.010)	(0.003)	(0.009)
No. of religions x How often contact religious leaders			0.004		0.008		0.001
			(0.003)		(0.004)		(0.003)
Catholic	0.23	0.042	0.042	−0.002	−0.003	−0.025	−0.025
		(0.007)	(0.007)	(0.008)	(0.008)	(0.007)	(0.008)
Protestant	0.13	0.010	0.011	0.005	0.005	0.010	0.010
		(0.009)	(0.009)	(0.010)	(0.010)	(0.009)	(0.009)
Pentecostal	0.05	0.017	0.015	0.030	0.037	0.027	0.027
		(0.012)	(0.013)	(0.014)	(0.014)	(0.013)	(0.013)
Muslim	0.21	0.063	0.063	0.015	0.015	0.007	0.007
		(0.007)	(0.007)	(0.008)	(0.008)	(0.008)	(0.008)
Completed secondary education	0.21	−0.006	−0.007	0.070	0.069	0.065	0.065
		(0.007)	(0.007)	(0.007)	(0.007)	(0.007)	(0.007)
Completed some university	0.05	−0.031	−0.033	0.086	0.084	0.079	0.079
		(0.014)	(0.014)	(0.013)	(0.013)	(0.012)	(0.012)
Urban	0.37	−0.028	−0.029	0.041	0.039	0.046	0.045
		(0.006)	(0.006)	(0.006)	(0.006)	(0.006)	(0.006)

Religious group activity and frequency of contact with religious leaders also had a more positive effect on support for democracy where there was more than one effective religious group than where there was one effective religious group. Looking at Model 2 for support for democracy, we find that religious group activity had a rather large negative effect on support for democracy at one effective religion. For every one-unit increase in religious group activity, the probability that one voted decreased by 1.9 percentage points where there was one effective religious group. However, where there was more than one effective religious group, each one-unit increase in religious group activity increased the probability that one expressed support for democracy by 1.5 percentage points. Similarly, frequency of contact with religious leaders had a negative effect on support for democracy at one effective religion. Where there was one effective religious group, every one-unit increase in contact with religious leaders decreased the probability that a respondent expressed support for democracy by 2.6 percentage points. However, where there was more than one effective religious group, contact with religious leaders had a slightly positive effect on support for democracy. Where there is more than one effective religion, every one-unit increase in religious group activity increased the probability that a respondent expressed support for democracy by 0.8 percentage points. In sum, religious group activity had a more positive effect on voting and support for democracy in religiously diverse settings than in religiously homogeneous settings. While frequency of contact with religious leaders had a much smaller effect, it too had a more positive effect on voting and support for democracy in more religiously diverse settings than in settings that were religiously homogeneous.

Although religious group activity and frequency of contact with religious leaders were shown to have a more positive effect on support for freedom of speech in religiously diverse societies than in religiously homogeneous societies, the difference was negligible. Where there was one effective religious group, religious group activity decreased the probability that a respondent expressed support for freedom of speech by 0.9 percentage points. Where there was more than one effective religion, every one-unit increase in religious group activity increased support for freedom of speech by 0.7 percentage points. Every one-unit increase in frequency of contact with religious leaders decreased the probability that one expressed support for freedom of speech by 1.5 percentage points where there was no more than one effective religious group. Where there was more than one, a one-unit increase in contact with religious leaders increased the probability that one supported freedom of speech by 0.1 percentage point. That was not exactly worthy of a newsflash.

We want to learn how increases in religious diversity affect the impact of religious group activity and contact with religious leaders on voting and support for democracy. We leave support for freedom of speech aside, since there is little evidence that increases in religious diversity determine in any way the impact that religious activity and contact with religious leaders have on support for freedom of speech. In Figures 4.1 and 4.2, we saw that, as the effective number of religious groups increased (i.e., the average of the INTER-RD and INTRA-RD scores), religious group activity and frequency of contact with a religious leader had an increasingly positive impact on voting. For every one-unit increase in religious group activity, the probability that one voted hardly changed where there was one effective religious group.

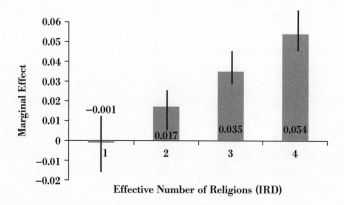

Figure 4.1 Marginal Effect: Change in Probability of Voting for a Change in Religious Group Activity (95% Confidence Interval)

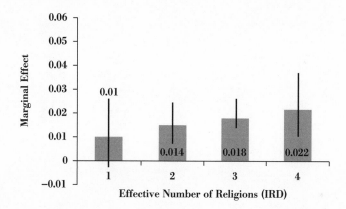

Figure 4.2 Marginal Effect: Change in Probability of Voting for a Change in Frequency of Contact with Religious Leader (95% Confidence Interval)

However, where there were two effective religious groups, every one-unit increase in religious group activity increased the probability that one voted by 1.7 percentage points.[8] In countries with three effective religious groups, the increase in voting that was associated with a one-unit increase in religious group activity was 3.5 percentage points; in countries with four effective religious groups, it was 5.4 percentage points. Essentially, this meant that when a Christian or Muslim went from a religious group activity score of 1, not a member of a religious group, to a religious group activity score of 4, an official leader of a religious group, the probability that he or she voted increased by almost 11 percentage points in countries where there were three effective religious groups and by more than 16 percentage points in countries where there were four effective religious groups. All the while, we control for age, educational attainment, and urban or rural environment so that we can be sure that what we were zeroing in on is the impact of religious group activity. As

Figure 4.2 shows, the change in the impact of contact with religious leaders on voting per change in effective number of religious groups was positive but less pronounced.

Figure 4.3 shows that, as the effective number of religious groups increased, religious group activity had a very positive impact on the probability that one supported democracy. In countries where there was one effective religious group, the impact of religious group activity was negligible. Where there were two effective religious groups, there was a 1.9 percentage-point increase in the likelihood that one expressed support for democracy for every one-unit increase in religious group activity. In countries with three effective religious groups, the increase in the probability that one expressed support for democracy increased by 3.5 percentage points for every one-unit increase in religious group activity and by 5.2 percentage points in countries with four effective religious groups. Figure 4.4 shows that contact with religious leaders also had a positive impact on the probability that one supported democracy. Where there were four effective

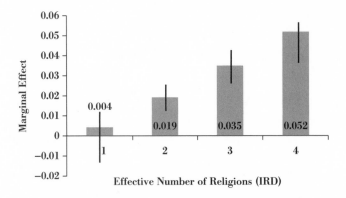

Figure 4.3 Marginal Effect: Change in Probability of Support for Democracy for a Change in Religious Group Activity (95% Confidence Interval)

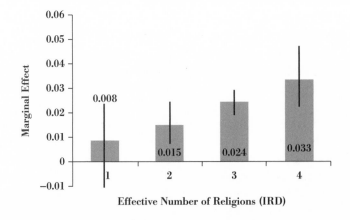

Figure 4.4 Marginal Effect: Change in Probability of Support for Democracy for a Change in Frequency of Contact with Religious Leaders (95% Confidence Interval)

religious groups, the probability that one expressed support for democracy increased by 11 percentage points as one moved from never having contacted a religious leader in the past year to having done so often.

MAKING SENSE OF THE RESULTS

We found that religious group activity and contact with religious leaders had a positive effect on voting and support for democracy where there was a higher effective number of religious groups. Even when controlling for religious identity (i.e., mainline Christian, Pentecostal Christian, or Muslim), gender, age, and education, the relationship holds.

However, we did not find such a relationship when it came to respect for freedom of speech. Neither religious group activity nor frequency of contact with religious leaders had much of an impact on support for freedom of speech, regardless of the effective number of religions. We need to do our best to make sense of these results. What did these results suggest?

The results suggested that Christian and Islamic religious communities were more effective at promoting political engagement in religiously diverse countries than in religiously homogeneous countries. These findings do conform to the expectations of the theory that I presented back in Chapter 2. In that theory, I had proposed that religious communities would tend to have a more positive effect on civic engagement and support for democracy in religiously diverse settings than in religiously homogeneous settings because, in religiously diverse settings, religious leaders encourage such engagement and support. This was because religious leaders wanted to ensure that the voices of their religious communities are not drowned out by the voices of other religious communities. In religiously homogeneous societies, religious leaders were typically less concerned with politically mobilizing their followers, largely because there were fewer religious rivals with which to be concerned. The question is, is such religious-based political participation good or bad for freedom?

Although we cannot conclude that Christian and Islamic religious communities were more conducive to respect for freedom of speech in religiously diverse settings than in religiously homogeneous settings, we also cannot conclude that Christian and Islamic religious communities were discouraging respect for freedom of speech in religiously diverse societies. This "non-finding" was significant since so much of the literature would have led us to expect the most religiously observant Christians and Muslims to be less supportive of freedom of speech in religiously diverse societies than in religiously homogeneous societies (Lipset 1959; Lijphart 1977; Rabushka and Shepsle 1972; Montalvo and Reynal-Querol 2003). We did not find evidence that Christian and Islamic religious groups are encouraging or discouraging respect for freedom of speech.

A word of caution is in order before drawing any hard conclusions from the results reported in this chapter. While the Afrobarometer data were very helpful, it was important to note that the Afrobarometer survey data were not ideal for our purpose. The Afrobarometer survey was designed especially to gauge support for and satisfaction with democracy and economic reforms. Although the fourth round of the survey did ask about religious group activity and frequency of contact with religious leaders, one might argue that these two measures of religious observance were insufficient for capturing religious engagement among Christians and Muslims. Perhaps more important, the Afrobarometer survey did not include a question about religious tolerance or respect for religious freedom.

What we needed was a survey devoted especially to assessing the relationship between religious engagement and political actions and attitudes. Such a survey would have more questions on religious observance than the Afrobarometer so that we would be able to develop a more comprehensive measure of religious engagement. The survey would also include at least one question on respect for religious freedom so that we might assess the relationship between religiosity and respect for such freedom. No institution besides the family was better placed to affect respect for religious liberty than religious institutions themselves. Perhaps the most profound effect that a religious community might have on the prospects for liberal democracy concerned the impact it had on religious tolerance and respect for religious freedom.

SUMMARY

In sum, we found some evidence that supported the theory I presented in Chapter 2 and some evidence that did not support that theory. Religious group activity and frequency of contact with religious leaders had a positive effect on voting and support for democracy in religiously diverse countries of sub-Saharan Africa. However, we did not find that religious group activity and contact with religious leaders had a positive effect on support for freedom of speech in religiously diverse sub-Saharan African countries. Nonetheless, this non-finding was significant since much of the literature led us to believe that religious diversity would decrease religious-based support for basic freedoms, such as freedom of speech.

While the results reported in this chapter were important in that they allow us to assess whether and to what extent religious diversity affected the political impact of Christian and Islamic religious communities in sub-Saharan Africa, they were based on analysis of a limited body of data. The Afrobarometer survey was not dedicated to assess the relationship between religious engagement and support for liberal democracy, and, as such, did not include questions that could be used to develop a more comprehensive measure of religious engagement. In addition, important indicators of religious engagement, religious group activity, and frequency of contact with religious leaders were insufficient for measuring religious engagement. There were a variety of ways in which Christians and Muslims might be religiously observant. We need to do our best to include as many of them as possible when developing a measure of religiosity that can actually get at just how religious people really are. A more comprehensive measure of religious engagement may lead to different results from those reported here. Additionally, the Afrobarometer did not include a question on support for religious freedom. Perhaps the most important contribution that a religious institution could make to the emergence of a liberal democratic political culture was to support religious freedom.

While a survey that was devoted especially to assessing the relationship between religious engagement and support for liberal democracy would be helpful, it was also important to recognize that survey data only took us so far. In order to understand whether and how religious communities affected the prospects for liberal democracy, we also need to take a closer look at individual countries. Besides comparing the effects of religious observance across countries, we need to examine the nature of religious communities within countries and how their political theologies had seemed to change across time. We need thicker description to get closer to establishing a causal relationship between the religious diversity of a setting and the extent to which Christian and Islamic religious communities were encouraging of a liberal democratic political culture. In the following chapter, I do just that. I take a closer look at three countries: religiously diverse Nigeria, predominantly Muslim Senegal, and predominantly Christian Uganda. I analyze how religious diversity appears to have affected the application of religion to politics in each country. Further, to assess the impact of religious observance on the emergence of a liberal democratic political culture, I use a survey designed especially to gauge how religious engagement affects political actions and attitudes across the three countries.

5

A Closer Look at Nigeria, Senegal, and Uganda

"Religion is a problem in this country because we are split," said Agnes, a Roman Catholic who resides in the Nigerian city of Kano. She went on to clarify, "Christians and Muslims are constantly trying to gain advantages over each other and this is why we get violence."[1] This is Agnes's experience of the situation in her country, and it is also the conventional wisdom concerning religion and politics in Nigeria. Although most observers have noted that ethnic divisions (apart from religious differences) were more disruptive in the first few decades of Nigeria's independence (achieved in 1960) (Laitin 1986; Kukah 1993), it is widely recognized that religious tensions have become increasingly pronounced and destructive since the late 1970s and early 1980s (Kukah and Falola 1996; Falola 1998; Paden 2012). Compared to other countries in the region that are more religiously homogeneous, whether predominantly Christian or Muslim, observers think that the "even split" puts Nigeria at a disadvantage when it comes to achieving political stability and liberal democracy. This is because competition for social and political influence between the two religions has often erupted into violence (Human Rights Watch 2013; Paden 2012). While countries that are less religiously divided may have their own challenges that dim the prospects for free and fair elections, tolerance for social and ideological differences, and respect for basic freedoms, religious diversity and the attendant competition are thought to present special challenges in Nigeria.

While religious diversity appears to lead to intense religious competition that results in extremism in Nigeria, it is important to remember that appearances may be deceiving. To this point, I have presented evidence to indicate that religious diversity may not be the obstacle to a liberal democratic political culture that many have supposed it to be. In Chapter 3, we found that Christian and Muslim religious leaders have tended to be more supportive of pro-freedom political theologies in religiously diverse settings than in religiously homogeneous settings. In Chapter 4, I pointed to evidence that suggests that religious-based support for some key indicators of a liberal democratic political culture (i.e., voting and support for democracy) is stronger in religiously diverse countries of sub-Saharan Africa than in religiously homogenous countries of the region.

With greater focus on and attention to national context, this chapter compares the political impact of Christian and Islamic communities in three countries: religiously diverse Nigeria, predominantly Muslim Senegal, and predominantly Christian Uganda. We find little evidence to support the assertion that Christianity and Islam are less supportive of a liberal democratic political culture in Nigeria than in Senegal and Uganda. In fact, we find that religious observance had, at the time of the survey, a more positive impact on key liberal democratic actions and attitudes in Nigeria than in Senegal and Uganda. In this chapter, I analyze survey research that I conducted in all three countries in 2006 and 2007. Before describing the survey and presenting the findings, I discuss each country's religious demography and consider how that demography appears to have affected the type of political theologies promoted by religious leaders and the impact that Christian and Islamic religious communities have had on the prospects for liberal democracy.

NIGERIA: WHERE DIVERSITY APPEARS TO SUBVERT PROSPECTS FOR LIBERAL DEMOCRACY

Nigeria is Africa's most populous country, with approximately 169 million people as of 2012.[2] It is also one of the world's most religiously and ethnically diverse countries, with an almost equal proportion of Christians and Muslims and about 250 distinctive ethno-linguistic communities (Paden 2008). Counting Christians and Muslims is a politically charged process; therefore, the official Nigerian censuses of 1991 and 2006 did not include questions on religious identity (Paden 2008: 5–6). Recent estimates of the percentages of Christians and Muslims are based on the Nigeria Demographic and Health Survey (DHS).[3] By all accounts, the country has a nearly equal percentage of Christians and Muslims. As of the mid-1990s, Barrett and colleagues (2001) estimate that 45 percent of Nigeria's population professed Christianity, and 43 percent professed Islam. As of 2010, the Pew Research Center estimates that 52 percent of Nigeria's population were Muslim, and 46 percent of the country's population were Christian.[4] Nigeria's inter-religious diversity score (INTER-RD) is 2.43, and its intra-religious diversity score (INTRA-RD) is 2.87. While there are other countries with a higher effective number of religions, few countries in sub-Saharan Africa or in the world, for that matter, come as close to having an equal percentage of Christians and Muslims as Nigeria.

Islam was introduced in what is today northern Nigeria as early as the tenth century, and Christianity came to southern regions of the territory during the mid-nineteenth century. From the north Islam spread southward and, from the south, Christianity spread northward. By the thirteenth century, long before the advent of Christianity in the area, Islam had become the religion of the Hausa, the Fulani, and the Kanuri ethnic groups of the north (Ohadike 1992: 102). Borno was established as an Islamic state in what is today northeast Nigeria as early as the ninth century, and the Sokoto Caliphate was established in the northwest during the early eighteenth century (Mahmud 2013; Paden 2005: 37–39). The Sokoto caliphate and the emirate state system spread southward and eastward to include much of what is today northern Nigeria, except for Borno (ibid.). Starting from about 1804, the Fulani succeeded in spreading Islam to as far south as the Niger River. From northern Nigeria, Muslim clerics, traders, and craftsmen carried Islam southward to the Yoruba, who called much of southwestern Nigeria home (Miles 2000: 210). Christianity spread as far north as central Nigeria with the expansion of British colonial rule, and, in an effort to promote a good working relationship with Muslim leaders, colonial administrators largely prevented the spread of Christianity farther north. Thus, the northern part of Nigeria is predominantly Muslim, the central part of the country (often referred to as the Middle Belt) includes a sizable population of both Christians and Muslims, the south central and southeastern regions are predominantly Christian, and the southwest is roughly half Christian and half Muslim (Paden 2005).

Since the colonial era and at least partly due to the ways in which the British administered Nigeria (separately administering north and south), there emerged three distinctive politico-cultural zones that have been defined largely by ethno-linguistic identities that have come to overlap with religious differences.[5] These zones include the north, where the largest ethnic group is the Hausa-Fulani (mostly Muslims), the southeast, where the Igbo (almost entirely Christians) is the largest ethnic group, and the southwest, an area that the Yoruba ethnic group (a mix of both Muslims and Christians) has traditionally called home. Concerned about the destabilizing potential of ethno-religious differences between north and south, the British administered the two regions separately. From the beginning of the Nigerian state, some kind of federation was thought necessary for purposes of conflict management and administrative efficiency. As early as 1946, it was decided (then by the British) that there should be three states, Northern, Eastern, and Western, which would correspond to the three major ethno-linguistic differences (Hausa-Fulani, Igbo, and Yoruba). Nonetheless, after independence in 1960, tensions mounted as leaders from the Igbo-dominated southeastern part of the country declared that region's independence from Nigeria. A three-year-long civil war followed. The Biafran War, 1967 to 1970, was, according to many observers, more about ethnic identity and economics than about religion. However, since most of the southeasterners were Christians and those leading the Nigerian state were not, religious appeals were used to rally southeasterners and to further the cause of cessation (Kukah 1993). Christians from the southeast claimed that separating from Nigeria would be the only way to avoid domination by northern Muslims (ibid.). Since the war's end, Nigeria has generally enjoyed greater national unity and, despite the inter-communal tensions that have existed since 1970, there has been little or no serious discussion of cessation. However, in the interest of preventing or confining further inter-regional and inter-communal conflict, Nigeria's three cultural zones have been carved up into several states, thirty-six in total as of this writing.

While Nigeria is roughly half Muslim and half Christian, there is a significant degree of pluralism within the country's Christian and Islamic communities. While the Roman Catholic and Anglican churches are the largest Christian denominations in Nigeria, when combined most Christians are members of other churches and sects. Barrett, Kurian, and Johnson (2001) estimate that 18 percent of Nigeria's Christian population identified as Anglicans and 12 percent as Roman Catholics in the year 2000. By almost all accounts, Evangelical Christianity and, more specifically, Pentecostalism, has been growing dramatically in Nigeria. Barrett, Kurian, and

Johnson (2001) estimate that approximately half of all Christians in Nigeria considered themselves Evangelicals or Pentecostals by the year 2000.[6] They indicate that there were seven Christian denominations or sects that included 10 percent or more of the Christian population as of the year 2000 (ibid.). Christian identity in Nigeria is rather fluid, as many Christians move from one church or sect to another. Therefore, there is a great deal of competition for adherents and influence within Christianity, particularly between the Roman Catholic, Anglican, and other mainline churches, on the one hand, and newer Evangelical and Pentecostal churches, on the other.

Nigeria's Muslim population, like the country's Christian population, is diverse. Although the competition between Islam and Christianity for adherents and influence is considerable, intra-Islamic competition for followers and influence is intense as well. The vast majority of Nigerian Muslims are *Sunni*, yet there are various movements and groups, all more or less *Sunni*, that have different visions for Nigeria and for Islam's place in Nigeria. While the Pew Research Center (2010) reports that 10 percent of Nigerians called themselves *Shi'a* in 2010, there is reason to think that the percentage of Muslims who are truly *Shi'a* (in a religious sense) is much lower than that. Those who call themselves *Shi'a* are essentially making a political statement and believe that there should be a greater integration of religion and state in Nigeria (Paden 2008). Within the last decade, there have been violent clashes between *Sunni* and the so-called *Shi'a* in northern Nigeria.[7]

Over the years, intra-Islamic tensions have mounted, pitting those whom Paden (2005, 2008) calls the anti-innovation reformists against the two major Sufi brotherhoods (i.e., the Qadiriyya and Tijaniyya). Reformists have focused on ridding Islam of errors and innovations that they associate with Sufism and promoting a greater role for Islam in Nigeria's governance.[8] The anti-innovation legalists stress the importance of returning to the basics of Islam, the Koran and the sayings of the Prophet, or *Hadith*, and call for the *Shari'ah* to be enshrined as the law of the land.

One anti-innovation legalist movement is the *Jama'at Izalat al-Bida wa Iqamat al Sunnah* (Society for the Eradication of Evil Innovations and the Re-establishment of the Sunnah), better known as *Izala* (Paden 2008: 29). The *Izala* began as an anti-hierarchical movement that was very critical of the emirs of northern Nigeria and the Islamic establishment in the country. It has contributed to a religious revival among northern Muslims, as it has accused Nigeria's Muslim elites of selling out to secularism and for failing to promote the integration of Islamic and state authority. The movement has split and splintered into a variety of groups, notes Paden (2013: 79). Because of *Izala*'s revivalism and pluralism, it is very similar to Pentecostalism in Nigeria (although probably not as popular among Muslims as Pentecostalism is among Christians). Just as many of Nigeria's Pentecostals criticize Roman Catholic and mainline Protestant churches for having strayed from the strict path put forth in the Bible, so the *Izala* groups accuse Muslim leaders and the *Sufi* brotherhoods of diluting Islam and not fighting hard to establish an Islamic state (ibid.). In this sense, the *Izala* and some Pentecostal groups are on a collision course in that they both promote anti-freedom political activism—one that affords special state-granted privileges to Islam and one that calls for a privileged place for Christianity vis-à-vis the state. In short, there has been a battle for the heart and soul of Islam in Nigeria, as well as Christianity, that has raged for several decades. These battles within both Christianity and Islam, often masked by the conflict between Christians and Muslims, have seemingly intensified during the first two decades of the twenty-first century. Within Islam, there are at least two competing political theologies. One political theology insists on the integration of religious and state authority and is championed by the anti-innovation legalists, and the other does not insist on such integration and is largely associated with the Sufi orders and Nigeria's Islamic religious establishment (i.e., emirs and other prominent Muslim religious leaders).

Two important flashpoints concerning Christian-Muslim relations in Nigeria include Nigeria's entrance into the Organization of the Islamic Conference (OIC), now the Organization for Islamic Cooperation, and the constitutional enshrinement of the *Shari'ah* in Nigeria's twelve northernmost states. Christian-Muslim tensions, already strained due to violence in northern Nigeria that took place in the early 1980s, worsened when it was announced, in 1986, that Nigeria had become a member of the OIC. Christian leaders across denominations expressed outrage and concern that the decision had been made without discussion and debate (Kukah 1993). Christian leaders claimed that joining the OIC was tantamount to declaring Islam to be the official religion of Nigeria (Kukah and Faolola 1996: 247–249). While some members of the government and Muslim religious leaders tried to soften the significance of the decision, suggesting that the move was no more significant than Nigeria having diplomatic relations with the Vatican or arguing that the decision to enter the OIC had more to do with the economic benefits of belonging to the organization than with religion, Christian leaders insisted that they would never agree to Nigeria's membership in the organization (ibid.). Despite the loud cries of protest from Christians, including Catholics, mainline Protestants, and Evangelicals, Nigeria has remained a member of the OIC.

The second flashpoint concerns the introduction of the *Shari'ah* in the constitutions of predominantly Muslim northern states. The constitutional enshrinement of the *Shari'ah* in northern Nigeria seems to have been driven largely by popular frustration with the lack of law and order. Many northern Muslims seemed frustrated enough with the "secular state" that they were ready to turn to their religion in hopes that it would bring the security and development that they desired (Mahmud 2013; Paden 2008). Whether a calculated decision made in order to boost lagging political support among the general population or a decision motivated primarily by religious conviction, governors moved to privilege the *Shari'ah* in the constitutions of their states. By the year 2003, the *Shari'ah* had been constitutionally enshrined in the twelve most northern states. Although the *Shari'ah* applies to Muslims only, this has led some Christians in those twelve states to claim that they have been relegated to second-class citizens in their own country (Falola 1998).[9] Tensions between Christians and Muslims continued to mount, and Christians began to talk about the importance of coming together to fight attempts to Islamize Nigeria (Kukah and Falola 1996: 237–238). Further, some Christians began to intensify their efforts to make Nigeria a "Christian country" (Marshall 2009).

With the inauguration of Nigeria's Fourth Republic, launched in 1999, Christian and Islamic groups began to very openly take mutually exclusive stances on the role of religion in public life. Through converting people to Christianity and adding to those who believe in Christ, some Christians, especially the growing number of Pentecostal Christians, have sought to make Nigeria a Christian country (Marshall 2009: 214–215). These efforts to evangelize have not sat well with Muslims, whether Islamists who promote a *Shari'ah*-based state, members of the more moderate Sufi brotherhoods, or the many unaffiliated Nigerian Muslims. These aggressive efforts to evangelize have led Christians into a direct confrontation with Islamists who have sought to impose the *Shari'ah* and make Nigeria an Islamic state (ibid.). Marshall (2009: 214) suggests that there has emerged in Nigeria greater religious polarization and two "competing theocratic projects" that are mutually exclusive.

Given the conflict between and within Christian and Islamic communities, it should come as no surprise that Nigeria is often considered the "poster child" for the argument that religious diversity, especially in developing countries undergoing political transitions, is bound to prompt religious competition and trigger religious extremism that is incompatible with liberal democracy. Since the 1980s, before Nigeria became a member of the OIC and before the *Shari'ah* came to be enshrined in the constitutions of northern states, there were numerous episodes of deadly inter-religious violence. Churches and mosques were desecrated and/or destroyed.[10] The Christian versus Muslim violence of the 1980s and 1990s claimed several thousands of lives (Quinn and Quinn 2003; Paden 2005). That violence continued, and Human Rights Watch estimates that more than 11,000 people were killed in religious and/or ethnic violence between 1999 and 2006.[11]

The religious competition and the Christian-Muslim violence that has engulfed parts of northern Nigeria and much of the country's Middle Belt have prompted "religious outbidding." By religious outbidding, I mean a dynamic whereby Christian and Muslim religious leaders seek to gain followers and influence among their co-religionists by claiming to be better at checking the social and political influence of the rival religion than other religious leaders. [12] The context drives both Christians and Muslims to the extremes. In Nigeria, there are Christian religious leaders who have sought to attract followers by portraying themselves as the true champions of Christianity. The true champions of Christianity, according to this line of thought, are uncompromising in their efforts to convert all of Nigeria to the Christian faith (Marshall 2009: 214–216). Muslim religious leaders have sought to attract followers by portraying themselves as the true champions of Islam, who will stop at nothing to prevent the so-called true champions of Christianity from succeeding. The true champions of Islam, as several Muslim leaders portray themselves, will never compromise in efforts to promote a social order that privileges the *Koran* and the *Shari'ah* (Falola 1998: 230–246; Paden 2008: 35–36). There has been a concurrent revivalism in Islam and Christianity, with fundamentalism in one seeming to feed off and stoke fundamentalism in the other (Campbell and Harwood 2011). As Kukah and Falola (1996: 112) note, "Both Muslims and Christians seem to think that by demonizing other groups, they will ensure the 'unity' of their constituencies. But the fossilization of feelings only expands the frontiers of bigotry and instills fear."

The Christian Association of Nigeria (CAN), an inter-denominational umbrella organization founded in 1976 to promote Christian values in society, has recently experienced divisions that are related to disagreements over how best to deal with Islam—the outbidding of which I just made mention. CAN is arguably the most socially and politically important Christian organization in the country. Originally founded by Roman Catholics and Anglicans, the Association has come to include Evangelical and Pentecostal Christians, and leaders from these churches have become increasingly influential (Loimeier 2007; Marshall 2009). As their percentage of the Christian population increases, Pentecostals have grown powerful in CAN. Pentecostal leaders have tended to be less compromising in their efforts to Christianize Nigeria than mainline Christian leaders, and this has created tension within CAN (Loimeier 2007). For example, one of the complaints lodged by some members of CAN against Archbishop (now Cardinal) John Onaiyekan, Catholic Archbishop of Abuja and President of CAN from 2007 to 2010, was that he was too soft on Islam. With the help of Pentecostal members of the association, Pentecostal Pastor Ayo Oritsejafor was elected President of CAN over Archbishop Onaiyekan in 2010. As leader of the Word of Life Bible Church and President of the Pentecostal Fellowship of Nigeria (PFN) with his own television program (*Hour of Deliverance*), Pastor Oritsejafor has a huge following across Nigeria. According to many observers, Oritsejafor took control of CAN in large part by appealing to the large numbers of Pentecostals and other Christians who thought that Onaiyekan was overly compromising in his approach to Muslims and was not dedicated enough to making Nigeria a Christian country.[13] Claiming that CAN's leadership was politically compromised, the Roman Catholic Church pulled out of CAN in January 2013.[14] Again, this is evidence of religious outbidding: Christian leaders competing for and winning popularity among fellow Christians by claiming that they will never compromise with Muslims. It appears that Nigeria's religious diversity and fears of an Islamic takeover of Nigeria have prompted this religious outbidding.

Among Muslims, religious leaders and religious movements compete with each other for followers and influence by capitalizing on perceptions of Christian domination and frustration with Nigeria's political, economic, and political status quo—a status quo thought by many Muslims to be more favorable to Christians than to Muslims. These groups include the so-called *Shiite* movement, mentioned above, and a group that calls itself the "Taliban," which is inspired by but has no direct connection to the Taliban in Afghanistan (Paden 2008: 35–36). More recently, *amā'at Ahl as-Sunnah lid-da'wa wal-Jihād*, or the Congregation of the People of Tradition for Proselytism and Jihad, better known as *Boko Haram* (often translated as "Western education is a sin"), has been at the forefront of Nigeria's violent Islamist movements. Founded in 2002 in the predominantly Muslim Borno state of northeastern Nigeria by *Salafi* teacher Mohammed Yusuf, *Boko Haram* began by seeking to make Borno a *Shari'ah* state.[15] Over the years, since Yusuf died in police custody in 2009, *Boko Haram*'s ambitions have grown and violent attacks have infamously increased.[16] *Boko Haram* seeks to make all of northern Nigeria a more purely Islamic society and has waged a campaign of terror in efforts to do so. Another militant Islamist group that has seemed to grow out of *Boko Haram* is *Jama'atu Ansarul Muslimina Fi Biladis Sudan* (Vanguards for the Protection of Muslims in Black Africa), which is known more commonly as

Ansaru. Founded in the predominantly Muslim city of Kano in 2012, the group has kidnapped and killed Nigerians and foreign nationals in Nigeria perceived to be a threat to Muslims and a truly Islamic way of life.

Since the 1980s, Islamist groups have gathered enough followers, have been sufficiently organized, and have attracted enough financial resources to inflict considerable destruction. In the last decade, *Boko Haram* has terrorized large parts of northern and central Nigeria (i.e., the Middle Belt). Besides promoting the complete integration of religious and state authority, *Boko Haram* opposes voting in elections. The group has claimed responsibility for a number of attacks that targeted those considered to be obstacles to a *Shari'ah*-based society in northern Nigeria. In August 2011, *Boko Haram* claimed responsibility for a deadly bomb attack on the United Nations compound in the federal capital, Abuja. During the same year, the group claimed responsibility for Christmas Day bombings of several churches throughout northern Nigeria. The Council on Foreign Relations estimates that *Boko Haram* was responsible for more than 1,700 deaths between July 2011 and February 2013.

Although there have been no openly religious-based political parties in Nigeria—and, in fact, such parties have always been illegal—political parties have been distinguished from each other largely by ethno-linguistic, regional, and, therefore, religious differences. Nonetheless, many observers note that ethno-linguistic and regional differences were more salient for party politics than religious differences for the first four decades of Nigeria's independence (Laitin 1986). Even at the dawn of the Fourth Republic in 1999, parties tended not to be distinguished from each other along religious lines. Because the Fourth Republic Constitution required the winning presidential candidate to obtain 25 percent of the vote in two-thirds of the county's states, Olusegun Obasanjo's People's Democratic Party (PDP) and the other major political party, the All People's Party (APP), had a strong incentive to mix their presidential tickets along regional, ethnic, and religious lines. Thus, Obasanjo, a Yoruba Christian from the southwest, had a northern Muslim running mate, Atiku Ababakar. The APP also fielded a presidential ticket that included a Christian from the southwest, Olu Falae, and a northern Muslim, Umaru Shinkafi. Although the 2007 election is widely regarded as a deeply flawed election, it was largely free of religious tension, as all three major political parties, the PDP, APP, and the Action Congress (AC), fielded Muslim presidential candidates who had Christian running mates.

Relations between Christians and Muslims in many parts of Nigeria appeared to worsen in the run-up to and aftermath of the 2011 election, as many Muslims became concerned that Christians were unfairly dominating the presidency of the country.[17] Although not a formal requirement, there has been an expectation that, within the PDP, which had become Nigeria's most powerful political party, the top of the presidential ticket would alternate between Christians and Muslims. This agreement to rotate the PDP's presidential candidates came to be commonly known as the "zoning system." After a Christian president, Olusegun Obasanjo, served two four-year terms (1999–2007), the PDP put forward Umar Yar'Adua, a Muslim. Yar'Adua was elected president in 2007. Having suffered from a serious illness, he died before he could finish his first term. Yar'Adua's vice president, Goodluck Jonathan, assumed the presidency in accord with Nigeria's constitution. Many Muslims expected that the PDP, also the party of Yar'Adua, would continue the zoning system and field a Muslim candidate for the presidency after Jonathan served the remainder of Yar'Adua's term. Instead, Jonathan sought the presidency in 2011 with the backing of the PDP leadership. Jonathan won the presidential election, defeating challenger Muhammadu Buhari, a Muslim backed by the Congress for Progressive Change (CPC). There were widespread allegations of electoral fraud. Violence between Christians and Muslims followed the election, particularly in the northern part of the country and the Middle Belt.[18] The fallout over the end of the zoning system within the PDP and allegations of electoral fraud in the subsequent general election have increased a sense of frustration among many Muslims that the PDP has become a party dominated by Christians and that Muslims are being deprived of their rightful voice in the governance of Nigeria (Campbell and Harwood 2011).

Despite the religious conflicts that have shaken parts of Nigeria, it is important to note that not all of Nigeria's Christian and Muslim religious leaders have promoted mutually exclusive political theologies. There have been and continue to be Christian and Muslim religious leaders who promote mutual respect across the religious divide, eschew violence, and seek to promote religious freedom for all. Further, there are organizations of Christians and Muslims devoted to peace and mutual respect. One such organization is the Nigeria Inter-religious Council (NIREC), which has focused efforts on training youth to promote coexistence and mutual understanding among Christians and Muslims.[19] Typically, the Sultan of Sokoto co-chairs NIREC, along with a prominent Christian leader. Another such organization has established the Inter-Faith Mediation Centre (IMC). The IMC brought calm to the northern city of Kaduna after deadly riots between Christians and Muslims broke out at various times between 2000 and 2004 (Paden 2005: 171). Both CAN and the National Supreme Council of Islamic Affairs (NSCIA) may be considered moderate umbrella groups as well. Despite the outbidding described above and extremists within both CAN and the NSCIA, each organization has played an important role in calling for tolerance and mutual respect between Christians and Muslims (Paden 2005: 171–178). Despite the inter-religious violence that has rocked Nigeria since 1980, it is worth noting that, compared to many other sub-Saharan African countries, there is evidence to suggest that Nigerian Christians and Muslims have tended to view each other more favorably. A survey conducted by the Pew Forum on Religion and Public Life in 2008–2009 found that 38 percent of Nigerian Christians viewed Muslims as more violent than Christians. This is a far lower percentage as compared to Chad (70 percent), Ghana (61 percent), Cameroon (57 percent), and a lower percentage than in Kenya, Zambia, Mozambique, Uganda, Tanzania, Democratic Republic of Congo, Liberia, and Ethiopia.[20] Further, just 13 percent of Nigerian Muslims viewed Christians as more violent than Muslims, which is 7 percentage points below the median for the sub-Saharan African countries included in the survey.[21] This suggests that, at least at the time of the Pew survey, Christian-Muslim relations in Nigeria may have been less tense than in several other African countries where violence between Christians and Muslims was less frequent or deadly.

Despite the efforts of Christian and Muslim leaders who promote pro-freedom political theologies and the Pew survey data showing that Nigerian Christian-Muslim relations have not been as bad as one might suspect, Nigeria is a religiously diverse country where mutually exclusive political theologies appear to dampen the prospects for liberal democracy. A sizable percentage of Christians and Muslims in the country have had seemingly irreconcilable differences on the proper role of religion in society and the separation of religious and state authority. According to the Pew Forum on Religion and Public Life (2010), 70 percent of Nigerian Christians supported making the Bible the law of the land, and 71 percent of Muslims supported making the *Shari'ah* the law of the land.[22] As noted above, some Christian and Islamic groups have encouraged, condoned, and/or excused violence in the cause of realizing their competing visions of one nation under God. It certainly appears that, in Nigeria, religious diversity has given rise to intolerant religion that diminishes the prospects for liberal democracy.

SENEGAL: A PREDOMINANTLY MUSLIM SOCIETY WHERE SUFISM APPEARS TO PROMOTE TOLERANCE

In contrast to Nigeria, Senegal is a predominantly Muslim country known for peaceful relations between religious groups and religious-based support for social and religious tolerance. Located on the West African coast, Senegal has a population of over 12 million and, as of the year 2000, Muslims made up at least 95 percent of the country's population.[23] While Islam in Senegal dates to the eleventh century, the majority of the Senegalese population converted to Islam between the seventeenth and the nineteenth centuries (Villalon 1995: 61). In Senegal, most Muslims belong to Sufi religious orders or brotherhoods—the same orders that, in Nigeria, are attacked by anti-innovation legalists for their supposed lack of orthodoxy and for their lack of commitment to a *Shari'ah*-based state. Sufism was introduced from North Africa during the eighteenth century. The small Christian minority, which traces its origins to the mid- and late nineteenth century, during the advent of the colonial era, is predominantly Roman Catholic. The Christian population is clustered primarily in Dakar, along the coast, and in the far southwestern region of Casamance. While there has been little or no significant inter-religious conflict in Senegal (Villalon 1995: 46), the Casamance region has been home to a Christian rebellion with ethnic and religious overtones. Nonetheless, the vast majority of Christians in Senegal, mostly Roman Catholics, seem to accept that they are part of a predominantly Muslim country with a culture shaped by Islam in many ways, and Senegalese Muslims largely respect the Christian minority's right to practice its faith freely.

Unlike in Nigeria, Muslims and Christians have not competed for political influence in Senegal, despite the fact that Senegal's first and longest-serving president (1960–1980), Leopold Senghor, was a Roman Catholic. There is no evidence to suggest that his presidency gave rise to fears that Christians would enjoy privileges at the expense of Muslims (ibid.). Christians and Muslims have enjoyed good relations. It has been so common for relatively wealthy Muslims in Dakar to send their children to

Catholic private schools that Muslims form the majority of students in such schools (Gellar 2005: 112). Villalon (1995: 46) notes, "the division between Muslims and the Christian minority has never been the basis of political action despite the fact that five percent of the population who are Christians have in fact been over-represented both in the state and in the modern sectors of the economy."

In Senegal, the Sufi brotherhoods have been very influential, and Sufism is often cited as the reason for the culture of tolerance and accommodation that has prevailed for so long in Senegal (Diouf 2013; Stepan 2013). The Sufi brotherhoods typically encourage concern for the interior or spiritual life of the believer and discourage social and political activism. Stepan (2013) notes that Sufism in Senegal "fosters rituals of respect by emphasizing those parts of the Koran that urge tolerance as a response to diversity." Meriboute (2009: 13) notes that Sufism is often considered as an "antidote" to political Islam because "it has a prose, grammar, and modern practices that circumscribe and support a space for pluralism and tolerance."[24]

The three most important Sufi orders in Senegal are the Qadiriyya, Tijaniyya, and Mouridiyya, with the majority of Senegalese belonging to either the Tijaniyya or the Mouridiyya. The Tijaniyya is the largest of the orders, including approximately half of the population. However, the Tijaniyya includes many sub-branches, and the Mouridiyya as a whole is larger than any one of the Tijani sub-branches (Villalon 2013: 164). Contrary to what we might expect, there is very little competition for followers or societal influence between the Mouridiyya and the Tijaniyya. Any differences that have existed have generally not been politicized. There is a great deal of intermarriage across orders, and Villalon (1995: 127) observes that it is not uncommon to find portraits of a religious leader, known as a *marabout*, from one order in the houses or shops of people who are members of another order. As the owner of one shop put it, "All *marabouts* are good (ibid.)." The differences between the orders are often blurred and, in some cases, we even find Senegalese who are members of more than one order at the same time. "Children are frequently sent to study the Koran with a local teacher or *marabout* without regard to order," observes Villalon (ibid.).

While there has been little in the way of serious competition between Sufi orders, *marabouts* compete with each other for disciples or *taalibes* (Gellar 2005: 111). There are thousands of *marabouts* in Senegal, each with his own group of *taalibes*. Many people look to *marabouts* for material support as well as spiritual guidance. It is not unusual for followers to switch *marabouts* if a *marabout* is unable to assist followers with a job, education, or financial support (ibid.). *Marabouts* exercise both spiritual and temporal powers, and their authority is based at least as much on their access to material resources and connection to a prominent and old maraboutic family line as on their reputation for "piety and knowledge in the religious sciences" (Villalon 1995: 134). While spiritual knowledge is to serve as the foundation for the authority that the *marabouts* exercise over their *taalibes*, the possibilities for an individual from outside one of the major maraboutic families to establish a following are quite limited.[25] Some *marabouts* have not only been objects of respect but of outright devotion. Many *marabouts* possess an extraordinary degree of power that is rarely enjoyed anywhere else by Muslim or Christian religious leaders. Many Senegalese believe that some *marabouts* possess magical powers that allow them to cripple (figuratively and literally) opponents and deliver miraculous favors for their followers.[26] However, it is important not to overstate the degree to which *taalibes* or followers are obedient to *marabouts*. With urbanization, economic development, and advances in education among their disciples, *marabouts* must be concerned about maintaining their legitimacy among their followers (Coulon 1981; O'Brien 1971; Villalon 1995). Gellar (2005: 111) notes that "more and more followers now see *marabouts* as primarily spiritual guides and do not feel obligated to follow their advice or orders in political and economic matters."

Despite efforts by some Muslim reformers during the 1950s and 1960s to cast the *marabouts* as collaborators with the colonial regime, *marabouts* and their descendants maintained their legitimacy and authority into the post-independence era. In fact, leaders of the Senegalese nationalist movement sought their support. Independent Senegal's first president, Leopold Senghor, a Roman Catholic, was supported by the most influential *marabouts*. Creevey (1986: 718) notes that the *marabouts'* support for Senghor largely explains the stability and the viability of his government. Further, the Mouridiyya formed the most important political constituency in support of the religiously neutral state (Berhman 1970; Coulon 1981; Cruise-O'Brien 1971, 1988).

Although the brotherhoods and Senegal's *marabouts* have promoted social and religious tolerance, it is debatable just how supportive they have been of democracy, and there is at least some reason to believe that democratization occurred despite their conservatism. *Marabouts* have been largely known for encouraging political quietism as they cooperated with the state in its development efforts. During the 1990s, the most influential Senegalese religious leaders refrained from explicitly giving political advice as opposition to the ruling party and popular unrest increased. According to Clark (1999: 162), "The *marabouts* were too intertwined with the government to criticize it openly; any challenge to the secular state and the existing order likewise represented a challenge to the religious leadership."

Since the 1990s, reformers who have promoted a more Islamist social agenda seem to have been receiving a greater hearing in Senegal. Both Creevey (1986) and Villalon (1995) suggest that this stems from a combination of greater interaction with Islamists in North Africa and the Middle East and dissatisfaction with the slow pace of economic development and democratization. The *Darhiratoul Moustarchadina wal Moustarchidaty*, which grew out of the Tijaniyya brotherhood, is known to be the first contemporary religiously based political movement in Senegal. It seeks to end the state's religious neutrality and to achieve a more prominent role for Islam in state and society. The movement, led by *marabout* Moustapha Sy, who comes from one of the most important Tijan families, verbally attacked President Diouf during the 1993 election campaign and was involved in post-election violence after Diouf's contested electoral victory (Villalon and Kane 1998). A similar movement, *Hiszbut Tarquiyyah*, emerged within the Mouride brotherhood. It started out as a student association at the University of Dakar and went so far as to question the appropriateness of hereditary maraboutic leadership within the Mouride order and to call for a more privileged place for Islam in state structures (Villalon 2013).

Since the advent of a more competitive political system in Senegal, there is evidence of a growing contest over the appropriate application of Islam to political life in Senegal. As Villalon (2013) notes, we are seeing that Sufism can be applied to politics in different ways. Two presidential candidates, Cheikh Abdoulaye Dieye and Ousseynou Fall, openly appealed to religion when campaigning (Villalon 2013). Dieye's campaign slogan was "God is One" and called into question the secular nature of the state (ibid.). It is worth noting that neither one of these candidates received much support in the election. However, the election of President Abdoulaye Wade in 2000 sparked debate over the secular nature of Senegal. In an apparent nod to Islamists, the first published draft of the new Senegalese constitution issued by Wade omitted the statement that Senegal is a secular state (*etat laique*) (Villalon 2007). There was such an uproar that Wade reinstated the affirmation of the secular state in Senegal's constitution. However, Villalon (2013) suggests that this controversy indicates that politicians, including Wade himself, sensed that there would be some kind of political advantage to leaving *laicite* (separation of religion and state) out of the constitution.

The advent of a more open political system has also been accompanied by intense debates over law regulating family life in Senegal. A group called the *Comite Islamique pour la Reforme du Code de la Famille au Senegal* (CIRCOF) formed in 2002 to push for reforms of the country's Family Code. Senegal's 1972 Family Code essentially mirrors France's law on family life. The CIRCOF sought to bring the 1972 Family Code in line with Islamic law and proposed a complete reworking of the law. The campaign waged by the CIRCOF drew an intense reaction from Senegal's secular elites, who were concerned that passing of the new family code based on Islamic law would be the first step toward an Islamic state—the integration of religious and state authority.[27]

Despite the evidence of growing debate over the application of Islam to public life, Senegal is a predominantly Muslim country where religion appears to have a stabilizing effect on public life and a moderating influence on political culture (Gellar 2005; Stepan 2013; Villalon 2013). Although Senegal's Muslim religious leaders are credited with promoting a culture of tolerance, just how much they have contributed to a liberal democratic political culture in Senegal is debatable. They have been a rather conservative political force in Senegal and have generally developed a cooperative and mutually beneficial relationship with the government of the day, which has not always been respectful of democratic processes.

Importantly, the powerful Sufi brotherhoods have not concerned themselves with calling for the state to enshrine the *Shari'ah* as the law of the land. Perhaps they see no need to do so in such a religiously homogeneous country. While over half of Senegalese support making the *Shari'ah* the law of the land (55 percent), this is a much smaller percentage than the percentage of Nigerians who supports the same (71 percent).[28] In contrast to Nigeria, there has been little or no inter-religious or intra-religious violence in Senegal. According to the Pew Forum on Religion and Public Life, a much smaller percentage of Senegalese Muslims is reported to be very or somewhat concerned with religious extremism (21 percent) than in Nigeria (50 percent).[29] Among the seventeen predominantly Muslim countries included in a survey that the Pew Forum conducted in 2005, Senegalese were the most optimistic about the prospects for democracy in their country and rejected the idea that democracy was simply a Western concept (87 percent).[30] While there are "anti-innovation reformists" who challenge the Sufi orders and call for a greater integration of religious and state authority, they have not disrupted social and political life thus far (Villalon 1995: 46; Quinn and Quinn 2003).[31] Smith (2013) notes that, in recent surveys conducted in Senegal, 78.3 percent of respondents stated that they have no problem with having neighbors of a different religion[32] and, surprisingly enough, 71 percent of those interviewed in this predominantly Muslim country believed that it is possible for Senegal to have a Catholic president.[33] Senegal is a religiously homogeneous country where both Islam and Christianity appear to promote political stability and the tolerance necessary for liberal democracy.

UGANDA: A PREDOMINANTLY CHRISTIAN COUNTRY WHERE RELIGION APPEARS TO HAVE HAD A MOSTLY POSITIVE EFFECT ON THE PROSPECTS FOR DEMOCRACY

Although Uganda is a predominantly Christian country where religion has not always been a stabilizing or liberalizing force, in recent decades the country's major Christian churches are thought to have mostly contributed positively to efforts to promote democracy and, to a lesser extent, respect for basic freedoms.[34] Christians make up at least 80 percent of Uganda's population of 37 million, and two Christian churches have dominated the religious landscape. These two churches are the Roman Catholic Church and the Church of Uganda (i.e., part of the Anglican Communion). However, Uganda has grown in intra-Christian diversity since 1986, when President Yoweri Museveni opened Uganda to other Christian groups.[35]

As of the year 2000, approximately 41 percent of Uganda's population was Roman Catholic and 39 percent belonged to the Church of Uganda (Barrett et al. 2001). The religious demographics have almost certainly changed since the year 2000, and there is good reason to think that Evangelical churches, especially Pentecostal or "Born-Again" churches, have grown largely at the expense of the Roman Catholic Church and the Church of Uganda. Exact figures are hard to come by, and often Pentecostals are lumped together with members of Charismatic movements that exist within the Catholic and mainline Protestant churches. According to the World Christian Database (2002), 20 percent of Ugandans were either Pentecostal or Charismatic as of the year 2000.

Although Muslims represent a sizable minority in Uganda and were estimated to make up 12 percent of the population in 2000, Islamic movements are thought to have played a negligible role in the country's politics since the fall of Idi Amin in 1979.[36] Amin was a Muslim who sought to promote Uganda as an Islamic state. Since the end of the 1970s, Uganda's Muslims have been divided by ethnic identity, issues of religious authority, and land ownership (Kokole 1995: 51). This lack of unity has impeded their political influence in the country. The growth of assertive Pentecostal Christianity that seeks to convert Muslims and the threat of the Somali-based Islamist movement *Al-Shabab* threatens to weaken the already tenuous Christian-Muslim relations in

Uganda. Unlike predominantly Muslim Senegal, where Christians and Muslims enjoy rather good relations, Christian-Muslim relations in predominantly Christian Uganda are more strained. While not nearly as contentious or violence-prone as in Nigeria, Christian-Muslim relations in Uganda can be described as painfully polite.

The Church of Uganda and the Roman Catholic Church trace their roots to 1877 and 1879, respectively. Muslims predated Christians in Uganda by about thirty years, arriving in the country from the East African coast during the 1840s. From the early 1880s and into the 1890s, missionaries representing the two Christian churches and Muslims engaged in an intense struggle for converts and to influence society and state. Religious leaders spent a great deal of energy on trying to win the favor of the *Kabaka*, or king, of the Baganda. The Buganda Kingdom (the kingdom of the Baganda people) was Uganda's largest, wealthiest, and most highly organized traditional kingdom. The Baganda traditionally called the shores of Lake Victoria and the central part of Uganda home, including the site of Uganda's current capital city, Kampala.[37] By the early decades of the twentieth century, the two Christian churches had clearly gained advantages over Islam, had experienced dramatic growth in terms of adherents, and had commenced a very heated contest with each other for more adherents and greater influence. At least when it came to political influence over the *Kabaka* and within the Buganda Kingdom, the Church of Uganda appeared to win that contest. Waliggo (1995: 208) notes that there was a clear social hierarchy in central Uganda that was largely defined along religious lines: Protestants came first, Catholics came second, Muslims were third, and those who followed African traditional religions were last.[38] Nonetheless, Roman Catholics grew in number relative to members of the Church of Uganda and never gave up attempts to win more political influence over the Buganda Kingdom and Uganda more widely.

In the run-up to Uganda's independence in 1962, it was clear that there continued to be intense competition for influence between the Catholic Church and the Church of Uganda (i.e., Protestant). Besides ethnic-based parties, Ugandans founded political parties along the Catholic-Protestant religious divide. The religious divide between Christians seemed more politically important than ethnicity, as Baganda Christians were split politically between Catholics and Protestants. Catholics formed the Democratic Party (DP), a predominantly Catholic party, and Protestants (i.e., members of the Church of Uganda) formed two parties, the *Kabaka Yekka* (i.e., "the King only") for Baganda Protestants and the Uganda People's Party (UPC) for non-Baganda Protestants. Unlike religious-based organizations in Nigeria, these organizations did not call for the integration of religious and state authority or for religious freedom to be curtailed for those who belonged to other churches or religions. Their platforms did not call for "a Catholic Uganda" or "a Protestant Uganda." In other words, these organizations did not promote mutually exclusive political theologies. Rather, these were essentially secular political parties whose leaders decreased the costs of political mobilization by organizing around ready-made religious institutions, each of which encompassed several ethnic groups, in such a way that they might help achieve electoral victory at the national level.

Between the late 1960s and the mid-1980s, competition between Catholics and Protestants was interrupted by political repression, civil war (which had little or nothing to do with religion), and the collapse of the state in most parts of the country. The repression began under Prime Minister Milton Obote and continued through the dictatorship of Idi Amin. Idi Amin came to power in a military coup in 1971 and, because Amin was a Muslim who openly stated that he intended to promote Islam, relations between Christians and Muslims worsened.[39] Kokole (1995: 53) notes that, in military and political circles, many Christians converted to Islam in order to keep their jobs. While Amin's rule first appeared to be a positive development for the status of Muslims, it became clear over time that Islam would be tarnished by his rule. As Amin's government became increasingly repressive, Muslim religious leaders tried to distance themselves from it. According to Pirouet (1980: 24–25), Uganda's Muslim religious leaders were concerned about how Amin's brutality would damage the reputation of Islam and, after his rule, would end up leading to severe discrimination against Muslims. Further, Pirouet (1980: 18) notes that ". . . being a Muslim did not necessarily guarantee anyone's safety." When it came to eliminating those considered a threat to his power, Amin did not discriminate based on religious identity. In addition to ordering the assassination of Christian leaders, Amin called for the assassination of several prominent Muslims (ibid.).[40]

Amin's harsh treatment of the Catholic Church and the Church of Uganda, as well as the brutality with which he treated Muslims who dared to question him, inadvertently resulted in Christian unity and some Christian-Muslim cooperation, aimed at finding a way to remove Amin from power. Christian and Muslim religious leaders expressed deep concern about the state of the country at various times throughout the 1970s. In the absence of political parties and respect for freedom of association, the religious leaders, particularly leaders of the Christian churches, formed the closest thing to an opposition party in Uganda. Despite their attempts to distance themselves from Amin, Muslims found life difficult in Uganda during the years following Amin's rule. Negative stereotypes and anti-Muslim feelings abounded (Kokole 1995).

Although Amin's misrule and the way he persecuted both Protestant and Catholic leaders unified Christians in a way that they had never been unified before, the old divisions between Catholics and Protestants (i.e., members of the Church of Uganda) resurfaced as the political system opened up again in 1980. The lifting of the ban on political organizations led to the return of the political parties that were divided along religious lines. The DP and the UPC were back in business. The UPC was the party of Milton Obote, who, having served as prime minister and president before Amin, returned to the presidency. Obote was at least as brutal with those who threatened his power as Amin. People in parts of the country that did not vote for the UPC and those who supported the DP were targeted for punishment and intimidation (Waliggo 1995: 114). Like Amin before him, Obote cared less about religion than about consolidating his power. Although he welcomed the support of the Church of Uganda, there was never a movement to use the law or to rewrite the constitution in order to make the Church of Uganda the *de jure* official church of Uganda or to limit the freedom of other religious bodies. However, the fact is that Obote's party, the UPC, was associated with the Church of Uganda, and the DP drew much of its support from Catholics. Catholic leaders were again frustrated. They believed that the large percentage of Catholics in

Uganda meant that the Catholic Church deserved a greater voice in government than it was getting (Ward 2005: 72).

As Yoweri Museveni's National Resistance Movement (NRM) forced Obote from power and officially formed a government in 1986, Christian leaders, particularly Catholic leaders, were jubilant (Waliggo 1995: 115). Museveni was neither a Catholic nor a member of the Church of Uganda. However, he included many Catholics from southwestern Uganda and members of the Church of Uganda from Buganda in the leadership of his movement. Upon coming to power, Museveni reached out to religious institutions, particularly the Catholic Church. One might argue that Museveni needed the Catholic and the Protestant churches. As the state fell into disrepair during the Amin and Obote years, these churches were holding Uganda together through the services they offered (e.g., spiritual, educational, and health-related services). While clergy never served in ministerial posts, several prominent Catholic and Protestant clerics did serve as advisors to Museveni.[41]

Because some Catholic and Protestant religious leaders were advisors to Museveni, particularly during the first decade of his presidency (i.e., 1986–1996), some analysts argue that the Christian churches have been slow to support the building of truly democratic institutions. Prominent religious leaders were reluctant to openly question Museveni's policies, even if privately they were concerned that he was not building democratic institutions and was not respectful of human rights.[42] For at least a while, it appears that Museveni managed to politically neutralize Uganda's major religious bodies by bringing some of their leaders into his inner circle.

Nonetheless, there is some evidence to suggest that, in recent years, Uganda's major Christian churches have become more openly critical of Museveni and more outspoken in their support of democratic institutions. The Uganda Joint Christian Council (UJCC) and the Inter-Religious Council of Uganda (IRCU) are two organizations of religious leaders that have served as vehicles for religious leaders to come together and speak out together on social, economic, political, and religious issues in the country. The UJCC, including representatives from the Church of Uganda, the Roman Catholic Church, and the much smaller Orthodox Church, was founded in 1963 and has grown stronger as relations between Christian churches have improved. The IRCU is an inter-religious organization that includes Christian and Muslim religious leaders. The Roman Catholic Church, the Church of Uganda, the Seventh-Day Adventist Church, the Orthodox Church, and the Uganda Muslim Supreme Council are members of the IRCU.

Through the UJCC and the IRCU, and as individuals, leaders of both the Catholic Church and the Church of Uganda called for an end to the "no-party" or "movement system" and a return to multiparty politics. In 2007, Museveni did act to reinstate political parties. However, that same year he also managed to convince Uganda's Parliament to amend the constitution to remove presidential term limits. Protestant and Catholic religious leaders came out strongly against the amendment to remove presidential term limits from Uganda's constitution. Emmanuel Cardinal Wamala, then Catholic Archbishop of Kampala, openly criticized this move by Museveni and the Parliament.[43] Since then, Archbishop Luke Orombi of the Church of Uganda and Catholic Archbishop Cyprian Lwanga have called for the reintroduction of term limits for the president.[44] These religious leaders have also accused Museveni of violating freedom of speech when he closed down radio stations and newspapers for publishing stories that were critical of his rule.[45] Despite their increasingly outspoken criticism of Museveni's attempt to remain in power and their efforts to promote freedom of speech, some have called into question just how supportive these religious leaders are of liberal democracy. In 2011 and 2012, the UJCC expressed its support for a very controversial "anti-gay law" that called for long prison sentences and even punishment by death for those known to engage in homosexual behavior.[46]

Although there has been little or no systematic violence between Christians and Muslims in Uganda for at least a hundred years, a relatively large percentage of each religious group tends to view each other unfavorably. According to the Pew Forum on Religion on Religion and Public Life (2010: 39), 30 percent of Ugandan Christians interviewed said that they believe all or most Muslims are hostile toward Christians. The same survey in Nigeria found that only 23 percent of Nigerian Christians said the same. Of Ugandan Muslim respondents, 20 percent indicated they believe all or most Christians are hostile toward Muslims, compared to 16 percent of Nigerian Muslims and 13 percent of Senegalese Muslims (ibid.). A higher percentage of Christians in Nigeria (53 percent) had a positive view of Muslims than in Uganda (32 percent), and a higher percentage of Muslims had a more positive view of Christians in Nigeria (63 percent) than in Uganda (37 percent). Perhaps even more strikingly, the same survey found that 50 percent of Ugandans (Christians and Muslims) were very concerned about religious extremism in their country—the exact percentage of Nigerian respondents who answered the same way (ibid.). In predominantly Christian Uganda, it is also noteworthy that a marginally higher percentage of respondents expressed fears of Christian extremism than Islamic extremism. With the rise of the Somali-based Islamist group *Al-Shabab*, and in the aftermath of *Al-Shabab*'s deadly attacks of July 2010 in Kampala and in nearby Nairobi in September 2013, there is good reason that the percentage of Ugandans who fear Islamic extremism has increased.

Despite the tensions between Christians and Muslims, the long history of competition between Catholics and Protestants, and Christian leaders' support of the proposed "anti-gay" law, Christianity appears to be mostly encouraging of a liberal democratic political culture in Uganda. There are no major Christian or Muslim religious leaders or movements that seriously call for the integration of religious and state authority. More like Senegal than Nigeria, Christianity and Islam would appear to mostly promote political stability and the prospects for liberal democracy in Uganda.

COMPARING THE EFFECTS OF
RELIGIOUS OBSERVANCE

Although it would appear that Christian and Islamic communities have had a more positive effect, or at least a less negative one, on prospects for liberal democracy in predominantly Muslim Senegal and predominantly Christian Uganda than in religiously diverse Nigeria, we have not yet considered the effects of religious observance on political actions and attitudes of individual Christians and Muslims. The Pew Forum data mentioned above are raw data that essentially compare the attitudes of Christian respondents with those of Muslim respondents. However, we cannot conclude that Christians answered a question in a certain way because of Christianity, or that Muslims answered a question in a certain way because of Islam. We do not know for sure whether and to what extent religious observance, rather than other factors such as education, income, age, and gender, influenced the ways in which respondents answered.

To get at the effect of religious observance on actions and attitudes that are conducive to liberal democracy, I conducted a survey in Nigeria, Senegal, and Uganda. That survey included mainline Christians (i.e., Roman Catholics, Anglicans, Methodists, Presbyterians), Pentecostal Christians (i.e., Assemblies of God and other independent churches associated with the "Born-Again" and "Saved" movements), and Muslims. The survey was administered face to face in the language of the respondent's choice and away from houses of worship, usually in or near the respondent's residence. The sample was purposive in that every effort was made to ensure that mainline Christians (i.e., Protestants and Catholics), Pentecostal Christians, and Muslims were represented equally and that there would be gender balance in the sample.

In order to understand whether religious observance has a systematically different effect on liberal democratic actions and attitudes across the three national settings, we need a good measure of religiosity and good indicators of liberal democratic actions and attitudes. In the previous chapter, we analyzed Afrobarometer survey data. As valuable as the Afrobarometer data are, I noted that the survey was not developed with the purpose of gauging the impact of religious observance on political actions and attitudes. Because the survey does not include many religiosity questions, it does not allow us to develop a very comprehensive measure of religious observance. For the survey featured in this chapter, I developed a relatively comprehensive measure of religious observance that combines indicators of communal religious engagement and personal religious devotion. These include (1) how frequently a person attends religious services, (2) how involved a person is in religious-based associations, (3) how frequently the individual contacts religious leaders, (4) how much an individual respects religious leaders, (5) how frequently a person prays, and (6) how important religion is in one's life. These variables are summed so that each respondent was assigned a religious observance score that ranged between a score of 22, indicating the most religiously observant, and a score of 0, indicating the least religiously observant.

The liberal democratic actions and attitudes that we are interested in explaining may be placed in two broad categories: political participation/civic engagement and tolerance/respect for freedom. Questions to determine whether a person of voting age *voted in last election, was interested in public affairs, participated in political discussions* with friends and neighbors, and *acted collectively to raise issues* with others in order to get something done in the community were used as measures of political and civic engagement. Attitudes conducive to liberal democracy include *belief in the importance of multiparty elections, tolerance of differences in opinion*, and *respect for freedom of religion.* As noted in the previous chapter, the Afrobarometer survey does not include a question on respect for religious freedom. Yet, there is reason to believe that Christian and Islamic religious communities are likely to have a profound effect on the prospects for liberal democracy, depending on whether they encourage or discourage support for religious freedom. By including such a question, this survey is likely to provide important data that will allow us to better discern the relationship between religious observance and support for liberal democracy.

The actual questions that Christian and Muslim respondents were asked in the survey are included in Table 5.1. In all cases, a higher value represents behaviors or attitudes that are more conducive to liberal democracy. It is important to note that, taken in isolation from the attitudinal indicators, any one of the participation measures is not indicative of a liberal democratic political culture. People may vote, but they may vote for those who openly promote anti-democratic values or campaign to curtail basic freedoms. Citizens may discuss politics frequently, but, in their discussions, may encourage illiberal and anti-democratic activities. They may raise an issue in order to get something done in that community, and that "something" may infringe

Table 5.1 Indicators of Liberal Democratic Values, Survey of Christians and Muslims in Nigeria, Senegal, and Uganda

Variable	Description
Voting	In the most recent election did you vote: (0 = no, 1 = yes)
Interested in politics	How interested are you in public affairs (0 = not interested, 1 = somewhat interested, 2 = very interested)
Raise an issue	How often do you get together with others to raise an issue. (0 = never, 1 = would do it if had the chance, 2 = once or twice, 3 = several times, 4 = often)
Discuss politics	How often do you discuss politics with friends or neighbors (0 = never, 1 = would do it if had the chance, 2 = once or twice, 3 = several times, 4 = often)
Accept Differences	A: In order to make decision in our community, we should talk until everyone agrees: B: Since we will never agree, we must learn to accept differences of opinion 1 = Agree very strongly with A, 2 = Agree with A, 3 = Agree with B, 4 = Agree very strongly with B
Support Multiparty Politics	A: Political parties create division and confusion in Nigeria B: Many political parties are needed 1 = Agree very strongly with A, 2 = Agree with A, 3 = Agree with B, 4 = Agree very strongly with B
Support Religious Liberty	Every religion and church should be allowed to promote its beliefs and values:1 = strongly disapprove, 2 = disapprove, 3 = neither approve or disapprove, 4 = approve, 5 = strongly approve.

on the rights of individuals or minority groups. Three attitudinal variables, "acceptance of differences," "support for democracy," and "support for religious freedom," may be considered stand-alone variables that even by themselves indicate support for democracy or liberal values. However, taken together with the "participation" measures, like voting, political interest, political discussions, and raising an issue in public to get something done in the community, they are much stronger indicators of a liberal democratic political culture. I have decided not to combine these components into one variable because that would mask the various ways in which religious observance may affect different components of a liberal democratic political culture. By keeping them separate, we are better able to assess whether religious observance has a positive or negative effect (or neither) on all, some, or none of the components of a liberal democratic political culture in any one of the three countries under consideration.

Because we are interested in how religious observance affected actions and attitudes of Christians and Muslims in each of the three national contexts, I allow the religious observance score to vary by religious identity and country. For example, I estimate the marginal effects of religious observance for Muslims in Senegal, Uganda, and Nigeria. I do the same for mainline Christians and Pentecostal Christians as well, although Pentecostals are not included in Senegal since we could not find enough Pentecostals to survey in that country. In other words, we assess the effect of religious observance on liberal democratic ideals *while allowing for impact to vary by religious affiliation and national context.* The full results of probit and ordered-probit analyses can be found in Appendix A. In the following sections I describe what we find and illustrate the results for voting, political discussions, and respect for religious liberty.

While the results suggest that the national context is not the only factor that mattered, and that religious observance was positively related with some components of a liberal democratic political culture in the religiously homogeneous countries (e.g., voting among Muslims and mainline Christians in Senegal and support for religious liberty among mainline Christians in Senegal), religious observance tended to have a positive effect, rather than a negative effect, on actions and attitudes conducive to liberal democracy in Nigeria. Further, the positive effect of religious observance tended to include members of all three religious groups in Nigeria. Religious observance was having a much more positive effect on the indicators of a liberal democratic political culture in Nigeria than in Uganda. Further, with respect to certain components of a liberal democratic political culture, such as political interest, political discussions, and respect for religious liberty, religious observance was also having a more positive effect in Nigeria than in Senegal.

In Figure 5.1, we see the results with regard to voting. Each bar represents the marginal effect of religious observance on the likelihood that one reports to have voted in the most recent general election for each religious grouping (i.e., Muslims, mainline Christians, and Pentecostal Christians) in each of the three countries (i.e., Nigeria, Senegal, and Uganda). Through each bar, there is a black line. This black line indicates the standard error for each marginal effect. Where the black line is shorter than the bar, the marginal effect is statistically significant. The marginal effect is insignificant

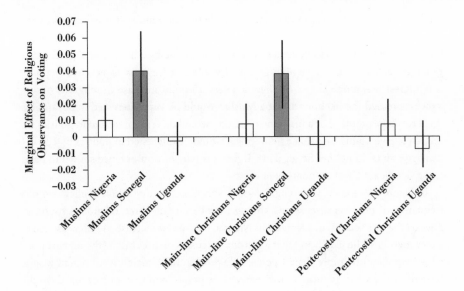

Figure 5.1 Religious Observance and Voting in Nigeria, Senegal, and Uganda

wherever the black line is as long as or longer than the bar. I indicate the most significant marginal effects by shading the bars. So, shaded bars indicate where and among whom (i.e., which religious group) religious observance has the most significantly positive effect on the given component of a liberal democratic political culture.

We see that religious observance had a more positive effect on the likelihood that Muslims and mainline Christians would have voted in Senegal than in Nigeria and Uganda. Every 10-point increase in religious observance score increased the likelihood that a Muslim in Senegal would have voted by a whopping 41 percentage points. The same increase in religious observance in Nigeria increased the likelihood that a Muslim would have voted by 11 percentage points. In Uganda, religious observance had no discernible impact on the likelihood that a Muslim would have voted. Moving to the right on the graph, we see the results pertaining to mainline Christians. We see that only in Senegal did religious observance have a positive effect on voting among mainline Christians. Every 10-point increase in religious observance increased the likelihood that a mainline Christian voted by 35 percentage points. Among Pentecostals, religious observance had no discernible effect on the likelihood of having voted in Nigeria or Uganda. Again, Senegal is excluded because Pentecostals were not surveyed there. In sum, religious observance was clearly having the most profoundly positive effect on voting in Senegal at the time of the survey than in Nigeria and Uganda.

However, when it comes to types of political engagement other than voting, we find a different story. For other measures of political engagement—such as raising an issue in public to get something done in the community, political interest, and the frequency of political discussions with family, friends, and neighbors—religious observance tended to have a more positive effect in Nigeria than in Senegal and Uganda. Only in Nigeria did religious observance increase the likelihood that one would have raised an issue in public to get something done in the community. The effect was small, but positive. In Nigeria, every 10-point increase in religious observance increased the likelihood that one would have raised an issue in public by a little over 1 percentage point for each of the three religious groups. The effect of religious observance on political interest was much larger. In Nigeria, every 10-point increase in religious observance increased the likelihood that a Muslim would be very interested in politics by 23 percentage points, that a mainline Christian would be very interested in politics by 15 percentage points, and that a Pentecostal would be interested in politics by 12 percentage points. In neither Senegal nor Uganda is religious observance shown to have had a significant effect on political interest.

In Figure 5.2, we see that religious observance had a more positive effect on the frequency of political discussions among members of all three religious groups in Nigeria than in Senegal or Uganda. In Nigeria, a 10-point increase in religious observance increased the likelihood that a Muslim discusses politics often (the highest possible frequency) by more than 4 percentage points, that a mainline Christian would have done the same by more than 5 percentage points, and that a Pentecostal would have done so by 3 percentage points. Religious observance had a positive effect on the frequency of political discussions in Senegal, but the effect was not statistically significant. In Uganda, religious observance had no effect on the frequency of political discussions regardless of the religious group. Of course, one can be politically engaged without being supportive of democracy or social tolerance. What about the effect of religious observance on these components of a liberal democratic political culture?

We find that religious observance had little or no effect on acceptance of differences of opinion or on support for democracy in any one of the three countries. Only in Nigeria did religious observance have a positive effect on acceptance of differences

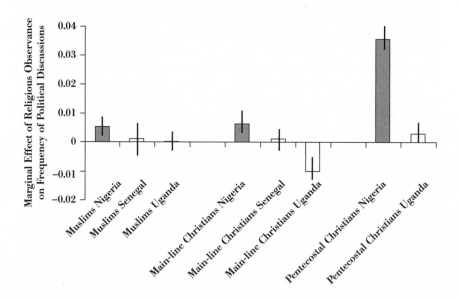

Figure 5.2 Religious Observance and Political Discussions in Nigeria, Senegal, and Uganda

among Muslims, and the effect was small. For every 10-unit increase in religious observance, the likelihood that a Muslim in Nigeria accepted differences of opinion to the highest possible level increased by 1 percentage point. In Uganda, religious observance had a slightly negative effect on acceptance of differences among Pentecostals. Among Pentecostals in Uganda, acceptance of differences of opinion decreased by 1 percentage point for every 10-unit increase in religious observance. When it comes to support for democracy, only among Nigeria's mainline Christians did religious observance have a positive effect. Yet, that effect was very small. For every 10-point increase in the religious observance score, the likelihood that a mainline Christian in Nigeria would have expressed the highest possible support for democracy increased by less than 2 percentage points.

Despite the inter-religious violence that has taken place in Nigeria, only in Nigeria did religious observance have a positive effect on support for religious liberty among members of all three religious groupings, Muslims, mainline Christians, and Pentecostals. Figure 5.3 illustrates the results. For every 10-unit increase in religious observance, the probability that a Muslim in Nigeria expressed the highest possible support for religious liberty increased by 2.5 percentage points. The same unit increase in religious observance had no impact on the probability that a Muslim would have done the same in Senegal or Uganda. While religious observance had a larger marginal effect on respect for religious liberty among mainline Christians in Senegal than in Nigeria, the difference was slight. In Nigeria, too, religious observance had a significant and positive effect on respect for religious liberty among mainline Christians. Every 10-unit increase in the religious observance score increased respect for religious liberty among mainline Christians in Nigeria by more than 4 percentage points and in Senegal by 5 percentage points. Only in Nigeria did religious observance increase the

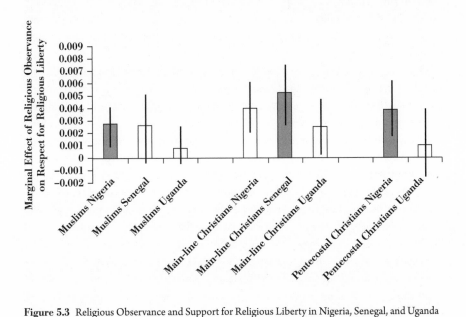

Figure 5.3 Religious Observance and Support for Religious Liberty in Nigeria, Senegal, and Uganda

probability that a Pentecostal Christian expressed the highest level of support for religious liberty, a 3.8 percentage-point increase in probability for every 10-unit increase in religious observance.

MAKING SENSE OF THE RESULTS

Although one might expect to find religious observance to have a more positive effect on liberal democratic political culture in Senegal and Uganda than in Nigeria, we find just the opposite. With the exception of voting, upon which religious observance has the most positive effect in Senegal, religious observance had, at the time of the survey, a more positive effect on interest in politics, raising an issue in public to get something done in the community, frequency of political discussions, and support for religious liberty in Nigeria than in Senegal and Uganda. This was largely true among members of all three religious groupings: Muslims, mainline Christians, and Pentecostals. In none of the three countries do we find religious observance having had an effect in one way or another on acceptance of differences of opinion and support for democracy.

The results with regard to voting are puzzling, especially in light of our analysis of Afrobarometer survey data in the previous chapter. In the previous chapter, we found that religious observance had a more positive effect on voting in countries that have a higher number of religions. However, in this chapter we find religious observance had the most positive effect on voting in Senegal, the country with the lowest number of religions. Perhaps there is something about the *maraboutic* system and the strength of the brotherhoods that explains the positive relationship between religious observance and voting in Senegal. *Marabouts* may be especially effective at getting their followers to vote. It is surprising that religious observance would not be having a more positive effect on voting in Nigeria, where competition between religious groups is intense and expected to drive up religiously motivated voter turnout. The results suggest that religious diversity is not the only factor that might affect the impact that religious observance has on voting.

Of course, voting is just one measure of political engagement. The results do suggest that religious observance had a more positive impact on forms of political engagement other than voting in Nigeria than in Senegal and Uganda. These forms of political engagement are political interest, the frequency of political discussions, and getting together to raise an issue in public to get something done in the community. Although voting in countries like Senegal, Nigeria, and Uganda is often time-consuming since it usually entails locating the correct polling station and waiting in long lines, it is important to recognize that there are forms of political participation that are more demanding than voting. Getting together with others to raising an issue in public typically requires more time, more effort, and more courage than voting. It is an action that can be dangerous, and there may be the possibility of physical harm, depending on the sensitivity of the issue raised. It is worth noting that religious observance had a more positive effect on raising an issue in public and the other two measures of political engagement, political interest and the frequency of political discussions, in Nigeria than in Senegal and Uganda.

Although we find that religious observance was positively related to support for democracy in countries with a higher number of effective religious groups when we analyzed Afrobarometer data in the previous chapter, we find little or no relationship between religious observance and support for democracy or acceptances of differences of opinion in the three countries under study in this chapter. Why might this be the case? I suspect that our analysis of the aggregated Afrobarometer data, pooled from many countries, masks differences between individual countries. This reveals the value of deeper analysis of individual countries and the pitfalls of analyzing pooled national-level data.

When it comes to the effect of religious observance on respect for religious freedom, there are important differences between Nigeria, Senegal, and Uganda. Surprisingly, religious observance had the most positive effect on respect for religious liberty in Nigeria. This positive relationship held true for Muslims, mainline Christians, and Pentecostal Christians. With the exception of mainline Christians in Senegal, among whom religious observance had a positive effect on respect for religious liberty, religious observance did not have a significant effect on respect for religious liberty in the other two countries. The results suggest that Christian and Muslim religious communities in Nigeria were actually encouraging respect for religious pluralism and were doing so more effectively than Christian and Muslim communities in Senegal and Uganda.

Although we find that religious observance tended to have a more positive effect on key components of a liberal democratic political culture in Nigeria than in Senegal and Uganda, we cannot say that we know why that was the case. We do not know whether religious observance was having a more positive effect on components of a liberal democratic political culture in Nigeria because of Nigeria's religious diversity, as the theory I put forward in Chapter 2 proposes, or because of other factors that distinguish these three countries. In order to discover whether religious diversity explains the different effects that religious observance has on components of liberal democratic political culture, we need to connect the effects of religious observance to the political theologies promoted by religious leaders. Further, we need to know whether the religious leaders are taking the religious landscape into account when deciding what types of political theologies to promote. We need religious leaders and ordinary members of the religious communities they lead to provide reasons for their own behaviors and attitudes.

SUMMARY

Although Nigeria's religious diversity appears to diminish religious-based support for liberal democracy, appearances are deceiving. There can be no doubt that religious extremism has been more of a problem in Nigeria than in Senegal and Uganda over the past several decades. However, the media headlines that feature religiously inspired intolerance and deadly violence between Christians and Muslims in Nigeria are presenting one side of the story. The results that I report in this chapter suggest that religious observance among Christians and Muslims was, at the time of the survey, having a more benign effect on key components of a liberal democratic political culture in Nigeria than in Senegal and Uganda.

We have answered the "what" question at a particular point in time (the time the survey was conducted, 2006–2007) across three countries: *What* effect does religious observance have on actions and attitudes conducive to liberal democracy in Nigeria as compared to Senegal and Uganda? We find that religious observance tended to have a more positive effect on some key components of a liberal democracy in Nigeria than in Senegal and a much more positive effect than in Uganda among Muslims and Christians. However, we have not answered the "why" question: *Why* did religious observance have a more positive effect on key components of a liberal democratic political culture in Nigeria than in Senegal and Uganda?

In the next chapter, I take a look at the curious case of Nigeria and attempt to get closer to an answer to both the "what" and the "why" questions. If religious diversity is the factor that sets Nigeria apart from the other two countries and explains why religious observance had a more positive impact on key components of a liberal democratic political culture, we would expect to find that this relationship held up across settings *within* Nigeria. We would expect to find that religious observance had a more positive impact on political participation, support for democracy, and respect for religious liberty in those settings of Nigeria that have been religiously diverse for the longest period of time than in those that have only recently become religiously diverse, as well as in those that are religiously homogeneous. Further, we need to supplement mass survey data with in-depth interviews and observations that help us to understand why religious leaders and members of the religious communities have made their decisions to engage in certain political behaviors and adopt certain political attitudes. The next chapter is devoted to doing just that.

6

The Curious Case of Nigeria

When it comes to explaining how religious observance affects key components of a liberal democratic political culture, we find evidence to suggest that country location has mattered a great deal. Religious leaders in sub-Saharan Africa tended to be more openly supportive of the pro-democracy movements of the 1980s and 1990s in those countries of the region that were the most religiously diverse. It is important to note that religious leaders in some religiously homogenous countries, such as some Catholic leaders in heavily Catholic Zaire/Democratic Republic of Congo, were outspoken in their support for democratic reforms during the 1980s and 1990s. However, we found that religious leaders were typically more vocal in their support for democratic change in religiously diverse countries than in religiously homogeneous countries. In using survey data to compare the effects of religious observance on civic engagement and religious tolerance across Nigeria, Senegal, and Uganda, we find that national setting mattered at least as much, if not more, than whether a religious community was Christian or Islamic, mainline Christian or Pentecostal Christian. Christian and Islamic religious communities were having, at the time of the survey, a more positive effect on the frequency of political discussions and respect for religious freedom in religiously diverse Nigeria than in predominantly Muslim Senegal and predominantly Christian Uganda.

However, we have yet to answer the "why" question. If religious leaders tended to be more supportive of pro-democracy movements in sub-Saharan Africa's most religiously diverse countries, we do not know for certain why this was the case. We cannot yet say whether religious observance was having a more positive effect on key components of a liberal democratic political culture in Nigeria than in Senegal and Uganda because of Nigeria's religious diversity or other factors that distinguish Nigeria from the other two countries. While we have answered the "what" question (i.e., What effect was religious observance having on political actions and attitudes of Christians and Muslims across Nigeria, Senegal, and Uganda?), we have not yet answered the "why" question (i.e., Why did religious observance have a more positive effect on actions and attitudes conducive to liberal democracy in Nigeria than in Senegal and Uganda?). Does Nigeria's religious diversity explain why religious observance had a more positive effect on civic engagement and religious tolerance there than in Senegal and Uganda, or are there other factors that distinguish Nigeria from the other two countries that explain why religious observance had a more positive effect civic engagement and religious tolerance in Nigeria?

One way to address the "why" question and to assess whether religious diversity is the key to explaining why religious observance had a more positive effect on civic engagement and religious tolerance in Nigeria than the other two countries is to dig more deeply into the case of Nigeria. If religious diversity explains why religious observance had a more positive effect on certain key components of a liberal democratic political culture in Nigeria than in Senegal and Uganda, we should find that religious observance had a more positive effect on liberal democratic political culture in Nigeria's more religiously diverse local settings than in the country's more religiously homogeneous local settings. If the theory I presented back in Chapter 2 is right, we should find that religious observance was having a more positive effect on political actions and attitudes that are conducive to liberal democracy in religiously diverse settings because religious leaders were more encouraging of such actions and attitudes in these settings. Further, we should find that religious leaders encouraged such actions and attitudes because they decided that doing so was the best way to accomplish their goals for their religious institutions in settings that, in their view, would be religiously diverse for the foreseeable future.[1]

In this chapter, I compare the impact of Nigeria's Christian and Islamic religious communities on key components of a liberal democratic political culture at the municipal level. The comparison at the municipal level focuses on two cities with minimal Christian-Muslim diversity (i.e., inter-religious diversity) and two municipal settings

Figure 6.1 Map of Religions in Nigeria and Sites of Survey

Christianity, Islam, and Liberal Democracy

with a great deal of inter-religious diversity. These cities are predominantly Muslim Kano, predominantly Christian Enugu, highly diverse Ibadan, and moderately diverse Jos. The cities where we conducted the survey are located on the map in Figure 6.1, which also shows which states have enshrined the *Shari'ah*, Islamic religious law, in their state constitutions, and which of Nigeria's thirty-six states are predominantly Muslim (where Muslims make up more than 75 percent of the population), predominantly Christian (where Christians make up more than 75 percent of the population), and religiously diverse (where neither Christians nor Muslims make up more than 60 percent of the population). As the map indicates, Kano is in the north-central part of Nigeria, Enugu in the southeast, Ibadan in the southwest, and Jos in the Middle Belt. I find that in the two settings with little inter-religious diversity, predominantly Christian Enugu and predominantly Muslim Kano, Christian and Islamic religious communities promoted voting and political interest, but not respect for religious liberty. In one of the religiously diverse settings, Jos, Christian and Islamic religious communities promoted more demanding forms of political activism (i.e., more demanding than voting), but discouraged support for religious liberty. In Ibadan, the other religiously diverse setting included in the comparison, Christian and Islamic religious communities had neither a positive nor a negative impact on the indicators of political participation included in the study, but a very positive effect on support for religious liberty.

When taken together with the results of interviews and narrative accounts of events over the last several decades, the findings reported in this chapter suggest that two inter-related factors are crucially important for explaining the impact of Christian and Islamic religious communities on key components of a liberal democratic political culture in Nigeria: (1) the length of time a setting has been religiously diverse, and (2) the degree to which a setting is religiously integrated. The city of Ibadan has included equally large Christian and Muslim communities since the late nineteenth century, and religious identities have come to cut across ethnic identities and even extended families. There is evidence to indicate that religiously inspired support for liberal democratic ideals in Ibadan is the result of a learning process that has taken place over time. Ibadan's Christian and Muslim religious leaders learned over time that it would be in the best interest of their religious communities to "live and let live" and to promote state neutrality in religious affairs. By promoting state neutrality in religious affairs, religious leaders allowed for greater Christian-Muslim integration.[2] In turn, this integration created a virtuous cycle. The mixing and mingling of religious groups decreased the likelihood that future religious leaders would promote intolerance or special privileges for their religious communities at the expense of others. This is because Christian religious leaders who might try to promote religious dominance, not to mention politicians who might play the religion card to gain power, would get no support from Christians who had Muslim neighbors, friends, schoolmates, coworkers, and family members. Muslim religious leaders and politicians who might try to do the same would also get nowhere with Muslims who had Christian neighbors, friends, schoolmates, and coworkers.

Interviews with religious leaders and ordinary Christians and Muslims in religiously diverse Jos suggest that religious observance has not had the same kind of positive effect on religious tolerance in that city as in the religiously diverse city of Ibadan because Christians and Muslims in Jos have been largely segregated from each other in a way that they have not been in Ibadan. This is in part due to a rapid increase in the Muslim population of Jos and other areas of Plateau State. While there has been a small but significant Muslim population in Jos since the colonial era, economic desperation in the north, aggravated by worsening environmental conditions over the last few decades, has driven tens of thousands of Muslims south to Jos, Plateau State, and other parts of Nigeria's Middle Belt (Griswold 2010; Paden 2012). The influx of Muslims has transformed Jos from a predominantly Christian city into a city that has a Christian majority and a very sizable and fast-growing Muslim minority.[3] Alarmed that they are losing influence over the city and afraid that Muslims will soon outnumber Christians in the area, Christian leaders have reacted by calling on Christians to defend themselves against what they consider to be efforts to Islamize Jos.[4] In this city, where religious demographics have rapidly shifted, Christians and Muslims are divided not only by religion but by ethnicity and indigene/settler status, with the vast majority of Christians belonging to ethnic groups considered to be indigenous to Jos, with the rights that come along with that status, and most Muslims belonging to ethnic groups considered to be latecomers or settlers, generally excluded from land ownership and other rights. As a result, Christians and Muslims have remained separated, occupying different areas of the city. For example, Jos North Local Government Authority (LGA) has been predominantly Muslim, and Jos South LGA predominantly Christian. Thus, religiously diverse Jos, unlike religiously diverse Ibadan, has been a highly segregated city—a city of religiously homogeneous blocs and fault lines, along which there have been repeated episodes of deadly violence. Evidence presented in this chapter suggests that religious observance did not have a positive effect on religious tolerance in Jos during the time of our survey largely because of Jos's religious segregation and the ways in which religion, ethnicity, and indigene/settler status overlapped and reinforced each other in the city, not because of its religious diversity. Religious fault lines, the existence of religiously homogeneous zones, not religious diversity, have been Jos's problem. The existence of religiously homogeneous zones is what distinguishes religiously diverse Jos from religiously diverse Ibadan and explains why religious communities in Jos have been less effective than religious communities in Ibadan at encouraging pro-freedom political theologies that espouse respect for religious liberty.

While focused on the case of Nigeria and survey research conducted at a particular point in time (2006), the results have far-reaching implications in that they reveal how national-level analysis, which looks at a country as a whole without taking into account the variation across settings within a country and the effects of religious observance on the attitudes and behaviors of individual Christians and Muslims, can be very misleading. If we simply look at the case of Nigeria as a whole and from a distance, we would likely assert, as others have, that religious diversity has been an obstacle to political stability, let alone liberal democracy. However, when we look within Nigeria we find variation across settings that does not support this assertion. Religious observance was having, at the time of the survey, a more positive effect on support for key liberal democratic ideals in the most religiously diverse of the four settings included in our study. Given our findings, we cannot very well conclude that religious diversity is itself an obstacle to a liberal democratic political culture. In fact, the evidence suggests that religious diversity, if followed by religious integration, increases the likelihood that Christian and Islamic religious communities promote religious tolerance, if not civic engagement. Such religiously based support for religious tolerance is crucially important for the future of liberal democracy in Nigeria.[5]

In the next section of this chapter, I call attention to the inter-religious violence that has occurred in Nigeria and to the fact that this violence has not been equally distributed across the country. Such violence has been highly localized. This indicates that there has been sub-national variation in religious-based support for a liberal democratic political culture and in the strength of local religious networks to effectively fight off attempts to promote less tolerant brands of Islam or Christianity. I go on to describe the survey that I developed to assess how variation in religious diversity at sub-national level affects the impact of religious observance on political actions and attitudes. I then present the results and discuss the findings in light of events and statements made by Nigeria's religious leaders in parts of the country where the survey was conducted. In the following section, I consider whether and how events that have occurred since the time of the survey (2006) have affected the impact of religious communities on political culture. I discern whether there is evidence that Christian and Islamic religious communities have continued to be more conducive to a liberal democratic political culture in religiously diverse locations than in religiously homogeneous locations. I do this by analyzing the results of the Afrobarometer survey conducted in Nigeria in 2012 and by engaging in qualitative comparative assessment of events that have occurred and statements that have been made by religious leaders across the four settings. The results suggest that, since 2006, religious leaders continued to promote political theologies that are more supportive of liberal democracy in more religiously diverse and integrated settings than in more homogeneous or segregated settings. They also suggest that religious observance continued to have a more positive effect on certain indicators of a liberal democratic political culture among Christians and Muslims in religious diverse locations than in those that are religiously homogeneous or segregated.

EVIDENCE OF SUB-NATIONAL VARIATION IN RELIGIOUS-BASED SUPPORT FOR LIBERAL DEMOCRACY

As indicated in the previous chapter, there has been a great deal of religious violence in Nigeria since 1980. Nigeria is the proverbial "poster child" for the argument that religious diversity is bad for political stability, let alone liberal democracy. Diversity is thought to prompt religious competition and heighten religious passions as people feel the need to defend their deeply held beliefs about God and to promote a society that upholds norms based on those beliefs. This kind of competition, along with the passions that accompany it, is thought to fuel the violence within and between

Christian and Islamic religious communities that we have seen in Nigeria over the past several decades. While violence is not the focus of this book, violence between religious communities indicates a lack of tolerance. Tolerance, including religious tolerance, is an important component of a liberal democratic political culture. In Nigeria, some Christians and Muslims have clearly been intolerant of each other and have promoted mutually exclusive visions of state and society. Some Muslims envision an Islamic state, at least where Muslims make up the vast majority of the population, and some Christians want a privileged place for Christianity in Nigeria. Mutually exclusive political theologies have contributed to violent clashes that have, since the early 1980s, claimed tens of thousands of lives (Paden 2005: 52; Quinn and Quinn 2003: 50). More recently, the deadly attacks by religious extremist groups like *Boko Haram* have increased fears and suspicions within the Islamic community and between Christians and Muslims (Campbell 2013). Even if most Nigerians are not religious extremists, religious diversity and the competition that it engenders seem to have prompted religious extremism that threatens the integrity of the Nigerian state and diminishes the prospects for liberal democracy.

However, when we look within Nigeria, we find that deadly inter-religious violence has not been equally distributed across the country. Without going into detail about each and every incident of inter-religious violence, let us consider the states where

Figure 6.2 Sites of Inter-Religious Violence in Nigeria

the violence has taken place. Of the 40 most significant episodes of Christian-Muslim violence that occurred between 1980 and 2006, almost two-thirds (i.e., 26 discreet episodes) occurred in the three states of Kaduna, Kano, and Plateau. This is shown in Figure 6.2. Between 2001 and 2006, there has been more inter-religious violence (i.e., 11 episodes) in Plateau State than in any other state. The Nigerian government issued a report in 2004 in which it estimated that 54,000 people died in inter-communal violence in Plateau State between 1999 and 2004 alone (Paden 2005: 52). [6]

While there have been religious leaders who have tried to promote tolerance and accommodation in Plateau, Kano, and Kaduna states, all too often their voices have not been heard over those who preach an illiberal brand of Islam or Christianity.[7] Imo (2008) observes that more than a few prominent Christian leaders in northern Nigeria and Nigeria's Middle Belt have interpreted scripture in ways that condone violence in defense of one's self and one's faith. One such religious leader is the Anglican bishop of Kaduna, the Right Reverend Ogboyemi. After what he considered to be Muslim attacks on innocent Christians, the Bishop is reported to have said that Christians have no cheeks left to turn (Imo 2008: 61). Ogboyemi voiced support for the position of the Evangelical bishop of Kano, the Right Reverend Nyam, who encouraged members of his flock to fight Muslims in self-defense. According to Imo (2008: 62), the Reverend David Laje, the head of the Church of the Good News of Jos, a member church of the Evangelical Church of West Africa (ECWA), told him, "Ordinarily I enjoin patience with Muslims. But . . . God speaks to us according to circumstances. At some point, God will want you to retaliate . . . for His name's sake."

At least three highly respected experts on Nigeria have pointed out that it is no accident that the most tolerant and peaceful settings of Nigeria are religiously diverse settings, and have suggested that the political culture that has prevailed in southwestern Nigeria is largely the result of the religious diversity that has prevailed for so long there. David Laitin (1986: 9) argues, "The Christian-Muslim divide in Yorubaland of southwestern Nigeria, far from fanning the flames of religious conflict, actually built the foundation for compromise." [8] Although religious diversity in Yorubaland might seem likely to generate high levels of conflict, John Paden (2005: 109) argues that the situation is closer to a "pax Yoruba" that promotes accommodation between Christian and Muslim groups. Toyin Falola (1998: 171) notes that the competition between Christians and Muslims for converts in the southwest has been intense, but "it is unlikely that violence of the scale seen in the north will occur in the southwest. . . leaders of both religions always emphasize accommodation."

According to Paden (2005: 100), Yoruba Muslim and Christian leaders have worked to moderate both religious and political matters. These leaders refer to themselves as "fathers of all" and often play a key role in conflict mediation and resolution. In Ibadan, the capital of Oyo State, in the heart of Yorubaland, Muslim and Christian leaders have stressed the need for tolerance, peace, and patience (Paden 2005: 102). Christian leaders are as likely to quote the Koran as the Bible, and Muslim leaders are as likely to quote the Bible as the Koran, notes Paden (2005: 102). At times, they have even attempted to play a role in Christian-Muslim reconciliation in other parts of the country. The place of the *Shari'ah* religious law has not been the major issue in south-western states that it has in the northern states and Middle Belt states.

The question is, why have religious leaders in southwestern Nigeria encouraged accommodation and compromise across the religious divide, while religious leaders in the Middle Belt and the north of Nigeria been less willing to or able to effectively encourage such accommodation and compromise? Perhaps what sets southwestern Nigeria apart from the north and the Middle Belt is shared Yoruba ethnic identity. After all, religious identity cuts across ethnic identity in much of southwestern Nigeria so that there is an almost equal number of Christians and Muslims among the Yoruba. In much of the north and the Middle Belt, religious identities tend to overlap with and reinforce ethnic identities. Have the people of southwestern Nigeria been any wealth-ier and better educated than people in other parts of the country, and, if so, might this explain why they have been more religiously tolerant? Or, have Christian and Muslim leaders been more encouraging of tolerance in southwestern Nigeria because the southwest has been more religiously diverse and integrated than other parts of the country?

Despite the cross-national evidence presented in Chapter 5 showing religious observance having a more positive effect on key components of a liberal democratic political culture in Nigeria than in Senegal and Uganda, there is reason to doubt that Nigeria's religious diversity is the reason. After all, some of Nigeria's religiously diverse settings, such as Plateau and Kaduna states, have been the sites of some of the most recurring episodes of deadly inter-religious violence.[9] In these settings, it appears that religious leaders have either been unwilling or unable to effectively promote the reli-gious tolerance necessary for liberal democracy. However, we have yet to explore the effect that religious observance has had in such settings. This is the task at hand: to take a closer look at the curious case of Nigeria.

THE IMPACT OF CHRISTIANITY AND ISLAM ON POLITICAL CULTURE IN NIGERIA

As described in the previous chapter, I conducted a survey in Nigeria, Senegal, and Uganda in order to discover whether national context affects the impact that Christian and Islamic religious communities have on components of a liberal democratic politi-cal culture. In Nigeria, the survey included 1,200 individuals among whom there were mainline Christians (i.e., Roman Catholics, Anglicans, Methodists, Presbyterians), Pentecostal Christians (i.e., Assemblies of God and other independent churches associated with the "Born-Again" and "Saved" movements), and Muslims. The survey was conducted in four cities during November 2006: predominantly Muslim Kano (98 percent Muslim), predominantly Christian Enugu (95 percent Christian), mod-erately diverse Jos (61 percent Christian and 37 percent Muslim), and highly diverse Ibadan (50 percent Christian and 49 percent Muslim).[10] The survey was adminis-tered face to face in the language of the respondent's choice and away from houses of worship, usually in or near the respondent's residence. Within each religious group (i.e., mainline Christian, Pentecostal, Islamic), the sample was random. Within each location, an equal number (i.e., 100) of Muslims, mainline Christians, and Pentecostal Christians were surveyed.

As described in Chapter 5, I used a measure of religious observance that combines indicators of communal engagement and personal devotion. These include (1) how frequently a person attends religious services, (2) how involved a person is in religious-based associations, (3) how frequently the individual contacts religious leaders, (4) how much an individual respects religious leaders, (5) how frequently a person prays, and (6) how important religion is in one's life. Each of these variables were summed so that each respondent was assigned a religious observance score that ranged between a score of 22, indicating the most religiously involved, and a score of 0, indicating the least religiously involved.

The liberal democratic ideals that we are interested in explaining include whether a person of voting age *voted in the last election, was interested in public affairs, participated in political discussions* with friends and neighbors, and *acted collectively to raise issues* with others in order to get something done in the community. These are all actions that represent components of a liberal democratic political culture if accompanied by

Table 6.1 Indicators of Liberal Democratic Ideals

Variable	Description
Voting	In the most recent election did you vote? (0 = no, 1 = yes)
Interested in Politics	How interested are you in public affairs? (0 = not interested, 2 = somewhat interested, 3 = very interested)
Discuss politics	How often do you discuss politics with friends or neighbors? (0 = never, 1 = would do it if had the chance, 2 = once or twice, 3 = several times, 4 = often)
Act Collectively to Raise Issue	How often have you got together with others to raise an issue to get something done in community? (0 = never, 1 = would do it if had the chance, 2 = once or twice, 3 = several times, 4 = often)
Accept Differences	A: In order to make decision in our community, we should talk until everyone agrees B: Since we will never agree, we must learn to accept differences of opinion (1 = Agree very strongly with A, 2 = Agree with A, 3 = Agree with B, 4 = Agree very strongly with B)
Support Multiparty Politics	A: Political parties create division and confusion in Nigeria B: Many political parties are needed (1 = Agree very strongly with A, 2 = Agree with A, 3 = Agree with B, 4 = Agree very strongly with B)
Support Religious Liberty	Every religion and church should be allowed to promote its beliefs and values (1 = strongly disapprove, 2 = disapprove, 3 = neither approve nor disapprove, 4 = approve, 5 = strongly approve)

tolerance for differences and respect for basic rights. Attitudes conducive to liberal democracy include *belief in the importance of multiparty elections, tolerance of differences in opinion,* and *respect for freedom of religion.* The actual questions that Christian and Muslim respondents were asked in the survey are included in Table 6.1. In all cases, a higher value represents behaviors or attitudes that are more conducive to liberal democracy.

Before assessing the effects of religious observance, let us take a look at attitudes and actions across the four municipal locations. We find that actions and attitudes conducive to liberal democracy were as common or more common in predominantly

Table 6.2 Descriptive Statistics by Location, Sample Means (Standard Deviations)

Variable	Kano (Predominately Muslim)	Enugu (Predominately Christian)	Jos (Religiously Diverse)	Ibadan (Religiously Diverse)
Voting	0.75 (0.43)	0.42 (0.49)	0.72 (0.45)	0.66 (0.48)
Interested in Politics	1.00 (0.78)	1.13 (0.79)	0.95 (0.78)	0.69 (0.70)
Discuss Politics	2.21 (1.31)	2.02 (1.21)	2.34 (1.25)	1.97 (1.42)
Act Collectively to Raise Issue	1.28 (1.10)	1.96 (1.19)	1.55 (1.96)	1.08 (1.20)
Accept Differences	2.38 (1.15)	2.91 (0.96)	2.86 (1.18)	2.24 (1.08)
Support Multiparty Politics	2.51 (1.04)	2.32 (1.00)	2.27 (1.18)	2.23 (1.14)
Support Religious Liberty	4.24 (0.81)	3.88 (0.90)	4.07 (1.28)	3.94 (1.15)
Age in Years	28.0 (8.3)	28.5 (10.8)	27.6 (9.3)	31.1 (10.9)
Income in 1,000s of Naira	12.0 (13.4)	29.1 (34.8)	10.8 (12.2)	14.2 (11.3)
Religious Observance Index	17.1 (2.6)	16.9 (3.2)	16.9 (3.1)	14.9 (4.8)
Observations	300	300	300	300

Christian Enugu and predominantly Muslim Kano as in religiously diverse Ibadan and Jos. As Table 6.2 shows, there was very little difference in terms of the mean scores for the key dependent variables. On average, voter turnout and political discussions were highest in the predominantly Muslim location of Kano and lowest in the largely Christian location of Enugu. Because we surveyed an equal number of Muslims, mainline Christians, and Pentecostal Christians in each city, the sample means hold constant the mix of religions across these cities and only reflect differences in the intensity of preferences. Interest in politics tended to be highest in Enugu and lowest in religiously diverse settings of Ibadan and Jos. Respondents in Enugu were on average more likely than respondents in the other locations to have reported acting collectively to raise issues in public to get something done in the community. They were also more likely to say they were accepting of differences of opinion. It might be surprising to some to see that expressed support for religious liberty was greater in predominantly Muslim Kano than in mostly Christian Enugu. People reported being more religiously observant in Kano than in Enugu and the two religiously mixed locations. In sum, we do not find evidence to suggest that respondents in the religiously diverse settings were more politically engaged and supportive of liberal democracy than respondents in religiously homogeneous locations. But, of course, we have not controlled for the impact of religious observance.

Now, let us assess the effects of religious observance for each of the three religious groupings across the four cities. While controlling for gender, age, education, and income, we want to know whether religious observance had any effect on voting, political interest, raising an issue in public to get something done in the community, the frequency of political discussions, acceptance of differences in opinion, support for democracy, and respect for religious liberty. Further, we want to know whether there is evidence that religious observance was having, at the time of our survey, a systematically different effect on such actions and attitudes depending on the city. The complete results of the analysis may be found in Appendix B. Here, let me describe the findings and point to charts that illustrate the results.

In short, we find that location mattered, and that it explains the variation in the political impact of religious observance to a far greater degree than the type of religious group in question. In other words, knowing the city helps us to discern the impact that religious observance was having on political actions and attitudes better than knowing whether respondents were Muslims, mainline Christians, or Pentecostal Christians. However, religious observance was not always more positively associated with liberal democratic ideals in the religiously diverse cities than in the religiously homogeneous cities.

As shown in Figure 6.3, religious observance tended to have a more positive impact on voting in predominantly Muslim Kano (labeled simply as "Muslim area" in the figure) and predominantly Christian Enugu (labeled simply as "Christian area" in the figure) than in the religiously diverse cities of Ibadan and Jos. This is true of all three religious groups: Muslims, mainline Christians, and Pentecostals. In Enugu, every 10-unit increase in religious observance was associated with a 52 percentage-point increase in the probability that a Muslim voted, a 48 percentage-point increase in the probability that a mainline Christian voted, and a 57 percentage-point increase in the probability that a Pentecostal

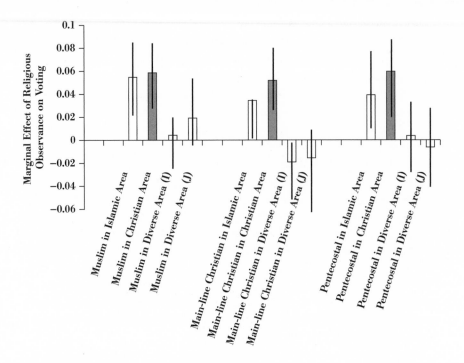

Figure 6.3 Religious Observance and Voting

Christian voted. In predominantly Muslim Kano, we also find that religious observance was boosting the probability that Muslims, mainline Christians, and Pentecostals voted. Religious observance had a positive but less significant impact on voting among Muslims in religiously diverse Jos, but not in religiously diverse Ibadan. Religious observance actually decreased the probability that a mainline Christian voted in Ibadan and had no effect on voting among mainline Christians in Jos. Religious observance had no impact on voting among Pentecostals in either Jos or Ibadan. In sum, religious observance had a much more positive impact on voting in the two religiously homogeneous cities than in the two religiously diverse areas.

When it comes to political interest, we essentially find the same pattern as with voting. Religious observance had a more positive impact on political interest among Muslims, mainline Christians, and Pentecostals in predominantly Christian Enugu and predominantly Muslim Kano than in religiously diverse Ibadan and Jos. What about other measures of political engagement, such as frequency of political discussions and raising an issue in public to get something done in the community?

Figure 6.4 shows that religious observance had a significant effect on the frequency of political discussions across Muslims, mainline Christians, and Pentecostal Christians in all four settings, but a marginally more positive effect in religiously diverse Ibadan than in the other three settings. This was true for Muslims, mainline Christians, and Pentecostal Christians. Every 10-unit increase in religious observance increased the likelihood that a Muslim in Ibadan would have reported to have engaged

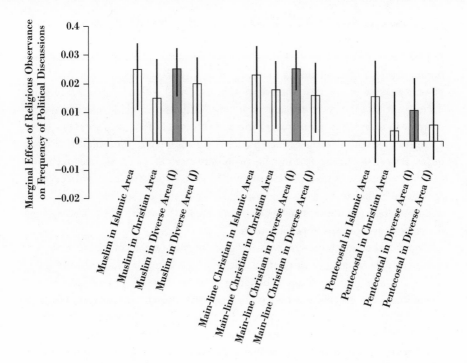

Figure 6.4 Religious Observance and Frequency of Political Discussions

often in political discussions by 20 percentage points, that a mainline Christian would have done the same by 18 percentage points, and that a Pentecostal also reported to have engaged often in political discussions by more than 7 percentage points.

Only in Jos did religious observance have an effect on raising an issue in public to get something done in the community, and the effect is positive. This is so across Muslims, mainline Christians, and Pentecostal Christians. Every 10-unit increase in religious observance increased the likelihood that a Muslim and mainline Christian would have raised an issue in public by 5 percentage points. Among Pentecostals in Jos, religious observance increased the likelihood by more than 3 percentage points. While Christian and Islamic religious communities in Jos did not appear to have much of an effect on voting, evidence indicates that they were effectively mobilizing their members to raise issues to get something done in the community between elections.

Of course, political engagement—whether voting, discussing politics, or acting collectively to raise an issue in public to get something done in the community—is not necessarily an indicator of support for liberal democracy. As we have noted previously, people may vote for candidates or parties that promise to cleanse their societies of vulnerable groups, be they racial, ethnic, or religious minorities. People may be politically engaged in the cause of bigotry or in an effort to curtail the rights of individuals who believe, look, and behave differently than they do. A basic level of social tolerance and respect for the rights of individual and minority groups is essential to what we call liberal democracy.

Because a basic level of social tolerance is essential in a liberal democracy, we include two indicators of tolerance. One is acceptance of differences of opinion, and the other is respect for religious liberty. We find that religious observance discouraged acceptance of differences of opinion among members of all three religious groups in Jos. Every 10-unit increase in religious observance was associated with a 45 percentage-point decrease in acceptance of differences among Muslims and a 24 percentage-point decrease in acceptance of differences among Pentecostals. Religious observance was also associated with a decrease in acceptance of differences among mainline Christians in Jos. Every 10-unit increase in religious observance decreased the likelihood that mainline Christians in Jos expressed support for differences of opinion by 14 percentage points. In Ibadan, religious observance did not decrease respect for differences of opinion among any one of the religious groups and had a positive effect on acceptance of differences among mainline Christians.

Arguably the most important way a religious institution can contribute to the formation of a liberal democratic political culture is by encouraging respect for religious liberty. It is one thing for non-religious actors to promote respect for religious liberty and quite another for religious leaders and religiously devout people to promote such respect. Where religious leaders, who stand to benefit the most from special privileges for their religious communities, do not focus their energy on achieving such special privileges for their religious communities and instead promote greater religious liberty

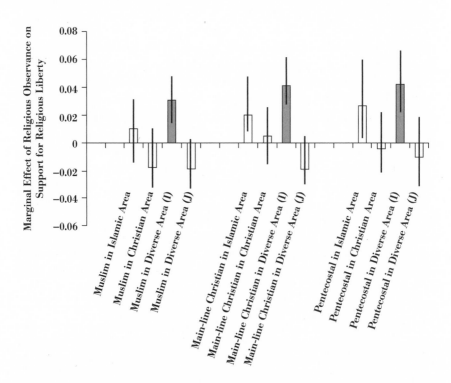

Figure 6.5 Religious Observance and Support for Religious Liberty

for all, members of their religious groups are more likely to be persuaded that religious liberty is desirable.

As can be seen in Figure 6.5, evidence suggests that religious observance had the most profoundly positive effect on support for religious liberty in religiously diverse Ibadan. This is true among Muslims, mainline Christians, and Pentecostals. In Ibadan, every 10-unit increase in religious observance is associated with a 28 percentage-point increase in support for religious liberty among Muslims, a 40 percentage-point increase in the support for religious liberty among mainline Christians, and a 43 percentage-point increase in support for religious liberty among Pentecostals. Although we find evidence to suggest that religious observance had a positive effect on support for religious liberty among mainline and Pentecostal Christians in predominantly Christian Enugu, the effect was twice as positive in religiously diverse Ibadan. While we might expect to find a more positive association between religious observance and support for religious liberty among Christians in predominantly Muslim Kano since Christians form a minority of the population there, we find no evidence that religious observance was affecting support for religious liberty among Christians in Kano.

When it comes to support for multiparty elections, we find little evidence that religious observance either promoted or impeded such support, regardless of the location and religious group, with the exception of mainline Christians in religiously diverse Ibadan. In Ibadan, religious observance had a positive impact on support for democracy among mainline Christians. For every 10-unit increase in religious observance, there is a 20 percentage-point increase in the probability that a mainline Christian expressed the highest level of support for a political system characterized by regular multiparty elections. We find that support for multiparty elections was already high among members of all three religious groups across the four locations, and religious observance, with the exception of mainline Christians in Ibadan, neither increased nor decreased such support.

EXPLAINING THE DIFFERENCE RELIGIOUS DIVERSITY MAKES

Taken together with evidence presented in Chapter 5, the results strongly suggest that context affected the impact that Christian and Islamic communities had on political participation, tolerance, and respect for religious liberty. While the theory I outlined in Chapter 2 proposes that religious diversity is a contextual factor that is likely to affect the impact of religious observance on political actions and attitudes, we find that religious observance was not always more positively associated with components of a liberal democratic political culture in the two religiously diverse cities than in the two religiously homogeneous cities in our study. Christian and Islamic communities had a much more positive effect on voting and political interest in predominantly Muslim Kano and predominantly Christian Enugu than in religiously diverse Jos and Ibadan. Further, there were real differences between our two religiously diverse settings. Christian and Islamic communities had a much more positive effect on collective action to get something done in the community in Jos than in Ibadan. However,

Christian and Muslim communities had a far more positive impact on respect for religious liberty in Ibadan than in Jos.

As is often the case, empirical reality does not always neatly conform to theoretical expectations, and there are important questions that need to be addressed. First, why did religious observance have a more positive impact on voting and political interest in Kano and Enugu, where there is little inter-religious diversity, than in Jos and Ibadan, where there is a great deal of such diversity? Second, is there any evidence that differences in religious diversity affected the degree to which Christian and Muslim religious leaders encouraged political activism and support for freedom? Third, is there any evidence that religious leaders in Ibadan have learned to live and let live to a greater extent than religious leaders in the other three settings? If so, how well does this explain the difference in the political impact of religious communities across the four settings?

VOTING AND POLITICAL INTEREST

As in the previous chapter, the results with regard to voting and political interest are puzzling. In the previous chapter we found religious observance to have had the most positive effect on voting in predominantly Muslim Senegal. In this chapter, we find religious observance had a more positive effect on voting in predominantly Muslim Kano and predominantly Christian Enugu than in religiously diverse Ibadan and Jos. This is surprising because there are a number of theoretical reasons that we would expect the findings to be just the opposite. In religiously diverse settings, we would expect that competition between religious groups for influence over policymakers would drive up religiously motivated voter turnout. We would expect religious leaders in religiously diverse settings to do all that they can to encourage people to vote for candidates who they expect to further the interests of the religious institutions they lead. In religiously homogeneous settings we would expect such religiously inspired voter mobilization to be less pronounced since the competition between religious groups for local political influence is less significant. The point here is that we do not find evidence of religiously driven voter turnout in the two most religiously diverse settings, Jos and Ibadan, where we would expect to find it. The results do suggest there was religiously driven voter turnout in the two most religiously homogeneous settings, Kano and Enugu, where we would expect religious leaders to be less concerned about getting out the vote. What might explain these results?

In an attempt to explain the results of statistical analysis, we turn to interviews conducted with leaders of religious majorities in Kano and Enugu. These interviews suggest that leaders of religious majorities in these two cities considered electing the right political leaders as necessary and sufficient for maintaining influence over these local settings. Many religious leaders in Enugu and Kano saw no need for political activism between elections and even considered such behavior as unnecessarily disruptive. For example, when asked whether it is important to get Muslims to be politically active, Ibrahim, a Muslim teacher (*Malam*) in Kano, said that it is important for Muslims to vote for good Muslims. He was not encouraging of political activism, which he associated with protest and violence:

Kano is a place where Islam has a special place. As long as Muslims vote for good Muslims and elect them to government, there are no worries. Protests are provocative and often lead to violence. With good Muslims in government, we can always ensure that the faith is respected.[11]

When asked if he thinks it is important for Catholics to be politically active, a Catholic priest in predominantly Christian Enugu said the following:

It depends on what you mean by politically active. I do not think it is right to protest all the time. I do not think that is the way to get things done. I believe it is important for us [Catholics] to vote and elect good leaders. We who are not in government do not always have the information we need to know what is best for government to do. If we elect good leaders, they will govern in ways that uphold our faith.[12]

Thus, a Muslim religious leader stated that voting is sufficient for maintaining Islamic influence in predominantly Muslim Kano, and a Christian religious leader said that doing the same is adequate for maintaining Christian influence in predominantly Christian Enugu. They were both concerned that political activism between elections could be destabilizing. They seemed to prefer the status quo and, at the time of the survey, they believed that voting would be the best way to maintain the status quo. These religious leaders encouraged their followers to vote for candidates who promised to uphold the faith in the public realm. And the very positive and significant coefficients in Figure 6.3 suggest that they were doing so quite effectively.

Interviews with leaders of religious minorities in Kano and Enugu are also revealing. While we might expect these leaders to have promoted more demanding forms of political participation because voting is clearly insufficient to gain influence where they represent such a small minority, interviews suggest that leaders of religious minorities in Kano and Enugu viewed anything more than voting in elections as dangerously provocative. Theo, a lay Catholic leader in Kano, put it this way:

If we [Catholics] are going to thrive here in Kano, we first must survive. In order to survive, we must get along with Muslims. In order to get along with Muslims, we must quietly go about our business. If we do that, we will survive and the Church will grow here. Catholics have been in Kano a long time. We have been patient. We must continue to be patient.[13]

Theo's statement suggests that there was a clear strategy. In order to grow in number and influence, Catholics in Kano were not to engage in political activism. This would draw attention and possibly trigger a backlash from some Muslims.

What about Pentecostals in Kano? While we might expect them to be more aggressive about winning converts and gaining influence than Catholics or other mainline Christians and, therefore, more encouraging of political activism, several Pentecostal leaders echoed the sentiments expressed by Theo. Johnson, a Pentecostal elder in Kano, said that he thought "Christians need to be patient."[14] He went on to add the following:

> We have no desire to cause trouble here. We simply want the freedom to worship the Lord Jesus Christ. While we do not enjoy the freedom to evangelize that we would like, we will bring destruction on our church and forfeit any chance to evangelize if we begin to protest. Our people should vote, yes. They should not be naïve about politics. But we need to be careful.[15]

It should be noted that there were other Christians, including Pentecostals or mainline Christians, who also thought that Christians should be more radical in their attempt to win converts and gain influence in Kano. However, where Christians were significantly outnumbered, there is good reason to think that these more aggressive Christians represented a minority within a minority. Most Christian leaders considered voting important and more demanding forms of political action, such as protests and demonstrations, imprudent.

Many Muslim religious leaders in predominantly Christian Enugu seemed to think the same way. Yusuf, a *Malam* based in Enugu, was largely representative of Muslim religious leaders in Enugu when he said the following:

> I am afraid to say that we are victims of discrimination here. However, we all must do a little suffering in life. We would do more suffering here if we started to organize rallies or protests to call for more respect for Islam. We are in Enugu. That is the way it is.[16]

MORE DEMANDING FORMS OF POLITICAL ACTIVISM

Although voting in a country like Nigeria is often time-consuming since it usually entails locating the correct polling station and waiting in long lines, it is important to recognize that raising an issue in public in order to get something done in the community is usually more demanding and may involve a risk to life or livelihood. It typically requires more time, effort, and courage than voting. Voting is an individual act, while raising an issue together with others in public is a collective act that necessitates coordination. In a country like Nigeria, this kind of coordination is not easily accomplished. As the leaders of religious minorities indicated in the quotes above, those who raise issues in pubic to call for local or federal governmental action often risk life, limb, or livelihood, depending on the sensitivity of the issues they raise.

There is good reason to think that Christian and Muslim religious leaders tend to encourage more demanding forms of political action in religiously diverse settings that are rapidly diversifying and where there is a great deal of uncertainty about the role of religion in public life than in settings that have been religiously diverse for long and where there is more certainty about the role of religion in public life. When and where there is certainty about the role of religion in public life, there is a generally agreed-upon norm about what is and is not the appropriate relationship between religion and state that all or most religious groups support. The agreement that is likely to satisfy all or most religious groups in a society is one that provides them with freedom and equal treatment before the law. In a location that has for long been religiously diverse, it is more likely that major religious groups have come to such an agreement. In a setting that has only recently become diverse, it is less likely that major religious groups have come to such an agreement.

Ibadan has been religiously diverse, with equally large Muslim and Christian populations, for more than one hundred years (Peel 2000; Laitin 1986). The Muslim population in Jos has been growing steadily over the past two decades and, according to the Nigeria Demographic and Health Survey of 2003, Christians represented a majority of the population (Paden 2008; Falola 1998). The dramatic growth in the Muslim population, largely due to migration, has turned a city where Christianity was dominant into a religiously diverse city in just a few decades. As noted earlier in the chapter, Christian and Muslim populations in Jos are segregated from each other to a far greater degree than in Ibadan. Religious communities in Jos have huddled together and have adopted defensive postures. Many Christians fear that Muslims mean to take over the city, and many Muslims, designated as settlers, express frustration and feel that they are the victims of discrimination.[17] Therefore, it may not be that surprising to find religious observance to have had a more positive effect on raising an issue in public in religiously diverse Jos than in any of the other three locations included in our study. In Jos, every 10-unit increase in religious observance is associated with a 5.1 percentage-point increase in the probability that a Muslim raised an issue in public, a 5.6 percentage-point increase in the probability that a mainline Christian did the same, and a whopping 38 percentage-point increase in the probability that a Pentecostal Christian would have raised an issue in public.

There is some anecdotal evidence to suggest that both Christian and Muslim religious leaders in Jos were encouraging followers to engage in collective action between elections because they thought it was crucial for advancing the interests of their religious communities. For example, Hussein, a Muslim religious leader in Jos, stated that he thought it crucially important for Muslims not only to vote, but to make their voices heard between elections:

> During elections and between elections, always, we must make sure that Muslims make their voices heard. Otherwise, I know the politicians, many [of whom] are Christians, will forget us. The politicians have got to know we are here and this is our home. This is not a Christian city. It is a city of Muslims and Christians.[18]

One Nigerian Catholic priest who was serving as the pastor of a large parish in religiously diverse Jos at the time of the survey indicated that the religious competition that exists in Nigeria, especially in Jos, means that it is crucially important that he and his fellow priests encourage Catholics to be politically knowledgeable and engaged:

There are so many competing voices. We need to work hard to keep them [Catholics] strong in their faith and encourage them to stand up for the Catholic Church in Nigeria.[19]

Interestingly enough, another Nigerian Catholic priest who served in Jos, but who had previously worked in predominantly Christian Enugu, noted how the difference in settings affects the work required of Church leaders:

Yes, we have to work harder here [in Jos]. In Enugu, there was a much stronger Christian and Catholic culture. We could take that for granted. Here, we cannot take anything for granted and we need to make sure our people are not shy about letting the politicians know that the Catholic Church is here. There are Catholic politicians here [in Jos], but they get pulled in many directions by different groups and often lose their way. We need to remind them of who they are.[20]

According to this Nigerian priest, where the Catholic Church represents a larger proportion of the population, he and other Catholic leaders need not work as hard at promoting the faith as they need to in areas where the Catholic Church represents a smaller percentage of the population. As his remark suggests, he is concerned about the Catholic Church's influence over the prevailing culture.

John, a Pentecostal pastor in Jos, stated that he also believes in mobilizing his flock for political action. According to John, Christians must be politically engaged if Christianity is to continue to influence the culture and politics of Jos:

Christians must speak up and be involved in politics. If we do not keep reminding politicians that we still form the majority of the population, we will lose our rights.[21]

There is good reason to think that religious communities in religiously diverse Ibadan had little or no impact on political mobilization because religious leaders were not encouraging political action. Ibadan has been religiously diverse for so long that most Christian and Muslim religious leaders had already arrived at a mutually acceptable position on the role of religion in public life. Therefore, religious leaders perceived less of a need to politically mobilize their followers than their fellow religious leaders in Jos. There is a religious-based culture of tolerance that has developed in Ibadan, and there is evidence to suggest that religious diversity and religious integration help explain the development of this culture of tolerance. John Paden (2005: 113) notes that interfaith mixing among members of the Yoruba ethnic group, who form the vast majority of the population in Ibadan, may help to depoliticize religion and to explain why Christian and Islamic communities have not played a significant role in mobilizing people for political action in Ibadan. Chief Olabode, retired navy commodore and military governor of Ondo, made the following statement in a Nigerian publication:

Let me tell you what we have in the South-West. My immediate elder sister is a Muslim. She was born a Christian, she married a Muslim from Lagos State. I gave her money to go to Mecca. I have another younger brother who married a Muslim from Lagos State. She is now so converted that she preaches the Bible. But all her family in the area are still Muslims. So, to us, it's nothing. There is hardly any Yoruba family you will go where you won't find a Muslim or a Christian in the South-West. There is hardly anyone.[22]

While it is important not to overstate the degree of Christian-Muslim integration in Ibadan (Laitin 1986: 141–144), evidence suggests that there is more of it there and in the southwest of Nigeria than in any other part of the country. Further, it is easy to understand why religion would not serve as a basis for political mobilization in a setting where religious communities are integrated to the degree they have been in the southwest of Nigeria.

LEARNING OVER TIME TO PROMOTE RESPECT FOR RELIGIOUS LIBERTY AND SEPARATION OF RELIGIOUS AND STATE AUTHORITY

When it comes to inter-religious tolerance and support for the separation of religious and state authority in Nigeria, interviews with religious leaders suggest that religious diversity affected the choices that religious leaders made. For example, Ezekial, a Pentecostal elder in the predominantly Christian Enugu, seemed to suggest that there is nothing wrong with trying to promote Christianity with state support if the conditions are right. "When Christians are in the majority, we should be allowed to make laws that uphold our faith and morals." Ezekial was quick to point out that this did not mean he was intolerant of Muslims or that they should not be welcome to live and work in Enugu:

Muslims are Nigerians too and they deserve to live anywhere they want in this country. However, if they want to live under their laws, they should move somewhere else.[23]

Thomas, also an elder in a Pentecostal church in religiously diverse Ibadan, stated that Jesus calls Christians to spread the faith. "However, I think we must be smart about how we spread the faith" he added. He went on to say:

We should not try [to spread the faith] through laws and government. This could really backfire on us. Muslims will try to spread their religion in the same way. There are many Muslims here and they are often more willing to fight for their religion than Christians. We may lose and this would be very bad. Instead of trying to use government, we should just make sure government allows us to worship in freedom.[24]

Although Thomas indicated that he fears some Muslim religious leaders may be more willing to promote the integration of religious and state authority than Christian religious leaders, there is evidence that this has not been the case in Ibadan and elsewhere in Yorubaland. The campaign to constitutionally enshrine the *Shari'ah* during the late 1970s and 1980s failed to gain much support among Yoruba Muslims. Paden (2005: 107) notes that Yoruba Muslim religious leaders "encouraged a separation of church or mosque and state and a religious pluralism." Laitin (1986: 9) notes that members of the Constituent Assembly (MCA) from the southwest who were charged with drawing up a new constitution for Nigeria during the 1970s were the least extreme on the issue of the place of the *Shari'ah*. In a survey of MCAs he conducted, Laitin found that 76 percent of MCAs from the southwest took moderate positions on the *Shari'ah* issue, whereas 80 percent of northerners and 77 percent of those from the Middle Belt took extreme positions (ibid.). Further, he found more renegade MCAs were from the southwest than from any other region of the country. Laitin defines a renegade as a Christian who did not unconditionally oppose a place for the *Shari'ah* in the public realm or a Muslim who did not insist on enshrining the *Shari'ah*. Twenty percent of MCAs from the southwest were renegades (ibid.). In predominantly Muslim Kano and other northern cities, such as Kaduna, Falola (1998) notes that Muslim leaders tended to do just the opposite. One such leader was Kaduna-based Abubakar Gumi (Kukah and Falola 1996: 152–153). "Gumi was relentless in his attempt to promote an Islamic regime in Nigeria. He did not think any Christian should be allowed to preside over Nigeria" (Falola 1998: 80). Falola (1998: 83) notes that these "pro-*Shari'ah* groups found themselves attacked by both Christians and fellow Muslims [in Ibadan and other areas of Yorubaland]."

If Christian and Islamic communities effectively encouraged religious tolerance in religiously diverse and integrated Ibadan, the question remains, did the religious tolerance or the religious diversity and integration come first? It would seem that a certain degree of tolerance is needed in the first place if a society is to grow in religious diversity (Alesina et al. 2003). On the other hand, how can there be tolerance of other religious groups in the absence of other religious groups? There is evidence to suggest that religious diversity came first in Ibadan and that it was the experience of religious diversity that eventually prompted religious tolerance. John Paden (2005: 113) notes that interfaith mixing among members of the Yoruba ethnic group, who form the vast majority of the population in Ibadan, has largely increased religious tolerance. In other words, religious diversity is not the result of pre-existing religious tolerance. Paden implies that religious tolerance is the result of religious diversity.

There is evidence to suggest that the culture of tolerance that has existed in Ibadan grew out of the experience of religious diversity. The culture of tolerance between Christians and Muslims evolved over time through repeated interaction and a process of learning. As Kukah and Falola (1996: 66) put it:

> . . . Islam failed to displace indigenous religion, and what was worse [from an Islamic perspective] Christianity began to spread after the 1840s and recorded phenomenal success. Christianity, too, did not succeed in displacing indigenous

religion or Islam. Thus, the three religions had to co-exist, with a great deal of tolerance.

In Ibadan and much of Yorubaland, religious diversity preceded the culture of tolerance that has existed between Christians and Muslims in Ibadan (Paden 2008; Laitin 1986). And it is important to note that Christianity collided with Islam, and indigenous religions, in the beginning. Although not as violent as the collision between Christianity and Islam in Jos today, the tensions were real and the competition intense. Peel (2003: 192) notes that, during the mid-nineteenth century, Muslim preachers in Ibadan warned Ibadan's rulers that "their lives would be cut short" if they allowed Christian missionaries into the area. Religious leaders fanned the flames of intolerance as Christians and Muslims tried to establish superiority in terms of numbers and influence (Peel 1967). Muslims portrayed members of the Anglican Church Missionary Society (CMS) as "enemies of the truth," and the CMS countered by calling Islam "the greatest obstacle to progress and civilization" (Laitin 1986: 129). At the very least, there was a war of words. Laitin (1986: ibid.) notes that Muslims complained that their children were under pressure to convert to Christianity as they pursued education in government-supported Christian schools, and they sought government support for their own Muslim schools. Up until the mid-twentieth century, Muslims complained that the Christian politicians were dominating governmental affairs in Nigeria's southwest and that Muslims were often the victims of discrimination (Kukah and Falola 1996: 84–85). Christians complained that it was unfair for the government to support Muslims so that they may make the *haj* or pilgrimage to Mecca (Laitin 1986; Kukah and Falola 1996). Although accommodation has not always marked the encounter between Christianity and Islam in religiously diverse Ibadan, it is difficult to imagine how such accommodation would have developed there if the encounter had never taken place.

What about Ibadan's ethnic homogeneity? It is important to note that there is variation in the extent to which religious and ethnic identities overlap or cut across each other in Nigeria, and one might expect this variation to be crucial for explaining the differences between Jos and Ibadan. In Jos, religious identity and ethnic identity have largely overlapped. In other words, most people in Jos have been divided by both ethnic *and* religious identities in a way that they have not been in Ibadan. Most Muslims have been members of the Hausa ethnic group, and most Christians have been members of other ethnic groups, including the Berom. The Berom, who are almost all Christians, are among the ethnic groups considered to be the indigenes or natives of the area. In fact, some observers have noted that the inter-communal violence in Jos and much of Plateau State has been less about religious differences than about who has the right to be considered "sons [or daughters] of the soil" and, thus, who has rights to land ownership and other benefits. Thus, the Berom Christians in the area have considered themselves indigenes and the Hausa Muslims to be transplants or settlers who are not deserving of the same rights. Nigeria's law backs up Berom claims, as have successive Plateau State governments, prompting Muslims in the area to claim that they are the victims of discrimination and are systematically denied rights in their own country.[25]

As Paden (2012: 76) notes, "There is. . . a dangerous mix of ethnic, religious, and land use factors in Plateau State that fuels tensions and conflicts."

In Ibadan and much of southwestern Nigeria, on the other hand, the population is largely made up of members of the Yoruba ethnic group and, among the Yoruba, we find an almost equal percentage of Christians and Muslims. Because Ibadan is in the heart of the Yoruba homeland, one might suspect that the religious tolerance in the city is due to the way religious identity cuts across ethnic identity there. Because many Muslims in Ibadan share Yoruba ethnic identity with Christians, perhaps we should not be surprised to find that Christians and Muslims are more tolerant of each other there than in Jos, where religious and ethnic differences overlap and reinforce each other. Perhaps the difference between Ibadan and Jos has less to do with the greater degree of religious diversity and integration of religious groups in Ibadan than with the fact that, in Ibadan, many more people who are divided by religion are united by ethnic identity.

If the higher level of religious tolerance that existed in Ibadan was due mostly or solely to the fact that many Christians and Muslims share Yoruba ethnic identity, we would expect to find the average level of support for religious freedom and acceptance of differences of opinion to have been higher in in Ibadan than in Jos. However, we do not find that this was the case. As Table 6.2 shows, the mean level of support for religious liberty was lower in Ibadan than in Jos. Religious observance had an effect on respect for religious liberty in Ibadan that it was not having in Jos. Religious observance increased support for religious tolerance in Ibadan and had little or negative effect on such tolerance in Jos. In other words, religious observance determined whether a respondent expressed the highest level of support for respect for religious freedom in Ibadan, rather than Yoruba ethnic identity or religious identity.[26] When taken together with the results of the in-depth interviews cited above, the evidence indicates that Ibadan's religious diversity and religious integration, rather than its high percentage of Yoruba or its ethnic homogeneity, explains why religious observance had a more positive impact on religious tolerance in Ibadan than in Jos, Enugu, and Kano.

A CHANGING CLIMATE

Although it is customary for social scientists to use the present tense when reporting the results of studies that have been conducted in the past, in this and the previous chapter I make a point of using the past tense. This is because the results discussed above are largely based on data gathered at a discreet point in time, and we know that time does not stand still. In fact, the main argument put forward in this book is that changes that occur across time, as well as differences that exist across space at the same point in time, affect the likelihood that Christian and Islamic religious communities effectively encourage or discourage a political culture conducive to liberal democracy. In other words, the conditions at a particular point in time may change, and these conditions affect how religious leaders and ordinary religious people apply their religious traditions to politics. Conditions vary by physical location as well, and the difference in conditions help explain why people who lead or belong to the same religious tradition apply that tradition to public life in different ways. While I find evidence to suggest that differences in religious diversity help explain the various ways in which Christian and Islamic religious traditions are applied to public life and the different ways in which communities affect key components of a liberal democratic political culture at a point in time, I have not assessed the impact of changes in religious diversity that have occurred across time. If most Christians or most Muslims were to leave Ibadan, making Ibadan a predominantly Muslim or Christian city, would religious observance have a less positive impact on religious tolerance? Even if a setting like Ibadan remains as religiously diverse as it was in 2006, is it not possible that other social, economic, and political changes would affect the degree to which religious observance has a positive effect on tolerance?

It is important to recognize that the findings reported in this book represent a snapshot of particular places at a given point in time. We are not able to say for certain that religious observance will forever and always affect actions and attitudes in the same way in all three religious grouping and across all four locations. Nonetheless, the results represent baseline data from which we can assess the effects of a changing climate on the impact that Christian and Islamic communities have on political culture. With additional data, we will be able to assess whether and how changes in religious diversity in any one of the four settings, as well as changes in the Nigeria's broader political, economic, and religious climate, affect the impact of religious observance on the political actions and attitudes of ordinary Christians and Muslims.

We do know that Nigeria's broader political and religious environment has changed since 2006, the year of our survey. If we were to conduct today the survey we conducted back then, we may not find that the results hold up so well. Inter-religious tensions in Nigeria have appeared to become more intense during recent years. Although we know that tensions existed before 2006 and there has been religious violence in the north and Middle Belt of Nigeria since the early 1980s, there is reason to think that matters have become worse. Since the founder of *Boko Haram*, Mohammed Yusuf, was killed in police custody in 2009, the group he founded has seemed to grow more aggressive and violent. *Boko Haram* has started to attack Christian churches in addition to government and United Nations installations. Mass abductions and the killing of civilians have heightened fears in northeastern Nigeria and the Middle Belt that the state there is collapsing. The April 2011 presidential election was followed by inter-religious violence, as some Muslims felt they were cheated out of the presidency (Paden 2012). Paden (2012: 3) observes that the post-election violence was the worst the country had seen since the 1967–1970 civil war. In many parts of the country, Christians have felt on edge because of Islamist militancy. More religious riots have occurred in religiously diverse but highly segregated cities like Jos and Kaduna, heightening tensions between Christians and Muslims and segregating cities that were already highly segregated along religious and ethnic lines.[27] The Council on Foreign Relations Security Tracker estimates that there were 785 deaths due to sectarian violence in the city of Jos between 2011 and 2013. The number of deaths is almost certainly higher (Human Rights Watch 2013; Paden 2012). More deadly violence also occurred in predominantly Muslims cities with significant Christian populations, like Kano.[28] After Christmas Day bombings in 2011 and the Nigerian government's declaration of a state of emergency in several northeastern and Middle Belt states, *Boko Haram* launched a campaign to cleanse northeastern Nigeria of all Christians (Paden 2012).

It is quite plausible that Christians and Muslims, even in relatively peaceful settings where adherents of these two religions have lived side by side for many years, are now looking at each other with more suspicion because of the deadly violence that has shaken other parts of the country repeatedly over the years. As Paden (2012: 95) notes, "[after the election of 2011] News of the ongoing violence began to eat away at the confidence of the entire country." Those promoting less tolerant brands of their religions have attempted to spread their ideology to parts of the country where Christians and Muslims have enjoyed good relations, including Ibadan and Lagos.[29] If we were to conduct a study at the time of this writing, we may find that poor relations between Christians and Muslims in Nigeria have become contagious and have spread from areas of the north and Middle Belt to other parts of the country. We may find that mutually exclusive political theologies have become more popular and that adherents of Christianity and Islam are adopting intolerant or illiberal applications of their religions, even in settings that have been religiously diverse for long periods of time and where there has been a great deal of mixing and mingling of Christians and Muslims. If so, we might find that religious observance has a less positive effect on components of a liberal democratic political culture today than in 2006. In recent years, we might find less religious-based support for religious tolerance in religiously diverse settings than in religiously homogeneous settings.

While we lack the kind of data that we need to thoroughly assess how the changes in Nigeria's broader religious and political climate have affected, if at all, the type of political theologies espoused by religious leaders and the impact of religious observance on the actions and attitudes of ordinary Christians and Muslims, there are some data to which we can turn for clues. Among other things, we can examine Afrobarometer data collected in 2012 to find out if there is any evidence that religious observance had, in 2012 as in 2006, a more positive impact on key elements of a liberal democratic political culture among Christians and Muslims in religiously diverse settings than in religiously homogeneous settings.

Nigeria's Afrobarometer survey of 2012 included 2,400 respondents randomly selected from across the country. Of the respondents, 55 percent were Christians and 44 percent were Muslims. The largest Christian denominations represented among the respondents were Roman Catholics (10.7 percent of all respondents), Pentecostals (12.1 percent of all respondents), and Anglicans (5.3 percent of all respondents). The overwhelming majority of Muslims included among the respondents identified as Muslims only, rather than with any Islamic subgrouping (37 percent of all respondents). Only a little over 2 percent of all respondents identified as *Sunni* and a little over 1 percent identified as *Shia*. Less than 1 percent of all respondents identified with one of the two major brotherhoods (i.e., Tijaniyya and Qadiriyya). Because the sample of Christians is not large enough to analyze the data broken down into specific Christian denominations by state, we separate Christians into mainline Christians and Pentecostal Christians. Therefore, we use the same religious groupings as we use above: mainline Christians, Pentecostal Christians, and Muslims.[30]

As noted back in Chapter 4, the Afrobarometer survey is especially dedicated to gathering information on African political and economic behaviors and attitudes. While not specifically designed to achieve a better understanding of how religious involvement is related to such actions and attitudes, the instrument does include questions about religious affiliation and religious activity that allow us to work toward exposing such a relationship. However, it is important to keep in mind that the Afrobarometer survey does not ask the same questions that I asked on the survey I conducted in Nigeria in 2006. For example, it does not ask many questions about religiosity. Thus, the measure of religious observance is less comprehensive than the one I used in the 2006 survey. The Afrobarometer also does not ask a question about respect for religious liberty, which I asked in the 2006 survey and which is, I propose, crucially important for understanding how religious communities are affecting support for basic freedoms and the prospects for liberal democracy.

There are two religiosity variables included in the fifth round of the Afrobarometer: religious group activity and the importance of religion in one's life. However, we must eliminate the importance of religion in one's life because there is a lack of variation in how people responded to the question. More than 90 percent of respondents stated that religion is very important in their lives. Therefore, we are left with religious group activity as our key independent variable of interest. That variable by itself is less than ideal. That's because this one question does not allow us to generate a measure of communal religious engagement that is comprehensive. The Afrobarometer asked respondents the following question: If you are a member of a religious group that meets outside of worship services, *could you tell me whether you are an official leader, active member, inactive member or not a member?*[31] Religious group activity is a qualitative variable that ranges from 1 to 4, with 4 representing the highest level of religious activity (i.e., that one serves as an official leader in a religious group) or highest frequency of contact. Despite the shortcomings for our purposes, the question does provide us with a measure of religious engagement, and we do find enough variation in how respondents answered this question to include it as our independent variable of interest.[32]

The key dependent variables of interest include *voting, support for democracy, support for elections, support for freedom of the media, and support for freedom of association.* I transform the key dependent variables into dichotomous variables that range from 0 to 1. When it comes to voting, only respondents who said they voted in the 2011 national election in their country received a score of 1. As regards support for elections, respondents who said that they agree very strongly that *"we should choose our leaders in this country through regular, open, and honest elections"* received a score of 1 and all others received a score of 0. Only those who said they agree very strongly with the statement, *"we should be able to join any organization whether or not the government approves of it"* received a score of 1, and all others received a score of 0.

Rather than compare the effects of religious observance by city, as I do earlier in the chapter, I compare the effects of religious observance for each of the three religious groups by state.[33] As displayed in the maps (Figures 6.1 and 6.2), I have assigned the states, excluding the Federal Capital Territory (i.e., the city of Abuja and environs), to three categories according to their religious diversity: those states that are over 75 percent Christian (13), those states that are over 75 percent Muslim (12) and those where neither Christians nor Muslims make up more than 60 percent of the population (11).[34]

While the results are not all that significant, they do indicate that religious group activity had a slightly more positive effect on support for regular elections and freedom of association in religiously diverse states than in religiously homogeneous states.[35] However, regardless of the religious diversity or homogeneity of states, religious group activity had no discernible effect, either positive or negative, on support for democracy and support for freedom of the media. In religiously diverse states, every 1-point increase in religious activity increased the likelihood that one expressed the highest possible degree of support for regular elections by 1.3 percentage points among mainline Christians and 10.4 percentage points among Pentecostal Christians. Among Muslims in religiously diverse states, religious-group activity had a positive effect on support for elections, but the effect is not statistically significant. However, the positive effect that religious observance had on support for elections is not confined to the most religiously diverse states. In predominantly Christian states, religious-group activity also had a positive effect on support for regular elections among members of all three religious groups. However, only in the case of Pentecostals is the effect significant. In contrast to religiously diverse and predominantly Christian states, activity in religious groups is shown to have had a negative effect on support for regular elections among mainline Christians and Muslims in predominantly Muslim states.[36]

In religiously diverse states, religious-group activity had a positive effect on support for freedom of association among Muslims, mainline Christians, and Pentecostal Christians, but only in the case of Pentecostal Christians was the effect significant. For every 1-unit increase in religious group activity, the likelihood that a Pentecostal Christian expressed the highest degree of support for freedom of association increased by 8.1 percentage points. In predominantly Christian states, religious-group activity had a negative effect on support for freedom of association. However, only among mainline Christians was the effect significant. In predominantly Muslim states, religious-group activity had a negative effect on support for freedom of association among mainline Christians but a positive effect among Muslims. Nonetheless, in neither case is the effect significant.

Although religious-group activity tended to have a more positive effect on voting in religiously diverse states than in predominantly Christian and Muslim states, none of the effects was statistically significant. In predominantly Christian states, religious-group activity was shown to have had a negative effect on voting among mainline Christians and Muslims and a slightly positive effect on voting among Pentecostals. Once again, the effects were not significant. In predominantly Muslim states, religious observance had a positive effect on voting among mainline Christians but a negative effect on voting among Muslims. In neither case was the effect significant.

While the results of the statistical analysis are not all that striking, the evidence suggests that engagement in a religious group that meets outside worship services among Christians and Muslims tended to have a slightly more positively effect on key components of a liberal democratic political culture in religiously diverse states than in religiously homogeneous states. Unfortunately, we do not have in-depth interviews from the period between 2006 and 2012. We do not know for certain whether Christian and Muslim religious leaders in réligiously diverse states have been more or less encouraging of actions and attitudes that are conducive to liberal democracy than religious leaders in religiously homogeneous states. Nonetheless, there is evidence that, in the most diverse states, Christian and Muslim religious leaders have been especially effective at organizing and presenting a united front to prevent the spread of anti-freedom political activism—an activism that seeks to discourage religious tolerance and promote the integration of religious and state authority.

Although those espousing anti-freedom political activism who promote less tolerant brands of Christianity and Islam have attempted to spread their political theologies among their co-religionists in religiously diverse settings that have a long history of inter-religious tolerance, they have been less successful there than in parts of the country that are predominantly Muslim or in settings that have rather recently and rapidly become religiously diverse.[37] For example, in 2010 an incident at the University of Ibadan threatened to sour Christian-Muslim relations.[38] That situation, however, was diffused as university officials and Muslim and Christian students came together to channel conflict and place the incident in perspective as they recommitted themselves to mutual respect and tolerance.[39]

There is evidence that religious social networks have been more effective at fighting off attempts to spread illiberal religious agendas in settings that have long been religiously diverse than in those that are religiously homogeneous or have only recently become religiously diverse. For example, in Ibadan, Christian and Muslim leaders have repeatedly issued joint statements and have collaborated to sponsor events designed to prevent episodes of inter-religious violence and heightened rhetoric from raising fears and acts of reprisal.[40] One Nigerian Catholic priest who had worked in Kaduna for many years before being assigned to Ibadan told me, "Christian and Muslim leaders are pro-active here [in Ibadan]. They work together more easily and they do so quickly to squash rumors that can spread and cause uneducated people to attack one another. There are people who love spreading rumors that Christians are attacking Muslims or Muslims are attacking Christians. In Kaduna, we [religious leaders] always seemed to be too slow. Rumors fly there and the next thing you know, people are fighting each other."[41] Although tensions between Christians and Muslims have appeared to increase in recent years even in settings that have for long been religiously diverse and integrated, it seems that Christian and Muslims leaders in such settings find it easier to work together and to effectively promote support for the tolerance and accommodation that are necessary for liberal democracy.

SUMMARY

While many observers claim that Nigeria's religious diversity is politically destabilizing and an obstacle to a liberal democratic political culture, in this chapter I point to quantitative and qualitative evidence to suggest that religious diversity is not necessarily destabilizing or an obstacle to liberal democracy. When comparing settings within Nigeria, I find that religious observance encouraged conventional political participation in Enugu and Kano, settings with little inter-religious diversity. However, religious observance had no impact on the acceptance of differences in opinion or respect for religious liberty in either of these predominantly Christian and Muslim locations.

In settings with a great deal of inter-religious diversity, Jos and Ibadan, I point to evidence to suggest that the effects of religious observance on political actions and attitudes depend on two inter-related factors. The first is the length of time a setting has been religiously diverse, and the second is the extent to which religious groups are integrated, the extent to which they mix and mingle. Ibadan has been religiously diverse for a much longer period of time than Jos. Ibadan's relatively long history of inter-religious diversity has given religious leaders time to learn that attempting to establish religious dominance through politics is literally a dead end. Religious leaders in Ibadan have learned that their religious institutions would be better served if they promoted respect for religious liberty and separation of religious and state authority. It is much less costly to their religious institutions to ensure that no religious institution enjoys special privileges over the others than to attempt to gain such special privileges. By promoting state neutrality in religious affairs, religious leaders allowed for greater Christian-Muslim desegregation.[42] This desegregation in turn created a virtuous cycle. The mixing and mingling of religious groups, made acceptable by religious leaders who began to actively support inter-religious tolerance and state neutrality in religious affairs, decreased the likelihood that future religious leaders would promote intolerance or special privileges for their religious communities at the expense of others. In Jos, religious diversity is a more recent phenomenon, and many Christian and Muslim religious leaders have not yet learned this lesson. Due to recent migration of Muslim groups from the north, religious identity overlaps with ethnic identity, and there is relatively little mixing and mingling of religious groups at the grassroots level. Violence between religious groups has also kept groups segregated. Thus, in Jos there is a vicious cycle: many religious leaders do not encourage tolerance or respect for religious liberty. Therefore, many Christian and Muslim communities do not mix and mingle. The fact that Christians and Muslims are largely segregated increases the likelihood that religious leaders continue to seek political and cultural dominance for the religious communities they lead.

Yet, if Ibadan's Christian and Muslim religious leaders learned over time that it was in the best interest of their religious communities to promote pro-freedom political attitudes if not actions, it is quite possible that Christian and Muslim religious leaders in Jos will do the same. There is evidence to suggest that some prominent Christian and Muslim religious leaders in Jos have responded to the deadly violence by promoting a "live and let live" attitude. For example, the Catholic

Archbishop of Jos, Ignatius Kaigama, and the Grand Khadi Kanam of Plateau State have joined forces to promote peaceful relations between Christians and Muslims. Though these two religious leaders were never known to have promoted religious intolerance, the deadly violence in Jos led them to be much more vocal and organized in the cause of religious liberty and peace. "Militancy, which is the use of force to foster one's religious values, contradicts the very essence of religion. True religion aims at promoting unity and harmony. Where mere geographical expansion or territorial domination become determining factors, God is certainly not the motivating factor behind it," writes Archbishop Kaigama (Kaigama 2006: 6). His Muslim counterpart, the Grand Khadi, has called for "Muslims to live with Christians in brotherhood" (ibid.: 16). Archbishop Kaigama collaborated with Grand Khadi Kanam to author a book devoted to promoting religious-based religious tolerance called *Dialogue of Life: An Urgent Necessity for Nigerian Muslims and Christians* (2006). In Kaduna, another Middle Belt city with religious demographics similar to those of Jos, except with a Muslim majority and a significant Christian minority, there is also reason for optimism. Although many Christian and Muslim leaders have discouraged tolerance, and great deal of deadly violence has occurred since the 1980s, some prominent Christian and Muslim religious leaders have changed their message from one of fight and defend to one tolerance. Based in Kaduna, Pastor James Wuye and Imam Muhammed Nurayan Ashafa have gone from encouraging violence to joining forces to condemn it. As Griswold (2010: 66–67) notes, they see their work to promote peaceful coexistence as the only way to ensure the mutual survival of their respective religious traditions in a religiously diverse society. Thus, there is reason to hope that Christian and Islamic religious communities will contribute positively to a liberal democratic political culture in Jos and other parts of the Middle Belt because Christian and Muslim leaders learn that it is the best way to address the needs of the people they are called to serve and the only way to ensure the survival of their religious traditions where they both exist in large numbers. If they do learn this important lesson, I propose that religious-inspired support for freedom will grow because of, rather than despite, the interaction that religious diversity makes possible.

7

Important Lessons and New Questions

In our search for explanations for why Christian and Islamic religious communities encourage or discourage actions and attitudes conducive to liberal democracy, we have focused on sub-Saharan Africa, and we have taken an especially close look at the case of Nigeria. Based on analysis of cross-national and aggregate-level data (in Chapter 3), we have found evidence of a positive relationship between religious diversity and the extent to which Christian and Muslim religious leaders have openly supported pro-democracy movements in sub-Saharan Africa. Further, when analyzing individual-level data and comparing countries included in Round 4 of the Afrobarometer survey (in Chapter 4), we found that religious observance was more positively associated with some key liberal democratic attitudes and behaviors in the most religiously diverse countries of sub-Saharan Africa than in the least religiously diverse countries of the region. In analyzing survey data from religiously diverse Nigeria, predominantly Muslim Senegal, and predominantly Christian Uganda (in Chapter 5), we found that religious observance was having the most positive effect on civic engagement and religious tolerance in Nigeria. In comparing four cities within Nigeria—Enugu, Kano, Jos, and Ibadan (in Chapter 6)—we found that Christian and Islamic religious observance was having the most positive effect on key liberal democratic ideals, especially respect for religious liberty, in Ibadan, the city with the longest history of religious diversity, where Christians and Muslims have gradually come to share neighborhoods, schools, workplaces, and biological family ties. Further, we found that Christian and Muslim leaders in Ibadan have tended to be more supportive of peaceful political participation and respect for religious freedom than in the other three settings. Many of these leaders justified such support based on Ibadan's religious diversity and integration.

Few topics have been subjected to as much over-generalization and over-simplification as the relationship between religion and politics, and, therefore, the last thing I want to do is more of the same. It is important to recognize, right from the start, that the results presented in this book are based on data taken from particular places (i.e., sub-Saharan Africa, Nigeria, Senegal, and Uganda) at discreet points in time. We should not try to generalize too broadly based on such a geographically and temporally limited body of evidence. While I have put forward a general theoretical framework for explaining religious-based support for a liberal democratic political culture back in Chapter 2, it will only be possible to thoroughly test such a framework with further research within and beyond sub-Saharan Africa. Nonetheless, the findings reported in the previous chapters do allow us to draw some important conclusions that call into question overly simplistic and mechanical explanations for how and why Christianity and Islam affect political culture. While the results presented in this book do not prove beyond the shadow of a doubt the soundness of the theory I put forward in this book, they do provide some support for the theory. Further, they raise important questions for future research. Ultimately, it is my hope that this book represents one step forward along the path that leads to a deeper understanding of the factors that increase the likelihood that Christian and Islamic communities contribute positively to a political culture that is characterized by civic engagement and social tolerance—one that I call a liberal democratic political culture. If we can identify conditions that increase the likelihood that Christian and Islamic religious communities contribute positively to peaceful political participation and social tolerance, we can focus energy on cultivating such conditions.

In this chapter, I present the key take-away points of this book and discuss what the results presented in the previous chapters do and do not allow us to conclude. In discussing what we are *not* able to conclude based on the results reported in this book, I suggest directions for future research. I bring this book to a close by underlining the practical importance and real-world policy relevance of efforts to develop an ever-deeper understanding of where, when, how, and why Christian and Islamic religious communities encourage or discourage peaceful political participation and social tolerance.

WHAT WE CAN CONCLUDE

Although based largely on one region of the world, sub-Saharan Africa, and on data collected at discreet points in time, the results presented in this book do allow us to draw important conclusions that promise to advance efforts to develop a better understanding of the ways in which Christianity and Islam are applied to public life. The findings call into question certain assumptions about how and why Christianity and Islam affect the prospects for liberal democracy. The results confirm the importance of social context and, more specifically, the extent to which the social context is religiously diverse and integrated. Further, this book reminds us that we cannot know how religious communities are affecting political actions and attitudes unless we analyze individual-level data and zero in on the effects of religious observance vis-à-vis other individual-level factors that may affect political actions and attitudes. This is something that should go without mention, but it warrants mention since it is still quite common for people to make assertions about how certain religious communities are affecting political culture based on the statements that some members of religious communities make, or the actions that relatively few members of religious communities take. All too often, observers assume that religious communities are affecting political culture in ways that encourage or discourage civic engagement and tolerance based on analysis of highly aggregated data and without considering how religious observance itself is affecting the actions and attitudes of the vast majority of individuals who belong to such communities. Too many people have taken analytical shortcuts and have leaped to conclusions concerning the impact of religion on public life. This book reminds us that there are no shortcuts allowed if we are to develop an accurate understanding of the rather complex ways that religious communities, particularly Christian and Islamic communities, affect political actions and attitudes. Finally, the findings reported in this book show that cross-national studies should be supplemented with sub-national comparative analysis. If we look at countries from a distance and only compare the effects of religious observance on political culture across countries, without recognizing the possibility that there is variation in the effects of religious observance across settings within countries, our conclusions about the effects of religious observance on political culture are likely to be incomplete at best, and totally wrong at worst. In other words, "the forest" we see when we observe countries from a distance can prevent us from recognizing "the trees," or the variation we find within a country when we take a closer look. Each of these important lessons deserves further discussion.

TIME AND PLACE MATTER

Stepan (2001) and others (Sisk 2011; Geertz 1973; Villalon 1995; Appleby 2000; Philpott 2007) have asserted that Christianity and Islam are not always and everywhere applied to public life in the same way, and each religious tradition is capable of generating different types of political theologies that are more or less conducive to liberal democracy. World religions as old, transnational, and transcultural as Christianity and Islam are multivocal (Stepan 2001). In other words, Christian and Muslim religious leaders and "ordinary" religious people have applied their scriptures and traditions in various ways across different social, cultural, economic, political, and religious contexts so that Christians and Muslims today may find theological justifications for various political positions. They may draw on their religious traditions to justify political activism or quietism, religious tolerance or intolerance. This does not mean that Christian and Muslim religious leaders can find theological sources to legitimately justify just any political position, attitude, or behavior. Although it may be more difficult to establish widely recognized boundaries of legitimacy in some religious traditions than others (e.g., Islam, without a universally recognized teaching authority, as compared to Roman Catholicism, with a centralized teaching authority that has the final word on what does and does not count as legitimately Roman Catholic behaviors and attitudes), all religious traditions and communities have parameters, and it is possible for religious leaders and ordinary religious people to be "out of bounds." Despite the boundaries that distinguish the legitimate from illegitimate ways of applying particular religious traditions to public life, it seems quite clear that religious leaders and ordinary believers have some discretion to apply religion to politics in ways they find most helpful for realizing their goals for their religious communities. In other words, they have options and they make choices about how to apply their religious traditions to politics—which attitudes to encourage and adopt, as well as which actions to promote and to take. They may choose to apply their religious traditions in ways that encourage or discourage voting, political discussions, and political protest. They may choose to cite religious sources to justify the integration or the separation of religious and state authority.

The evidence presented in this book confirms this assertion; religious leaders, as well as "ordinary believers," were making choices about how to apply their religious traditions to politics that varied by national and local context. Even within one region of the world, such as sub-Saharan Africa, and within one country in that region, namely Nigeria, we have found religious leaders of the same faith tradition choosing to espouse different types of political actions and attitudes. We have found that sub-Saharan Africa's mainline Christian religious leaders have not always and everywhere encouraged actions and attitudes conducive to liberal democracy, just as the region's Muslim religious leaders have not always and everywhere discouraged actions and attitudes conducive to liberal democracy. We have found variation across time and place. This variation leads us to conclude that, in the sub-Saharan African countries included in our study, time and place were more important than the type of religious community itself for explaining why religious leaders encouraged actions and attitudes conducive to liberal democracy. Although the conventional wisdom would lead us to expect mainline Christian communities everywhere to have been encouraging actions and attitudes conducive to liberal democracy, we did not find this to be the case in Nigeria. In some settings, mainline Christian communities were having no effect on actions and attitudes conducive to liberal democracy, while in other settings, at the same point in time, they were having a positive effect. Additionally, we did not find Nigeria's Islamic religious communities everywhere promoting the same type of political theology, one that discourages social tolerance and respect for religious freedom, which I call anti-freedom political activism (as the conventional wisdom would lead us to believe). In some settings, Islamic religious communities were effectively encouraging actions and attitudes conducive to liberal democracy, while in other settings, at the same point in time, they were having no effect on such actions and attitudes.

All three religious groupings included in our study of Nigeria—mainline Christians, Pentecostal Christians, and Muslims—moved together in a rather remarkable way depending on the setting. For example, religious observance had a positive effect on respect for religious freedom among members of all three religious groupings in religiously diverse Ibadan (see Figure 6.5). In predominantly Muslim Kano and predominantly Christian Enugu, we found that religious observance had no effect on respect for religious freedom, regardless of the religious grouping in question. In Jos, religious observance had a consistently negative effect, albeit statistically insignificant, on respect for religious freedom among members of all three religious groupings. The point here is that, contrary to the expectations of the conventional wisdom, religious observance was not having qualitatively different effects on respect for religious freedom, depending on the religious group in question. In other words, we did not find religious observance encouraging respect for religious freedom among mainline Christians in Ibadan but discouraging respect for religious freedom among Ibadan's Muslims or Pentecostal Christians. Religious observance had a positive effect on members of all three religious groupings in Ibadan, albeit to varying degrees. Additionally, we did not find religious observance having a negative effect on respect for religious freedom among Muslims in Jos, but a positive effect among Jos's mainline Christians and Pentecostals. Among Muslims and mainline Christians, as well as Pentecostals, religious observance had a negative effect, albeit a statistically insignificant one, on respect for religious freedom in Jos. If setting mattered and shaped the effect that Nigeria's Christian and Islamic religious communities had on the political actions and attitudes of those who belonged to them, as I propose, this raises an important question: What is it about the setting that mattered?

RELIGIOUS DIVERSITY MATTERS
(IN A SURPRISING WAY)

There are several factors that distinguish some national or local settings from others. Although there is a tendency for observers to lump all of sub-Saharan African countries together, there are important differences when we compare the national and sub-national contexts in the region. Besides different colonial legacies and histories, with some more violent and some more peaceful than others, sub-Saharan African countries vary in terms of their levels of human development, economic inequality, economic growth, educational attainment, political and civil freedoms, ethnic diversity, and religious diversity. It is not very easy to determine the relative effect of any one of these factors on the political impact of Christian and Islamic religious communities. However, while controlling for a number of factors that distinguish sub-Saharan African countries from each other (i.e., human development, education, level of political repression or democracy, ethnic diversity, and religious diversity), we have found that religious diversity stands out as a factor that matters a great deal and in a surprising way. Although many observers have suggested that religious diversity makes societies less tolerant and more prone to destabilizing violent conflict, particularly those societies of the so-called developing world (Lipset 1959; Easterly and Levine 1997; Karatnycky 2002; Montalvo and Reynal-Querol 2003; Quinn and Quinn 2003; Esteban and Mayoral 2011), the evidence from sub-Saharan Africa, and in particular Nigeria, to which we point in this book, indicates that the likelihood that Christian and Islamic communities effectively encouraged certain actions and attitudes conducive to liberal democracy tended to be greater in religiously diverse and integrated settings than in religiously homogenous settings or religiously diverse but segregated settings.

We have found evidence that religious diversity and integration increased the likelihood that Christian and Islamic communities encouraged civic enagegement and respect for religious freedom in Nigeria *because* of how these conditons affected the ways in which Christian and Muslim religious leaders decided to achieve their goals for their religious institutions. As I proposed in Chapter 2, these goals are (1) to grow their religious communities as large as they can, and (2) to influence the wider society according to the norms and values of their religious communities. In-depth interviews with Christian and Muslim religious leaders across the four Nigerian settings included in our study reveal that they were basing their decisions to encourage (or not) certain types of political participation (i.e., voting or more demanding forms of political participation, such as raising an issue together with others in public to get something done in the community), and religious tolerance on the level of religious diversity in their particular setting.

Where Christians were in the minority, such as in predominantly Muslim Kano, most Christian leaders, both mainline Christians and Pentecostals, said that they did not encourage political activism because they feared it would trigger a religious conflict that their religious communities would probably lose. In other words, to encourage political acitivism in such an environment would likely undermine their ability to survive and realize their goals of growth and greater influence. Where they formed a majority, such as in Enugu, most Christian leaders noted that they saw no need to do more than encourage Christians to vote in elections. Where Muslims formed a majority, as in Kano, most Muslim leaders echoed the sentiment. They reported having encouraged Muslims to vote, but saw no need to do more than that. In settings where they formed the vast majority of the population, most Christian and Muslim religious leaders decided that encouraging members of their religious communities to vote was the most desirable way to realize their goals of continued growth and influence. However, in religiously diverse but highly segregated Jos, most Christian and Muslim leaders said they believed it very important to encourage their followers to act together to raise issues in public, since otherwise they believed their communities would lose their freedom to grow and influence social life. Christian religious leaders in predominantly Christian Enugu and Muslim religious leaders in predominantly Muslim Kano noted that they saw nothing wrong with constitutionally enshrining their religious law as the law of the land or making laws that privilege their faith traditions over others as long as members of their faith traditions formed the majority of the population. In Jos, where Muslims represented a fast-growing minority, Christian leaders noted the importance of encouraging political action. Some even encouraged violence so as to maintain or achieve greater Christian dominance over the social and political life of Jos, a city that they considered to be theirs.

In Ibadan, most Christian and Muslim religious leaders said they did not see the need to encourage much political activism and noted that they believed neither Christianity nor Islam should be socially or politically privileged. Unlike in areas where Christians formed a majority (i.e., Enugu) or where Muslims formed a majority (i.e., Kano), religious leaders in religiously diverse Ibadan said they believed that the state should treat both religions equally. Christian and Muslim religious leaders said they encouraged tolerance of the other religion and rejected the suggestion that they should seek to achieve dominance over social and political life for their respective religious communities. To attempt to achieve state-sanctioned superiority, they noted, would bring the destruction of their religious communities and/or would undermine their authority among Christians and Muslims who had lived side by side and even shared biological family ties for as long as they can remember. In such a religiously diverse and integrated setting as Ibadan, Christian and Muslim religious leaders decided that the best way for them to grow their religious communities and influence the wider society would be to encourage religious tolerance and the separation of religious and state authority.

While there is some question as to whether religious diversity causes religious tolerance or religious tolerance explains religious diversity, we find evidence from Nigeria to indicate that the causal arrow there has run from diversity to tolerance. When we look at Ibadan, the most religiously diverse of the four settings included in our study, we find that Christianity and Islam collided upon first encounter. As described in Chapter 6, there was a great deal of conflict between Christians and Muslims as religious leaders sought to supplant the other religious group and to establish social and political superiority over the area. Neither Christianity nor Islam seemed to be encouraging much religious tolerance and, instead, Christian and Muslim leaders attempted to gain a privileged social and political position vis-à-vis the other. Neither Christian nor Muslim religious leaders were great champions of religious freedom, unless, of course, that freedom was limited to the religious communities they were leading. Peel (2003: 192) notes that, during the mid-nineteenth century, Muslim preachers in Ibadan warned Ibadan's rulers that "their lives would be cut short" if they allowed Christian missionaries into the area. Religious leaders fanned the flames of intolerance as Christians and Muslims tried to establish superiority in terms of numbers and influence (Peel 1967). Muslims portrayed members of the Anglican Church Missionary Society (CMS) as "enemies of the truth," and the CMS countered by calling Islam "the greatest obstacle to progress and civilization" (Laitin 1986: 129). Laitin (1986: ibid.) notes that Muslims complained that their children were under pressure to convert to Christianity as they attended government-supported Christian schools, and they sought government support for their own Muslim schools. Up until the mid-twentieth century, Muslims complained that Christian politicians were dominating governmental affairs in Nigeria's southwest and that Muslims were often the victims of discrimination (Kukah and Falola 1996: 84–85). Christians complained that it was unfair for the government to support Muslims so that they could make the *haj*, or pilgrimage to Mecca (Laitin 1986; Kukah and Falola 1996). Thus, the culture of tolerance between Christians and Muslims evolved over time through repeated interaction and a process of learning. As Kukah and Falola (1996: 66) note, religious leaders realized that they would not be able to displace the other religions and made a practical decision to get along.

It is quite obvious that growing religious diversity in Nigeria has not automatically prompted religious-based support for peaceful political participation and religious tolerance. We need only look as far as Nigeria's Middle Belt and the near north of Nigeria and to the cities of Jos and Kaduna to underscore this point. The Middle Belt has become more religiously diverse over the past several decades as many Muslims moved south into what had been predominantly Christian territory, where Muslims had long been present but where Christians had for long constituted a clear majority. As the area has become more religiously diverse, there has been little in the way of religious integration. Many Christians have responded with alarm to the growing Muslim presence. They have expressed fears that they will lose their land and that Muslims will dominate social life and political affairs. As indicated in Chapter 6, some Christians have responded to the growing religious diversity in their area with violence against Muslims. Christians have cleansed certain areas of Muslims, and the city of Jos has been largely "balkanized" along religious lines, with Local Government Authority (LGA) North becoming almost exclusively Muslim and a no-go zone for

Christians, and LGA South becoming an exclusively Christian zone and a no-go zone for Muslims. Complicating matters in the Middle Belt and the city of Jos is the fact that religious identities overlap with ethnic identities and indigene/settler status, with those considered indigenes being mostly Christians and those considered settlers being mostly Muslims. This gives Muslims in the area a sense of being second-class citizens in their own country. Assuming that there will be population growth among Christians and Muslims and that Muslim migration into the area from northern states will continue, the situation is not sustainable. Christian and Muslim religious leaders may continue to seek to dominate the other or, alternatively, may recognize that the communities they lead would be better off if they eschewed attempts to dominate each other and instead agreed that no religious community should dominate the other.

Although the learning process has been slower than many would like, there is reason to believe that many Christian and Muslim religious leaders in Jos and other areas of Nigeria's Middle Belt are coming to terms with the growing diversity and are recognizing that the status quo threatens the future of their religious communities. They are coming to see that their religious institutions would be better off if they promoted a live-and-let-live ethic and agreed that neither Christianity nor Islam should enjoy special privileges over the other (Paden 2012). In Kaduna, another Middle Belt city with religious demographics similar to Jos, except with a Muslim majority and a significant Christian minority, there is also reason for optimism. Although many Christian and Muslim leaders have discouraged tolerance and a great deal of deadly violence has occurred since the 1980s, some prominent Christian and Muslim religious leaders have changed their message from one of fight and defend to one of tolerance.[1] Based in Kaduna, Pastor James Wuye and Imam Muhammed Nurayan Ashafa have gone from encouraging violence to joining forces to condemn it. As Griswold (2010: 66–67) notes, they see their work to promote peaceful coexistence as the only way to ensure the mutual survival of their respective religious traditions in a religiously diverse society. Thus, there is reason to hope that Christian and Islamic religious communities will contribute positively to a liberal democratic political culture in Jos and other parts of the Middle Belt because Christian and Muslim leaders will learn that it is the best way to address the needs of the people they are called to serve and the only way to ensure the survival of their religious traditions where they both exist in large numbers. Time will tell whether and how growing religious diversity will affect how religious leaders decide to apply their religious traditions to politics in the Middle Belt and in cities like Jos. As I suggest later in this chapter, future research would do well to study whether and how changes in religious diversity, as well as other social changes and political developments in the area, affect political actions and attitudes that the Middle Belt's Christian and Muslim religious leaders choose to encourage.

While religious diversity alone does not supply a complete explanation for why Christian and Islamic religious communities promote a political culture conducive to liberal democracy, the evidence presented in this book suggests that attempts to explain the various ways in which Christian and Islamic communities affect political actions and attitudes that ignore religious diversity may fail to capture an important, often crucial, factor. In this book I have provided evidence from sub-Saharan

Africa and, in particular, Nigeria that supports Roger Trigg's (2014: 157) assertion, "Diversity of belief has always been a driving force for greater religious freedom."

INDIVIDUAL-LEVEL ANALYSIS MATTERS

While observers all too often look at the religious make-up of a country (i.e., whether it is predominantly Christian or Muslim or religiously diverse) and the political culture or level of inter-religious violence that prevails in a country to draw conclusions about how religious communities must be affecting political culture, this book shows that, when we control for religious observance at the individual level, we often find evidence to call such conclusions into question. For example, when we look at Nigeria from afar, we would likely assert that the country's religious diversity explains the inter-religious strife in the country. We might expect to find that Nigeria's Christian and Islamic religious communities have discouraged religious tolerance. After all, Nigeria is religiously diverse, and there has been much more inter-religious violent conflict in Nigeria than in neighboring countries that are less religiously diverse. However, as shown in Chapter 5, we actually find that religious observance among both Christians and Muslims was having a more positive effect on respect for religious freedom in Nigeria than in two religiously homogeneous countries that have been largely free of inter-religious violence of late, predominantly Muslim Senegal and predominantly Christian Uganda. This book reminds us that we cannot know how Christian and Islamic religious communities are affecting the prospects for liberal democracy until we zero in on the effects of religious observance on political actions and attitudes. Until we assess the effects of religious observance on political actions and attitudes relative to the effects of other differences that exist between individual Christians and Muslims that may affect their political actions and attitudes, such as gender, age, income, and education, we cannot claim to know how religious communities are affecting political culture.

SUB-NATIONAL ANALYSIS MATTERS

Besides underlining the importance of individual-level analysis, this book reveals how critically important it is to supplement an examination of differences across countries with an examination of differences within countries. It is crucial to recognize sub-national variation. As we have already noted, if we simply look at the case of Nigeria as a whole and from a distance, we would likely assert, as others have, that religious diversity has been an obstacle to political stability, let alone liberal democracy. However, when we look within Nigeria we find variation across settings that does not support this assertion. Religious observance was having, at the time of the survey we conducted, a more positive effect on support for key liberal democratic ideals, including frequency of political discussions and respect for religious freedom, in the most religiously diverse of the four settings included in our study. Given our findings, we cannot very well conclude that religious diversity is itself an obstacle to a liberal democratic political culture in Nigeria. In fact, the evidence suggests that religious diversity, if followed by religious integration, increases the likelihood that Christian and Islamic religious communities promote religious tolerance if not civic engagement. Such religiously based support for religious tolerance is crucially important for the the future of liberal democracy.[2]While these findings are based on the analysis of data from Nigeria, there is good reason to expect that an examination of sub-national and individual-level data in other religiously diverse societies would also call into question conclusions based on national-level data alone.

CONCLUSIONS WE CANNOT MAKE AND DIRECTIONS FOR FUTURE RESEARCH

Based on the evidence presented in this book, it is tempting to make generalizations about how Christianity and Islam affect the prospects for liberal democracy. As noted, plenty of observers have made such generalizations and continue to do so based on data taken from certain parts of the world at particular points in time. We all would like to claim that we have revealed something that is universal—something that explains a great deal across time and place. When it comes to this book, it is tempting to conclude that religious diversity eventually leads Christian and Muslim religious leaders to encourage civic engagement and religious tolerance always and everywhere. It is also tempting to conclude that religious diversity tends to be the most important factor for helping us to explain the political theologies espoused by Christian and Muslim religious leaders. While we may very well find support for these assertions, we do not yet have evidence that would allow us to make such claims. In fact, one reason I have repeatedly used the past tense when presenting the results in Chapters 4, 5, and 6 is to make clear that these results pertain to particular points in time. In a spirit of humility, it is important to review the conclusions that we *cannot* make based on the findings reported in this book and to propose how future research might put us in a better position to draw such conclusions or, depending on the evidence, conclude otherwise.

We Cannot Conclude That Religious Diversity Matters *Everywhere* and *Always* in the Same Way

Based on the evidence presented in this book, we cannot conclude that religious diversity matters everywhere and always in the same way. While we found evidence to indicate that sub-Saharan Africa's Christian and Muslim religious leaders were more openly supportive of the pro-democracy movements of the late 1980s and early 1990s in the region's most religiously diverse countries than in the region's religiously homogenous settings, this does not necessarily mean that we would find the same to be true beyond the region or even within the region today. Although we found evidence that religious observance had a more positive effect on civic engagement and respect for religious freedom in Nigeria than in Senegal and Uganda, we cannot say for certain that we would find the same to be true when comparing the same three countries today. Even within Nigeria, it is important to recognize that there are limits to what we can reasonably claim, since we conducted our survey only four settings at particular point in time. While we found that religious observance was having a more positive effect on religious tolerance in religiously diverse and integrated Ibadan than in religiously diverse but segregated Jos and the more religiously homogeneous cities of Kano and Enugu, we do not know whether we would find the same if we compared these four Nigerian cities today.

One big question for future research is, does religious diversity tend everywhere and always to increase the likelihood that Christian and Islamic communities encourage actions and attitudes that are conducive to liberal democracy? Have we found an interesting relationship that pertains only to a particular region and country at a particular point in time, or are we onto something that is generally true—that religious diversity and integration tend to increase the extent to which Christian and Islamic communities effectively encourage a political culture conducive to liberal democracy always and everywhere? The argument I put forward in Chapter 2 aspires to be a general theory that would explain the variation in the extent to which Christian and Islamic communities encourage actions and attitudes conducive to liberal democracy, regardless of the geographic setting or point in time. I propose that religious diversity, which varies across time and space, helps explain whether Christian and Islamic communities effectively promote a political culture conducive to liberal democracy and that diversity eventually increases the likelihood that Christian and Muslim leaders effectively encourage civic engagement and religious tolerance. In order to more thoroughly test the argument, we would need to conduct research that, among other things, includes more countries and more settings within countries that vary in terms of their religious diversity.

While we cannot go back in time to gather the individual-level data necessary to understand how religious observance was affecting political actions and attitudes in other countries, we can go back in time and across the world to discover whether there is any evidence that religious leaders tended to be more openly supportive of democratic institutions and religious tolerance in more religiously diverse settings than in religiously homogeneous settings. While a much deeper comparative analysis is necessary, we do find some reason to think that religious diversity helps explain the variation across time and space in the extent to which Christian communities have been supportive of democracy and religious freedom. For example, in his book, *Rendering unto Caesar* (1998), Anthony Gill argues that Catholic bishops were much more outspoken against authoritarian rule and in favor of democratic change where the Catholic Church faced a great deal of competition from Protestant groups than where the Catholic Church faced very little of such competition. Where Catholic attempts to retain membership and influence over the wider society turned to concern for the poor or popular classes, which was most often the case where they faced stiff competition from Protestants, Catholic bishops more openly opposed dictatorship and promoted democracy. According to Gill, countries where Catholic bishops were most openly supportive of pro-democracy movements of the 1970s and 1980s had relatively high growth in the percentage of the population belonging to Protestant groups between 1900 and 1970 (Gill 1998: 106). These countries are Brazil, Chile, El Salvador, Nicaragua, and Panama. In countries where the Catholic bishops were neutral or took pro-authoritarian political positions during the 1970s and 1980s, such as Argentina, Bolivia, Honduras, Paraguay, and Uruguay, there had been relatively little growth in Protestants between 1900 and 1970 (ibid.). "Religious competition is the best predictor of episcopal opposition to authoritarian rule [during the 1970s and 1980s] as compared to other potential explanations," writes Gill (1998: 104).[3]

In her book, *Religious Liberties: Anti-Catholicism and Liberal Democracy in Nineteenth Century U.S. Literature and Culture* (2011), Elizabeth Fenton proposes that American-Protestant support for liberal democratic ideals is largely the product of the encounter with Catholicism. Fenton (2011: 46) argues that ". . . The U.S. liberal democratic tradition did not spring fully formed out of Anglo-Protestant America but, rather, emerged from debates about Catholicism's role in the hemisphere and the world at large." Of course, there is good reason to think that those debates would not have taken place had there not been a growing number of Catholics and Catholic educational institutions with which to contend. As eminent sociologist of religion Peter Berger noted in an interview conducted in 2013:

> The United States started out with [religious] pluralism. Some didn't like this at all. The Puritans in New England hanged Quakers on Boston Common. They were not tolerant of other religions. They had to become tolerant because there were too many of these other people. You couldn't hang them all. You couldn't convert them all.[4]

In a cross-national and worldwide study, Alesina, Devleeschauwer, Easterly, Kurlat, and Wacziarg (2003) have found evidence of a positive relationship between religious diversity and indicators associated with greater tolerance.[5] While Alesina and colleagues find it difficult to believe that greater religious diversity may result in more tolerance and suggest that the causal arrow must run from tolerance to greater religious diversity, that some societies are more religiously diverse precisely because they were/are more tolerant societies to begin with, they provide no analysis to support this causal assertion (ibid.). While we cannot know at this point which way the causal arrow of their study runs, the findings reported in this book suggest that we should not summarily rule out the possibility that the causal arrow runs from religious diversity to greater tolerance.

Undoubtedly, we need to gather more data if we are to reasonably conclude that religious diversity tends to always and everywhere increase the likelihood that Christian and Islamic religious communities contribute positively to the prospects for liberal democracy. In accord with what I noted earlier in this chapter, we need to control for religious observance, we need studies that include a variety of Christian and Islamic religious communities, and we need longitudinal studies that allow us to assess whether and how changes in religious diversity or other socio-political changes that occur across time affect changes in religious-based support for a liberal democratic political culture across time. We need to conduct research that assesses whether and how the types of political theologies that religious leaders espouse change across time depending on changes in religious diversity and other socio-political changes that occur across time. Longitudinal studies that help us to discern whether and how changes in religious diversity and other socio-political changes affect the impact that religious observance has on the political actions and attitudes of individual Christians and Muslims are also necessary if we are to more thoroughly test the theory I propose in this book.

While this book does provide evidence to suggest that differences in religious diversity do affect the content of preaching among both Christian and Muslim leaders, I propose that further study focus especially on discerning any relationship between changes in religious demography across time and the political content of preaching. While there have been some studies on the content of preaching, they have often been limited to one country or one religious tradition and have not attempted to systematically relate the changes in local environment to differences in content (Reeber 1993; Nelson and Blizzard 1975; Beatty and Walter 1989). Although there have been some studies devoted to the impact of preaching with political content, few attempt to explain the variation in the content in the first place. Those that have done so have focused on differences between denominations rather than differences in the environment. In other words, little attention has been focused on the variation we find within denominations that may be explained by studying differences in social, economic, political, and religious conditions across settings or changes in such conditions across time in the same setting.

Longitudinal studies are necessary if we are to deepen our understanding of how religious diversity and other social conditions affect whether and the extent to which Christian and Islamic communities promote actions and attitudes conducive to liberal democracy. It is important to recognize that the findings from Nigeria reported in this book provide snapshots of how religious observance was affecting political attitudes and behaviors at particular places at a given point in time. Nonetheless, the results represent baseline data from which we can assess the effects of a changing climate on the impact that Christian and Islamic communities have on political culture. With additional data, we will be able to assess whether and how changes in religious diversity in any one of the four settings, as well as changes in the Nigeria's broader political, economic, and religious climate, affect the impact of religious observance on the political actions and attitudes of ordinary Christians and Muslims.

Further, studies intended to promote understanding of the variation in the political content of preaching across time and in various parts of the world would do well to integrate analysis of qualitative and quantitative data. As noted, it would be important to carefully collect the content of sermons and preaching with attention to nuances and an appreciation for the cultural context. Despite the headline-grabbing religious leaders who openly take extreme positions and denigrate other religions, it is reasonable to assume that most Christian and Muslim preachers and teachers do not openly and directly discourage religious tolerance, encourage the religious cleansing of particular geographic areas, or call for the integration of religious and state authority. It is quite possible that messages that promote intolerance, violence against religious others, or the integration of religious and state authority are veiled in language and figures of speech that would not be readily understood by outsiders not familiar with the cultural context. Thus, cultural proficiency is necessary if we are to collect the solid qualitative data needed to develop the understanding we want to achieve. In order to conduct the type of comparative analysis that would allow us to discern any trends and patterns, it would also be necessary to have a large enough sample of preachers and locations. Ideally, the sample of preachers spans many countries, several regions of the world, various socioeconomic conditions, and different religious traditions. A study like this would build on the work reported in this book and promises to contribute greatly to our understanding of the relationship between the environment and the political content of preaching. However, rather than simply focusing on the preaching, such a longitudinal study should also focus on the impact of such preaching on the attitudes and behaviors of ordinary Christians and Muslims, the congregations and audiences whose actions and attitudes such preaching is intended to affect. A longer temporal dimension that follows across time religious leaders and those who belong to the religious communities they lead would allow us to arrive at a more complete explanation for why Christian and Islamic communities encourage or discourage (or have no effect at all) on civic engagement and religious tolerance.

We Cannot Conclude That Every Society Shares the Same "Tipping Point" of Religious Diversity

As noted, religious diversity initially triggered conflict between Christians and Muslims in Ibadan as Christian and Muslim religious leaders attempted to gain superiority over each other. However, evidence indicates that Ibadan's Christian and Muslim religious leaders eventually halted their attempts to establish social and political hegemony for their respective religious tradition at the expense of the other. They eventually realized that they would be better able to grow their religious institutions and influence the wider society by promoting peaceful political engagement and respect for religious liberty. Although we currently lack the evidence needed to generalize, there is reason to believe that the same has been true in other parts of sub-Saharan Africa and beyond, such as in Latin America (Gill 1998), North America (Gill 2008; Fenton 2011; Trigg 2014), and South Asia (Varshney 2002). There is evidence to suggest that the experience of growing diversity has eventually prompted religious leaders to change the way they have sought to grow their religious communities and influence the wider society. The question then is, what does "eventually" mean? If religious leaders and ordinary religious people learn over time that the best way to achieve their goals for the religious communities they lead in religiously diverse settings is to encourage civic engagement and religious tolerance, how long does it typically take? Can we say that once a religious minority makes up a certain percentage of the population, religious communities begin encouraging actions and attitudes that are conducive to liberal democracy? Is the tipping point 20 percent, 30 percent, or 40 percent? Can we say that once a setting has been diverse and integrated for a certain period of time, religious leaders give up trying to establish hegemony for their religious communities and begin promoting liberal democratic values? How long must a setting be religiously diverse before religious leaders begin to encourage rather than discourage support for liberal democratic ideals? Is it five years, ten years, or longer?

Perhaps the "tipping point" has less to do with time than with events and, more specifically, violent events. Violence often leads to more violence and to a cycle of revenge. In the name of God, people seek to settle scores with people of different religions or those they consider hostile to their worldviews, whom they call aggressors (Juergensmeyer 2003). However, the ongoing experience of inter-religious violence that never seems to give one religious group a clear victory may lead to exhaustion so that religious leaders agree to disagree and to live and let live. To some extent, this seems to have been the case in the most religiously diverse areas of Western Europe, where political leaders and religious leaders finally decided, as in the Treaty or Peace of Westphalia of 1648 and the Act of Toleration of 1689, that religious wars would produce no clear winner and would continue to shatter lives and economies, leaving everyone, both Protestants and Catholics, worse off than they would be if they simply agreed to tolerate each other to at least some extent (Trigg 2014; Gill 2008).

Although we found that religious diversity and integration increased the likelihood that Christian and Islamic communities encouraged actions and attitudes conducive to liberal democracy in sub-Saharan Africa, particularly in Nigeria, we cannot conclude that a certain level of religious diversity and integration is necessary or that a setting has to be diverse for a certain specific length of time before the communities begin effectively encouraging such actions and attitudes. While there is very good reason to think that the degree of religious diversity and the amount of time a setting has been religiously diverse matter, we cannot say for certain how much religious diversity is necessary, or for how long a setting must be religiously diverse before religious communities are transformed by those who belong to them into institutions that promote rather than impede a political culture conducive to liberal democracy.

It seems unreasonable to think that there is one "tipping point" for all societies when religious diversity begins to prompt religiously inspired support for liberal democratic ideals. Among other factors, history is likely to matter. We cannot dismiss the history of relations between religious groups in a society. History teaches us that people do not easily forgive or forget violence perpetrated on them because of their social identities, particularly when religious identity is part of the mix (Horowitz 1985). A long cycle of violence and revenge between religious groups may be difficult to break. A society may be religiously diverse for a considerable period of time, but, if there is a long history of inter-religious violence, religious communities may impede rather than promote respect for religious liberty and support for the separation of religious and state authority. Comparative historical studies that help us to understand deeply when and why religious diversity prompts religious leaders to promote pro-freedom political activism would represent a significant contribution.

It is important to recognize that the forces of globalization may mean that a certain degree of "virtual" religious diversity exists even in the most religiously homogeneous of settings, and future research might assess how this new virtual religious diversity affects the political application of Christianity and Islam. Greater Internet access means that even historically dominant religious institutions do not have the monopoly over religion that they once enjoyed. Leaders of long-dominant religious majorities, Christians or Muslims, may react defensively to solidify state-granted privileges and to push for the passage of legislation that curtails freedom of media access and freedom of religion. It seems likely that long-dominant religious majorities would find it more difficult to check the growth of virtual religious diversity than to check the growth or "real religious diversity" or the emergence and flourishing of new and different religious communities. One question for further study concerns whether this new virtual religious diversity results in "real religious diversity" and, if so, whether this real religious diversity increases or decreases the extent to which leaders of the long-dominant religious majority and the fast-growing religious minorities encourage peaceful political participation and tolerance.

The Practical Importance and Policy Relevance of Developing a Greater Understanding

The results discussed in this book do have policy implications, and future research focused on how social conditions, including religious diversity, are likely to affect the political application of Christianity and Islam is important because of its policy relevance. If we find that certain social conditions, such as religious diversity and integration, increase the likelihood that Christian and Islamic communities encourage civic engagement and social tolerance, then we can propose that policymakers find ways to cultivate such conditions. If we find that certain conditions, such as religious homogeneity or the segregation of religious groups, increase the likelihood that Christianity and Islam are applied in ways that discourage religious tolerance and lead to violence against those who believe differently, then we can propose that energy and resources be spent on changing those social conditions.

At the very least, this book calls into question the wisdom of policies that espouse the creation or maintenance of religiously homogeneous political units as always and everywhere the best way to prevent religious institutions from negatively affecting political stability and the prospects for liberal democracy. In fact, the evidence presented in this book suggests that, in the long run, Christian and Islamic religious institutions are more conducive to actions and attitudes that enhance political stability and the prospects for liberal democracy in religious diverse and integrated settings than in religiously homogeneous settings or diverse but segregated settings. If anything, this book intimates that policymakers would do well to promote integration rather than the segregation of religious groups as a way to increase the likelihood that religious groups come to encourage civic engagement and social tolerance.

The evidence from Nigeria presented in this book calls into question the wisdom of religiously based federalism. While some observers have claimed that Nigeria would be more peaceful and religion would have a more benign effect on political culture were the country divided into more religiously homogeneous states, the evidence presented in the preceding chapters calls such claims into question. What if Nigeria were divided into two states, one predominantly Muslim state to the north and one predominantly Christian state to the south? Or, as a less extreme solution, what if Nigeria's federal system were made to conform more accurately to religious demography? What if the Nigerian constitution were changed to officially allow voters in each state to decide whether Christianity or Islam is to be the official religion of their state? Although we can only guess how creating more religiously homogenous states and zones, or even two states, would affect how Christianity and Islam are applied to political culture, the evidence presented in this book suggests that the results would not be desirable—that the two religions would be applied in ways that discourage rather than encourage social tolerance. Although we can only imagine how a "two-state solution" for Nigeria would affect tolerance of the Christian minority in the north and Muslim minority in the south, there is good reason to think that they would be victims of discrimination and would be deprived of the freedoms afforded to members of the religious majority. While there is no way to know for certain what would happen, one could easily imagine a mass exodus of Christians from the north and Muslims from the south.[6] While there is no way of knowing for sure, it is also possible that we would end up with two countries separated by religion that would be constantly in conflict with each other. That conflict could be violent at times, as the predominantly Muslim country to the north fights with the predominantly Christian country to the south over territory in Nigeria's Middle Belt or in the southwestern part of the country, where neither Christians nor Muslims form a clear majority. In fact, it is difficult to know where the southwest of Nigeria would belong, given that it is religiously diverse and integrated. Although there is no way of knowing, there is good reason to think that most southwesterners would feel uncomfortable in either the predominantly Christian or Islamic state. While I am not suggesting that separating religious groups that have long been in violent conflict with each other is never appropriate, I am suggesting that we should be aware of the unintended negative effects of religious-based federalism.

Based on the evidence presented in this book, I propose that attempts to increase the likelihood that Christianity and Islam in Nigeria are applied in ways that are benign by separating rather than integrating Christians and Muslims would be very misguided.[7] The findings presented in the preceding chapters suggest that segregation, rather than diversity, is "the problem" in Nigeria. If anything, the results indicate that what is needed is greater integration of religious groups, rather than less, and that such integration, if carefully cultivated, would increase the likelihood that Christianity and Islam are eventually applied in ways that are conducive to political stability, peaceful political participation, and religious tolerance.

If we find that religious diversity and integration consistently increase the likelihood that Christian and Islamic religious communities promote peaceful political participation and tolerance, this would naturally lead us to make policy recommendations. We might recommend that state actors pass and enforce laws that open the way for geographic territories to become more religiously diverse and integrated. We might also recommend that public schools and other institutions, such as the military, be religiously integrated. Since concern for their own popularity and the desire to be elected and re-elected may prevent politicians in religiously homogeneous zones from passing and enforcing laws that make their societies more religiously diverse and integrated, it may be more realistic to expect civil society groups to be at the forefront of the movement to promote religiously diverse and integrated societies. Examples of such efforts include those of Catholic Archbishop of Jos, Ignatius Kaigama, and the late Grand

Khadi Kanam, as well as those of Pastor James Wuye and Imam Muhammed Nurayan Ashafa, based in Kaduna, also known as "the Imam and the Pastor." The Interfaith Mediation Centre, founded by Wuye and Ashafa, is an example of an institution that has proven very effective at bringing Christians and Muslims together to build a foundation for an application of religion to public life that encourages mutual respect for the freedom of both Nigeria's Christians and Muslims wherever they are in the country (Paden 2012; 2005). Present at the grassroots level and led by those who are more likely to have an incentive (both spiritual and material) to promote pro-freedom political theologies, these types of inter-religious efforts and voluntary associations tend to promote mutual understanding and tolerance, and, therefore, we might argue that they deserve greater attention and support than they have typically received.

CONCLUSION

While we know that Christians and Muslims apply religious ideas to politics in various ways in Nigeria, in sub-Saharan Africa as a whole, and in other regions of the world, we have more work to do before we can say that we understand and can explain this variation very well. As I try to make clear in this final chapter, more research is needed. However, my hope is that this book represents a step forward along the path that leads toward greater understanding and evidence-informed policy prescriptions. The research presented in this book suggests that social conditions, particularly the degree to which societies are religiously diverse and integrated, systematically affect the impact that Christian and Islamic religious communities have on political actions and attitudes of those who belong to them. Assuming that religion will continue to be an immensely powerful social force in many parts of the world, we would do well to redouble our efforts to identify and foster social conditions that increase the likelihood that the world's two largest and most transnational religions, Christianity and Islam, are applied in ways that encourage the peaceful political participation and the social tolerance necessary for human flourishing.

Appendix A

Religious Observance and Liberal Democratic Ideals in Nigeria, Senegal, and Uganda

Marginal Effects (Standard Errors)

Dependent Variable and [Estimation Method]

Covariates	Voting [Probit]	Interested in Politics [Ordered Probit]	Raise an Issue [Ordered Probit]	Discuss Politics [Ordered Probit]	Accept Differences [Ordered Probit]	Support Multiparty Politics [Ordered Probit]	Support Religious Liberty [Ordered Probit]
				Model (1)			
Religious Observance	0.0071**	0.0051*	0.0233***	0.0013**	-0.0014	-0.00018	0.0027***
	(0.0025)	(0.00213)	(0.0060)	(0.0004)	(0.0023)	(0.0004)	(0.00058)
				Model (2)			
Religious Observance Muslim Nigeria	0.0119*	0.0239***	0.0016**	0.0047***	0.00077*	0.00534	0.00256*
	(0.00472)	(0.00406)	(0.00061)	(0.0009)	(0.00045)	(0.00074)	(0.00103)
Religious Observance Muslim Senegal	0.0415***	0.0030	0.0013	0.00052	0.00120	0.00015	0.00240
	(0.00885)	(0.00663)	(0.001)	(0.0014)	(0.00076)	(0.00129)	(0.00179)
Religious Observance Muslim Uganda	-0.0019	0.00119	0.00063	-0.0001	-0.0028	-0.00032	0.00074
	(0.00397)	(0.00306)	(0.00043)	(0.0006)	(0.00035)	(0.00058)	(0.00081)

Religious Observance M-Christian Nigeria	0.00589 (0.00498)	0.0155*** (0.0043)	0.0016* (0.00064)	0.0054*** (0.0010)	−0.00076 (0.00048)	0.0017* (0.00081)	0.00427*** (0.00113)
Religious Observance M-Christian Senegal	0.0355*** (0.00747)	−0.0059 (0.0058)	0.00024 (0.0008)	0.0008 (0.00121)	−0.000123 (0.00065)	0.00157 (0.00115)	0.00531** (0.00156)
Religious Observance M-Christian Uganda	−0.00389 (0.00656)	−0.0056 (0.0051)	.0006 (0.00071)	−0.0093 (0.00105)	−0.00108* (0.00059)	0.009561 (0.0096)	0.00229* (0.00135)
Religious Observance P-Christian Nigeria	0.00586 (0.00647)	0.0122* (0.0055)	0.0019* (0.000)	0.0033** (0.00115)	−0.00045 (0.00061)	0.00105 (0.00101)	0.00384** (0.00156)
Religious Observance P-Christian Uganda	−0.00565 (0.007380)	−0.0016* (0.0060)	0.0004 (0.0063)	0.0024* (0.00124)	−0.00066 (0.00068)	−0.001683 (0.0011)	0.00121 (0.00159)

Note: M-Christian denotes mainline Christian; P-Christian denotes Pentecostal Christian.

*P-value < 0.10; ** P-value < 0.05; ***P-value < 0.001.

Appendix B

Religious Observance and Liberal Democratic Ideals in Kano, Enugu, Ibadan, and Jos

Dependent Variable and [Estimation Method]

Covariates	Voting [Probit]	Interested in Politics [Ordered Probit]	Raise an Issue [Ordered Probit]	Discuss Politics [Ordered Probit]	Accept Differences [Ordered Probit]	Support Multiparty Politics [Ordered Probit]	Support Religious Liberty [Ordered Probit]
				Model (1)			
Religious Observance Index	0.0106** (0.0045)	0.0154*** (0.0034)	0.0018** (0.0007)	0.0142*** (0.0021)	-0.0049 (0.0032)	0.0036 (0.0027)	0.0161*** (0.0037)
				Model (2)			
Muslim in Kano (ISLAMIC)	0.0520** (0.0152)	0.0457*** (0.0104)	0.0000 (0.0018)	0.0189*** (0.0059)	-0.00131 (0.0086)	-0.0049 (0.0079)	-0.0140 (0.0114)
Muslim in Enugu (CHRISTIAN)	0.0553*** (0.0134)	0.0246** (0.0094)	0.0016 (0.0017)	0.0100* (0.0054)	-0.0224* (0.0087)	-0.0044 (0.0073)	0.0075 (0.0099)
Muslim in Ibadan (VDIVERSE)	0.0023 (0.0089)	0.0181*** (0.0066)	0.00014 (0.0011)	0.0203*** (0.0048)	-0.00249 (0.0062)	0.0044 (0.0054)	0.0279*** (0.0062)
Muslim in Jos (SDIVERSE)	0.0205* (0.0123)	0.0339*** (0.0084)	0.0051** (0.0015)	0.01528*** (0.0046)	-0.0452*** (0.0081)	-0.00180 (0.0066)	-0.0151* (0.0084)

M–Christian in Enugu (CHRISTIAN)	0.0479*** (0.0133)	0.0156* (0.0092)	0.0017 (0.0017)	0.0130** (0.0052)	–0.0086 (0.0087)	0.0035 (0.0071)	0.0231* (0.0098)
M–Christian in Kano (ISLAMIC)	0.0323* (0.0158)	0.0291** (0.0110)	–0.0023 (0.0020)	0.0166** (0.0064)	0.0138 (0.0103)	0.0031 (0.0071)	0.0026 (0.0124)
M–Christian in Ibadan (VDIVERSE)	–0.0201** (0.0086)	–0.0069 (0.0070)	0.00188 (0.0012)	0.0188*** (0.0042)	0.0176** (0.0057)	0.0196** (0.0057)	0.0401*** (0.0066)
M–Christian in Jos (SDIVERSE)	–0.0169 (0.126)	0.0084 (0.0084)	0.00555** (0.00173)	0.0118* (0.0051)	–0.0143* (0.0085)	0.0098 (0.0072)	–0.0151 (0.0093)
P–Christian in Enugu (CHRISTIAN)	0.0570*** (0.0148)	0.0194* (0.0101)	0.0013 (0.0018)	0.0028 (0.0058)	–0.0162* (0.0096)	–0.0086 (0.0080)	0.0267* (0.0111)
P–Christian in Kano (ISLAMIC)	0.0423** (0.0160)	0.0310** (0.0114)	–0.0018 (0.0021)	0.0066 (0.0065)	–0.0037 (0.0011)	–0.0080 (0.0089)	–0.0041 (0.01280)
P–Christian in Ibadan (VDIVERSE)	0.0028 (0.0117)	0.0068 (0.0077)	–0.0046 (0.0015)	0.0076* (0.0044)	0.00217 (0.0082)	–0.00233 (0.0062)	0.0426*** (0.0097)
P–Christian in Jos (SDIVERSE)	–0.0028 (0.0127)	0.0109 (0.0093)	0.0383* (0.00171)	0.004 (0.0052)	–0.0246** (0.0091)	–0.0086 (0.0089)	–0.0103 (0.0128)

Note: M-Christian denotes mainline Christian; P-Christian denotes Pentecostal Christian.

*P-value < 0.10; ** P-value < 0.05; ***P-value < 0.001

Notes

Chapter 1

1. This quote is taken from an interview conducted by the author in Ibadan, Nigeria, on November 10, 2006.
2. This quote is taken from an interview conducted by the author in Enugu, Nigeria, on November 7, 2006.
3. Separation of religious and state authority should not be confused with separation of religion and state. As I explain in the book, separation of religious and state authority is necessary in a liberal democracy. Separation of religion and state is not, as it is possible for there to be state-religion cooperation in a liberal democracy, as long as one religion is not singled out unfairly for special treatment or people of minority religious institutions are not victimized by state-approved discrimination (see Stepan 2000; Driessen 2014).
4. This does not necessarily mean that people who "live and let live" believe that all religions are equally valid or that one religion is as good as any other. It is assumed that, if people belong to a religious institution and observe the prescriptions of that religious institution, they believe that it is closer to the truth than the alternatives.
5. As Leege (1993: 9) writes, "Religious groups and religious beliefs are at the foundation of a culture. Religious worldviews consist of values that lay unique claim to truth while rationalizing social relationships and community objectives." Diamond (1994: 20) notes, "Given that religion is an important source of basic value orientations, we can expect that it can have a powerful impact on political culture and thus democracy."
6. Dogan and Pelassy (1984) observe that in political systems characterized by authoritarian rule, religious organizations have been the only institutions capable of offering host structures, leadership, and means of expression distinct from those controlled by the state. Phiri (2001: 131) argues that this has been the case in African countries since shortly after they achieved independence. As governance degenerated into authoritarian rule in Africa, Phiri argues that churches emerged as the only formidable opposition to the state. As Aminzade and Perry (2001: 16) find, "[religious institutions] often sustain a level of commitment required for high risk political activism." "The ability of religious institutions to appeal to the other worldly has implications for commitment processes, challenges to authority and logics of collective action," writes Wald (1987: 29–30). Smith (1996: 17–18) observes, "Shared religious beliefs can provide a sense of trust and loyalty that facilitates the type of communication and solidarity that expedites the process of coming to a shared definition of [their] situation."
7. These assertions are based on analysis of Afrobarometer survey data (www.afrobarometer.org). In a survey conducted in 2008 and 2009, the Pew Forum on Religion and Public Life (2010) found that a much higher percentage of respondents said that religion was very important in their lives in sub-Saharan Africa than in any other region of the world.

8. It is important to note that Woodberry and Shah (2004) do recognize that Protestantism is no panacea, particularly in sub-Saharan Africa.

9. Lipset (1959) notes that religion may serve as a functional alternative to politics. This implies an inverse relationship between religious devotion and political participation.

10. As Gill (2006) argues, religious values and norms do not arise in a vacuum but are shaped by incentives facing individuals at a particular time and in a particular place.

11. Through much of the nineteenth century and into the twentieth century, the Roman Catholic Church was officially opposed to democracy and liberalism. The *Syllabus of Errors* (1864) made it clear that it was an error to believe that the Roman Catholic Church could condone democracy or freedom of religion.

12. This quote is taken from an interview with a Pentecostal pastor in Jos, Nigeria, on November 7, 2007.

13. For example, leaders of the Catholic Church have attempted to prevent the entry of new religious groups in some Latin American countries (see Gill 1998), and the leadership of the Russian Orthodox Church has been focused on doing its best to keep other Christian churches out of Russia (see Anderson 2003).

14. It is important to distinguish between the separation of religious and state *authority*, on the one hand, and religion and state, on the other. In religiously diverse settings, religious leaders may call for a cooperative relationship between religion and state. However, I propose that religious leaders are more likely to call for religious neutrality (i.e., equal treatment of all or most major religions) in the most religiously diverse settings than in settings that are more homogeneous or where one group forms a religious majority. If leaders of religious majorities expect to enjoy majority status for long, I propose that they are unlikely to be as supportive of state neutrality in religious affairs as they would be in more diverse societies. In homogeneous societies, leaders of religious majorities are more likely to promote the continuation or the establishment of a special relationship with the state that provides them with more influence over and access to the state than minority religious institutions. Leaders of religious majorities may demonize other religions in the process, prompting bigotry and increasing the likelihood of violent conflict between religious groups.

15. In his book *Religious Diversity: Philosophical and Political Dimensions* (2014: 157), Roger Trigg writes, "Yet the history of fights for religious liberty suggests that diversity is not just a result of freedom. People like Thomas Helwys and Roger Williams, to take just two examples, did not come to their beliefs because of freedom. Their beliefs drove them to demand freedom that was sometimes a long time in coming. Religious minorities did not originally flourish because they lived in a free society."

16. Sen (2006) warns against treating culture as immutable, static, and independent of social context.

17. In her book *The Tenth Parallel: Dispatches from the Fault Line Between Christianity and Islam* (2010), Eliza Griswold describes the encounter between Christians and Muslims in sub-Saharan Africa and elsewhere. She describes the tensions and conflicts that accompany the encounter.

Chapter 2

1. Interview conducted by the author with John Waliggo, July 21, 2003, Kampala, Uganda.
2. Interview conducted by the author in Mbarara, Uganda, on July 15, 2006.

3. Interview conducted by the author in Lagos, Nigeria, on November 13, 2006.

4. Interview conducted by the author in Kano, Nigeria, on November 20, 2006.

5. Interview conducted by the author in Ibadan, Nigeria, on November 11, 2006.

6. According to the conventional wisdom, there are also differences in the extent to which Western Christian denominations and religious movements are expected to support a liberal democratic political culture. For example, mainline Christianity is thought to be more conducive to liberal democracy than Roman Catholicism and Pentecostal movements. However, the conventional wisdom holds that just about all of the Western Christian churches are more conducive to liberal democracy than Islam.

7. This would especially be the case for many Protestant churches as compared to the more hierarchically and less democratically organized Roman Catholic Church.

8. See page 445 of de Tocqueville, *Democracy in America* (New York: Harper and Row, 1988).

9. Toft, Philpott, and Shah (2011) point out that the Arab portion of the Islamic world, the Middle East and North Africa, lacks one electoral democracy or "free" country. They claim that Islam has not seemed to play a strong role in the global democratization of the past generation. Between 1981 and 2001, not a single Muslim country jumped into the group of "free" countries, while two Muslim countries departed from the "partly free" group and ten moved into the "not free" cluster.

10. Bernard Lewis (2003: 46), who is not known as an apologist for Islam, writes, "In modern Parlance, Jews and Christians in the classical Islamic state were what would be called 'second class citizens,' but second-class citizenship. . . was far better than the total lack of citizenship that was the fate of non-Christians and even some deviant Christians in the West."

11. Sen (2006: 66) points out that the Jewish philosopher Mairmoindes was forced to emigrate from intolerant (and Christian) Europe to the more tolerant (and Muslim) Arab world.

12. The case of Iran is illustrative. Although it is not considered a democracy by most standards, there are religiously based pro-democracy movements in the country (see Esposito 1996: 52–60). This reminds us that we must do more than simply observe whether a democratic or non-democratic regime prevails in a predominantly Muslim country. We must look *within* a country to truly discern whether and what type of effect religion has on political culture. Among other things, we must compare the most religiously observant with the least religiously observant and take note of the different types of religiously inspired or sanctioned social or political movements that exist in a country.

13. Anderson (2003) and Hoffman (2004) also point to evidence to indicate that Muslims are as supportive of democracy as Latin Christians.

14. This data appeared in Pew Research Center's report, *The World's Muslims: Religion, Politics, and Society* (2013).

15. The Pew Research Center (2006) suggests that one may be involved in Pentecostal worship and still remain nominally Roman Catholic.

16. In the book *To the Ends of the Earth: Pentecostalism and the Transformation of World Christianity* (New York: Oxford University Press, 2013), Allan Heaton Anderson does an excellent job of synthesizing the most plausible explanations for the growth in Pentecostal Christianity in the world since the early twentieth century.

17. Some religious leaders chose to promote such liberties discreetly and behind the scenes. Others chose a more direct and confrontational strategy, as in Poland during the 1980s. Most religious leaders chose a combination of the two strategies. The strategy chosen depends to at least some extent on the political opportunity structure or the extent to

which religious leaders perceived that open confrontation would trigger a violent reaction from the state.

18. I should note here that I am in no way suggesting that the intolerance espoused by the Taliban is in any way equivalent to the efforts of Catholic and Protestant leaders in Central-Eastern Europe to gain official recognition and established-religion status.

19. Note that the separation of religious and state authority is not the same as separation of religion and state. Established religions remained the norm for some time in Europe.

20. This quote taken from interview conducted by the author in Ibadan, Nigeria, November 10, 2006.

21. For example, in South Africa and Nigeria, 18 percent of Pentecostals reported that they had formerly been Roman Catholics. In Kenya, 20 percent reported the same. In Brazil, 45 percent of Pentecostals reported that they had formerly been Roman Catholics (*Spirit and Power: A 10-Country Study of Pentecostals*, Pew Forum 2006).

22. The case of Rwanda is the most obvious example. The intra-church division between Hutu and Tutsi ultimately undermined the effectiveness of some church leaders in their attempts to prevent or end the genocide of 1994, not to mention the political influence of the Roman Catholic Church in post-genocide Rwanda.

23. Interview conducted by author in Lagos, Nigeria, on October 16, 2011.

24. Exceptions to this might be when and where the state in which the clearly dominant religious institution is situated is hostile toward the religious institution, as in Poland during the Communist era, or when and where the government of the day proposes policies that threaten a religious institution's legal standing or that are antithetical to values espoused by the religious institution. Under these circumstances, leaders of a clearly dominant religious community do have an incentive to encourage members to political action.

25. Anthony Gill (1998) shows that the Catholic hierarchy in many predominantly Catholic countries of Latin America responded in this way in areas where Protestant churches began to grow.

26. For example, the Catholic Church was much slower to support democracy and religious liberty in predominantly Catholic countries of Europe, particularly Spain, Portugal, and Italy, than in other parts of Europe, such as Germany, the Netherlands, and Belgium.

Chapter 3

1. Quote taken from an interview with John Maina, conducted by the author in Nairobi, Kenya on July 31, 2010.

2. Perhaps the most dramatic example would be the introduction of the vernacular in the liturgy of the Roman Catholic Church after the Second Vatican Council (1962–1966). We can only imagine that many Africans found the pre-Vatican II Roman liturgy, with its use of the Latin language, interesting and mysterious but not necessarily intelligible and meaningful.

3. Article 11 of the Brussels Declaration states, "[Signatories] will protect and favor, without distinction of nationality or of religion, the religious, scientific or charitable institutions and undertakings created and organized by the nationals of the other Signatory Powers and of States, Members of the League of Nations, which may adhere to the present Convention. Scientific missions, their property and their collections, shall likewise be the objects of special solicitude. Freedom of conscience and the free exercise of all forms of religion are

expressly guaranteed to all nationals of the Signatory Powers and to those under the jurisdiction of States, Members of the League of Nations, which may become parties to the present Convention. Similarly, missionaries shall have the right to enter into, and to travel and reside in, African territory with a view to prosecuting their calling."

4. While the British generally allowed the Catholic Church to flourish in their African territories, there were often formal or informal benefits to belonging to the Anglican Church or other Christian churches favored by the colonial administration.

5. The raw data used by Alesina et al. (2002) to generate the Religious Fractionalization Index are taken from the *World Christian Encyclopedia* (Barret et. al. 2001).

6. The raw data used by Montalvo and Reynal-Querol (2000) are taken from several sources, including the *World Christian Encyclopedia, L'etat des Religions dans le Monde*, and *The Statesman's Yearbook*.

7. See *Tolerance and Tension: Islam and Christianity in Sub-Saharan Africa* (Pew Forum on Religion and Public Life, April 2010).

8. Posner then calculated the PREG index by adjusting the population denominator in the weight of each group so that the population of politically relevant ethnic groups would sum to 100 percent. These newly pooled population counts were entered into the final formula to compute the PREG index.

9. This is because the British often found Muslims living under the authority of emirs, with whom they established a good working relationship. British colonial officials did not want Christian missionaries disturbing the good relations enjoyed with the emirs.

10. While Haynes (1995) points to the fact that most mainline Christian leaders were European at the time to explain the difference, I suggest that a more convincing explanation concerns the fears that mainline Christian leaders had over what independence would mean for the future work of mainline churches in education and health.

11. Although nationalization was attempted in several countries after independence, it became clear that there was a lack of state capacity and governmental commitment. After attempts to nationalize, governments in several countries sought to partner with the mainline churches or invited them to reclaim complete ownership and control of educational and healthcare institutions (Gifford 1998; Haynes 1996).

12. State coffers were largely empty due to a combination of reasons, including unfavorable markets for the agricultural products in which these countries exported, corruption in government, and, by the early 1990s, severe decreases in foreign aid because of the end of the Cold War.

13. Thus "independent" churches were not financially independent. They were independent in the sense that they were not part of an international religious institution or network. Independent churches are churches that are homegrown Christian churches. An example of one such church is the Africa Inland Pentecostal Church of Africa (AIPCA). The Archbishop of the AIPCA clearly endorsed the rather authoritarian tactics of President Daniel Moi. At a rally to mark the anniversary of the church, the Minister of Lands and Settlement granted the church title deeds for land. The Archbishop of the AIPCA then announced that the church would hold a fundraising event at which the president himself would be the guest of honor (*Daily Nation*, February 10, 2001). In Zambia, President Chiluba invited international Pentecostal leaders to hold crusades in Zambia at his government expense. Churches that supported Chiluba received presidential discretionary grants (Phiri 2008).

14. Though Toft, Philpott, and Shah base their categorization on a period that begins in the year 1972, it is important to note that, in most sub-Saharan African countries, there were no significant pro-democracy movements during the 1970s. While there were liberation movements in South Africa, Southern Rhodesia (i.e., Zimbabwe), Mozambique, and Angola, not all of these movements were calling for liberal democracy. In most countries, significant movements for liberal democratic change did not emerge until the late 1980s and early 1990s. By that time, communism was collapsing in parts of the world where it had seemed firmly established, the Cold War was clearly coming to an end, and Western powers announced that they would no longer support dictatorships that they had once supported in order to counter Soviet-communist influence.

15. Interview conducted by the author on November 8, 2006 in Ibadan, Nigeria.

16. From an interview conducted by the author on July 25, 2011.

17. The HDI is a composite measure of development that combines life expectancy, educational achievement, and income (see United Nations Development Program website for explanation http://hdr.undp.org/en/statistics/hdi/).

18. For the analysis, we use the average level of political repression, measured as the combined Freedom House political rights and civil liberties scores for years 1980, 1990, 2000, and 2005. Freedom House provides a measure of respect for political rights and civic liberties for each country. For each of these two categories the scale is 1 to 7, with 1 being the most free and 7 being the least free. For more on the Freedom House measures, see http://www.freedomhouse.org/report/freedom-world-2013/methodology.

19. We use the average Polity IV democracy measure for each country for years 1980, 1990, 2000, and 2005 Polity IV Prohect used a measure of the exercise of political authority that ranges between −10 and +10, with +10 being a fully institutionalized democracy and −10 being a hereditary monarchy with no meaningful popular political participation. For more on the Polity IV measure, see http://www.systemicpeace.org/polity/polity4.htm.

20. It is also worth noting that these findings are similar to those of Anthony Gill (1998), who found that the level of political repression was not a good explanation for the variation in the extent to which Latin America's Catholic bishops were openly critical of authoritarian regimes of the 1970s and 1980s.

21. It is also possible that religious leaders believe that the freedoms associated with liberal democracy will make peaceful inter-ethnic relations more likely rather than less likely, and that authoritarian rule has soured inter-ethnic relations in their society.

22. Although there were some individual Christian leaders who did speak out against the authoritarian status quo before the late 1980s, churches did not tend to speak out as institutions in support of democratic reform until the late 1980s or early 1990s.

23. There are country years with data missing for explanatory variables, such as the human development index and average years spent in school. These country years are excluded from the analysis since the missing variables would end in results that would be misleading. Thus, the total number of countries years included in the analysis is 52.

24. The dependent variable is the variation in the role that religious leaders play with respect to pro-democracy movements. Religious leaders categorized as having played a leading or supporting role in pro-democracy movements between 1972 and 2009 according to Toft, Philpott, and Shah (2011). Countries where religious leaders played a leading or supporting role receive a score of 1, all other countries receive a score of 0. N = 52 country years. "Country years" are 1980, 1990, 2000, and 2005. Thus, data for each year are included

for each country. Independent variables (i.e., Human Development Index [Human Development Report], Average Years Spent in School [World Development Reports], and POLITY IV scores) are taken for each of these years separately. Years with missing data are excluded from the analysis.

Chapter 4

1. Quote taken from interview conducted by the author in Jos, Nigeria, on November 2, 2006.
2. Quote taken from interview conducted by the author in Kampala, Uganda, on July 17, 2006.
3. See www.worldvaluessurvey.org. In *Sacred and Secular: Religion and Politics Worldwide* (2004), Ronald Inglehart and Pippa Norris draw on World Values Survey data and note that the median level of popular support among countries included in the World Values Survey as of 2001 was 92 percent and that support was high among Muslims in predominantly Muslim and Muslim-minority countries. More recently, the Pew Research Center (2012) showed high levels of support for democracy among Muslims across the world. The same report showed that majorities of Muslims think that Islam should influence political life.
4. Almond and Verba (1963) argue that there are certain behaviors and norms that are necessary in order for a political culture to be called a "civic culture." Political participation and respect for norms that uphold the rights of individuals and minority groups to disagree with the majority are important features of a liberal democratic political culture.
5. In the previous rounds of the Afrobarometer, respondents were pretty much prompted to identify themselves according to three very broad categories: Christian, Muslim, or Traditional.
6. To test this prediction, I include an interaction term between the number of effective religions and the two religious activity variables (i.e., religious group activity and contacting religious leaders). If the theory is correct, we would expect a positive and statistically significant coefficient on the interaction.
7. The marginal effects are calculated by using the logistical model along with their standard errors. To isolate the effects of religious activity on liberal-democratic ideals, we need to examine the coefficients on two variables: the variable itself and the coefficient on the interaction with IRD. Specifically, the marginal effect for religious activity in the voting equation from column (1) is $-0.019 + 0.018 \times IRD$.
8. If n is the IRD score, I calculate the impact of changes in the IRD score (i.e., religious diversity) on the effect of religious activity by taking the marginal effect of religious activity in Table 4.3. I add it to the interaction of the marginal effects of religious activity and the IRD score multiplied by the effective number of religions (1 through 4). In this way, we get the change in the probability that one voted and supported democracy for every one-unit change in our religious engagement variables of interest at each level of religious diversity.

Chapter 5

1. This quote is taken from an interview conducted by author in Kano, Nigeria on November 21, 2006.
2. See World Bank population figures at http://data.worldbank.org/country/nigeria.

3. The DHS is conducted ever five years. The data are widely respected. See DHS reports for Nigeria at http://www.measuredhs.com/Publications/Publication-Search.cfm?ctry_id=30&country=Nigeria.

4. See *Tolerance and Tension: Islam and Christianity in Sub-Saharan Africa* (Washington, DC: Pew Research Center, 2010).

5. Paden (2008: 7) notes that there are six semi-official geo-cultural zones dating to the before the British colonial period. British administrative policy has played a key role in the creation of three politico-cultural zones to which I refer in this book (i.e., north, southwest, and southeast). The British amalgamated northern and southern regions of Nigeria into one political unit in 1914.

6. The Pew Forum on Religion and Public Life estimated that 18 percent of Nigeria's population belonged to Pentecostal churches in 2006 (*Spirit and Power: A 10-Country Study of Pentecostals*, Pew Forum on Religion and Public Life, 2006).

7. "Nigerian *Shi'a* Base Knocked Down," BBC, August 1, 2007.

8. Sufism was introduced from North Africa during the eighteenth century and stresses the importance of spiritual-mystical experience. It incorporates music, dance, and other cultural components that are frowned upon by Muslims who consider such practices un-Islamic.

9. It should also be noted that many claim that it violates Article 10 of the Constitution of Nigeria's Fourth Republic (dating to 1999), which states that "[t]he Government of the Federation or of a state shall not adopt any religion as a state religion."

10. Before 1980, reports of inter-religious violence are rare. It would appear that the Christian-Muslim violence began in earnest in 1980. This raises the question, why did such inter-religious violence begin to become more common and deadly in 1980? Further, if religious diversity leads to inter-religious violence and Nigeria was almost evenly split between Christians and Muslims well before 1980, why did we not see more inter-religious violence before 1980? We address these questions in Chapter 6.

11. See 2013 Human Rights Watch report "Leave Everything to God: Accountability for Inter-communal Violence in Plateau and Kaduna States, Nigeria." The International Society for Civil Liberties and the Rule of Law estimate that more than 13,000 people were been killed in ethno-religious violence between 1999 and 2010 (International Society for Civil Liberties and the Rule of Law, 2010).

12. Whereas there has been little written on "religious outbidding" per se, Rabushka and Shepsle (1972) and Horowitz (1985) write extensively about "ethnic outbidding" in ethnically divided societies.

13. In interviews, several Nigerian Christians, Catholics and non-Catholics alike, suggest that Oritsejafor was elected president of CAN by members of the Association who thought that CAN needed to take a more aggressive stance with respect to spreading Christianity and Christian values. They claimed that many Pentecostal members of CAN believed that Cardinal Onaiyekan had become too friendly with the Sultan of Sokoto and other Muslim leaders to adequately promote Christianity and defend the Christian faith.

14. See "Catholic Pullout of CAN Is Dangerous for the Body of Christ." In *Vanguard*, January 27, 2013.

15. While it not easy to pinpoint the exact year that *Boko Haram* was founded, it is generally thought to be 2002, when the movement began to get a great deal of attention beyond Maiduguri (International Crisis Group, "Curbing Violence in Nigeria: The Boko Haram Insurgency." Crisis Group Africa Report No. 216, 3 April, 2014; see also Walker 2012).

16. See International Crisis Group Report, "Curbing Violence in Nigeria: The Boko Haram Insurgency." Crisis Group Africa Report No. 216, April 3, 2014.

17. See Darren Kew's 2012 testimony before the US Sub-Committee on Africa, Global Health, and Human Rights, "The Crisis in Christian-Muslim Relations in Nigeria."

18. See "Elections Fuel Deadly Clashes in Nigeria," *New York Times*, April 24, 2013. See also "Nigeria Election: Riots over Goodluck Jonathan Win," BBC, April 18, 2011.

19. See Paden (2012) and see also the website for NIREC at www.nirecng.org.

20. See Pew Forum on Religion and Public Life, *Tolerance and Tension: Islam and Christianity in Sub-Saharan Africa* (2010).

21. Ibid.

22. See *Tolerance and Tension: Islam and Christianity in Sub-Saharan Africa* (Pew Forum on Religion and Public Life, 2010: 11).

23. See Barrett, Kurian, and Johnson (2001).

24. In the introductory chapter of *Tolerance, Democracy, and Sufis in Senegal* (2013), Mamadou Diouf provides an excellent review of how scholars have characterized Sufism.

25. While the charisma of a certain leader might explain the rise of the first *marabouts*, there is good reason to think that charisma is not enough for a *marabout* to gain a significant following (see Villalon 1993: 80)

26. For example, during the 1960s and 1970s, many insisted that Al Hajj Ibrahima Niasse had magically crippled one political opponent and caused another to be burned alive (see Creevey 1986: 717).

27. See Brossier, Marie. 2004. "Les debats sur la reforme du Code de la Famille au Senegal." DEA Etudes Africaines, options science politique.

28. See *Tolerance and Tension: Islam and Christianity in Sub-Saharan Africa* (Pew Forum on Religion and Public Life, 2010: 11).

29. See *The World's Muslims: Religion, Politics, and Society* (Pew Forum on Religion and Public Life, 2010: 68).

30. See 2010 Pew Research Center report, *Tolerance and Tension: Islam and Christianity in Sub-Saharan Africa*.

31. According to Villalon (2013), these movements have generally been most popular on university campuses. These groups include the *Jama'atou Ibadous Rahmane*, which led to the creation of the Mouvement des Eleves et Etudiants Jama'atou Ibadou Rahmane (MEEJIR) (ibid.).

32. See Richard Vengroff, Lucy Creevy, and Abdou Ndoye, "Islamic Leaders' Values and Transitions to Democracy: The Case of Senegal," Unpublished ms, University of Connecticut (2005).

33. It is interesting to note that the same survey found that only 48 percent thought it possible for Senegal to have a female president.

34. In 2012 and 2013, the position of Christian leaders on proposed legislation that would punish homosexual behavior with imprisonment and even death in Uganda has called into question their churches' support for basic freedoms and human rights. Otherwise, Uganda's two largest Christian churches, the Catholic Church and Church of Uganda, have been rather vocal in their support for free and fair elections, freedom of speech, and freedom of association.

35. President Idi Amin barred Christian missionaries from churches other than the Roman Catholic and Anglican churches in 1977.

36. This figure is the percentage reported by the Uganda Population and Housing Census (UPHC) of 2002.

37. While both the Church of Uganda and the Roman Catholic Church are found in just about every part of Uganda, there are some regions of country where one church is stronger than the other. Roman Catholics are more numerous than members of the Church of Uganda in the southwestern regions of the country, along the borders with Rwanda and the Democratic Republic of the Congo, and in areas of northern Uganda. The Church of Uganda is especially strong in parts of south-central Uganda along the shores of Lake Victoria, from Entebbe to Mukono, and in eastern Uganda toward the border with Kenya. Uganda's Muslims are rather concentrated in parts of central and eastern Uganda. Along with Roman Catholics and members of the Church of Uganda, there is a significant Muslim presence in the capital city of Kampala.

38. Ward (2005: 102) notes that, although technically there was no established church, the Church of Uganda was "unofficially the official church" of the Buganda Kingdom and, to a lesser extent, all of Uganda. It was simply assumed that the *Kabaka* must be a member of the Church of Uganda. Official functions, such as marriages, baptisms, funerals, and coronations took place at the Anglican Cathedral at Namirembe (i.e., in the Luganda language, *place of peace*) in Kampala.

39. According to Kokole (1995), there were strong incentives for non-Muslims to convert to Islam during the early years of Amin's reign.

40. Pirouet (1980: 18–22) writes, "Thousands attended the funeral of Fr Clement Kiggundu, editor of the Luganda Catholic newspaper, Munno, who was murdered in late 1972, and whose body was found in his burnt out car in the Mabira Forest. People turned to the churches when they found themselves in trouble, and the churches became involved in caring for widows and orphans, and so increasingly found themselves cast in the role of the opposition. Perhaps it is more accurate to say that they provided alternative structures and foci of loyalty at a time when most structures had broken down. . . .. Anglican Archbishop Luwum was murdered. Four bishops went into exile. The Anglican Church was forbidden to hold any special services for the Archbishop, and his body was hastily buried by the military.. . . The Chief Kadhi telephoned Amin soon after the murder of the Archbishop and reproved him for it. A few days later his car was involved in an accident, and it was reported that the Kadhi was seriously ill in the intensive care unit of Mulago Hospital."

41. For example, prominent academic and Catholic priest, Fr. John Waliggo, played a very important role in writing Uganda's 1995 constitution. He then went on to serve as Chair of the Uganda Electoral Commission. All the while, he remained a priest in good standing.

42. This assertion is based on an interview with Fr. John Waliggo, conducted by the author, on July 21, 2003. Fr. Waliggo himself expressed misgivings concerning Museveni's rule and neglect of the northern part of the country. However, he noted that it was best to try to work with the government to promote change than to disturb the political stability and economic development that much of Uganda was experiencing under Museveni.

43. See *Daily Monitor*, "Cardinal Meets Politicians over Life Presidency" (August 9, 2007).

44. See *Daily Monitor*, "Archbishop Rallies for Smooth Power Transfer" (March 28, 2012).

45. See *Daily Monitor*, "Respect Press Freedom, Says Church" (April 28, 2010).

46. See *Daily Monitor*, "Bishops Want Shelved Anti-Gay Bill Dusted" (June 12, 2012).

Chapter 6

1. As I have proposed, these goals are two: (1) to attract and retain adherents, and (2) to enhance the influence of their religious institutions on the norms and values in the wider society.

2. I propose that this religious integration takes place quite naturally when and where religious leaders are not seeking cultural and political domination for the religious groups they lead.

3. The Nigeria Demographic and Health Survey of 2003 estimated that Christians made up 61 percent of the population of Jos and that Muslims made up 37 percent of the population. The same survey estimated that 50 percent of Ibadan's population was Christian and 49 percent was Muslim.

4. See Philip Ostien, "Jonah Jang and the Jasawa" in *Muslim-Christian Relations in Africa* (August, 2009). Governors of Plateau State have encouraged the formation of vigilante groups of Christians as a solution to Christian-Muslim violence that has shaken the area (see *ThisDay*, September 11, 2011).

5. This would be true in any highly religious society.

6. Other major cities of the Middle Belt where inter-religious violence took place include Kaduna and Yelwa (see Falola 1998; Mahmud 2013).

7. Some of these leaders include Aminu Kano, Abubakar Balewa Maitama Sule, and Shehu Shagari, who are known for promoting moderation and tolerance.

8. Laitin (1986: 9) observes that of those who made up the Constituent Assembly in 1976, charged to draw up a new constitution for Nigeria, the Yoruba were least extreme on the religious issue. "Seventy-six percent of them took moderate positions. . . more Yoruba delegates suggested new compromises than any other group in the Constituent Assembly. . ."

9. Since the 1990s, Middle Belt cities where such violence has been most deadly are Jos, Kaduna, and Yelwa (see Human Rights Watch Report 2005, "Revenge in the Name of God").

10. According to the Nigeria Demographic and Health Survey of 2003, Christians made up 95 percent of the population in Enugu, and Muslims made up less than 1 percent of the city's population. Kano was a reverse image of Enugu that year, according to the NDHS, with Muslims making up 98 percent of the population and Christians making up less than 1 percent. According to the same survey, Christians made up 49 percent of the population of Ibadan, and Muslims made up 50 percent of that city's population. Jos was at an intermediate level of religious diversity as of 2003, not as diverse as Ibadan and more diverse than Kano and Enugu. It was estimated that Christians made up 61 percent of Jos's population, and Muslims made up 37 percent.

11. Interview conducted by the author on November 21, 2006.

12. Interview conducted on October 17, 2006.

13. Interview with the author on November 15, 2006.

14. Interview with the author on November 15, 2006.

15. Interview with the author on November 15, 2006.

16. Interview with the author on November 7, 2006.

17. See Human Rights Watch 2013 report, "Leave Everything to God: Accountability for Inter-Communal Violence in Plateau and Kaduna States, Nigeria" (New York: Human Rights Watch). See also United States Institute of Peace report of July 2012, authored by Aaron Sayne, "Rethinking Nigeria's Indigene-Settler Conflicts."

18. Interview conducted by the author on November 10, 2006.

19. Interview conducted on October 15, 2011.

20. Interview conducted on October 17, 2011.

21. Interview conducted by the author on November 11, 2006.

22. "If Nigeria Breaks Everyone will Suffer," *Kaduna Weekly Trust*, August 2, 2003.

23. Interview conducted by the author on November 12, 2006.

24. Interview conducted by the author on November 8, 2006.

25. See United States Institute of Peace report of July 2012 authored by Aaron Sanye, "Rethinking Nigeria's Indigene-Settler Conflicts," for a good description of the law with

regard to indigene and settler status in Nigeria. See also *Africa Security Brief* [No. 14] of July 2011 by Chris Kwaja, "Nigeria's Pernicious Drivers of Ethno-Religious Conflict" and the International Crisis Group report of December 2012, "Curbing Violence in Nigeria (I): The Jos Crisis, Africa Report 196" (Brussels: International Crisis Group).

26. There are Yoruba religious leaders who have called for violence. They are typically found in the north or the Middle Belt. One such religious leader is Anglican Archbishop Akinola (Griswold 2010: 53–57). Thus, this adds to the argument that ethnic identity per se is a less reliable predictor of whether religious leaders apply their religious traditions in ways that encourage or discourage religious tolerance and peaceful coexistence than the location of the religious leader. Archbishop Akinola's attitudes were forged in the north of Nigeria, where Muslims formed a majority or where religious communities were highly segregated from each other.

27. See *Vanguard*, "Post-Election Riots in Kaduna, Baurchi, Yobe, and Niger," April 19, 2011. See also "Jos Riots: So Close Yet so Far Apart," January 30, 2011.

28. See *Sahara Reporters*, April 18, 2011. See also Human Rights Watch, "Nigeria: Post-Election Violence Kills 800," May 7, 2011.

29. See *Sahara Reports*, "Muslims Students Paralyze University of Ibadan over Student Preacher," August 16, 2010. See also *Nairaland Forum*, "Religious Battle Looms in Ibadan," March 8, 2010. While much of the tension appears to be on university campuses, it threatens to spill out into the wider community of Ibadan.

30. However, there were not enough Pentecostal Christians interviewed in predominantly Muslim states to include them in the analysis. Therefor, in predominantly Muslim states, we only look at mainline Christians and Muslims.

31. This question is different from the question asked in the fourth round of the Afrobarometer in 2008. The question asked on the 2008 survey simply asked if respondents were active in religious groups. The 2013 survey asks respondents how active they are in religious groups that meet outside worship services.

32. Nonetheless, 90 percent of respondents indicated that they are either active or inactive members (60 percent active and 30 percent inactive) of religious groups that meet outside of worship services.

33. The city-level sample is often too small to conduct meaningful statistical analysis. Even at the state level, we have problems with the sample size. For example, a very small number of Pentecostal Christians were interviewed in many predominantly Muslim states.

34. The categorization is based on percentages of the population from the Nigeria Demographic and Health Survey (NDHS) of 2008 and cross-checked with the listing of religious patterns in Nigeria's states by John Paden in *Muslim Civic Cultures and Conflict Resolution* (2005).

35. The complete results of logistical regression analysis can be found in Appendix B.

36. The number of Pentecostals interviewed by the Afrobarometer in predominantly Muslim states was not sufficient to include Pentecostals in the analysis of data from predominantly Muslim states.

37. Such attempts are described in "Religious Battle Looms in Ibadan," in *Nairaland Forum*, March 10, 2010 and "Muslim Students Paralyze University of Ibadan over Student Preacher," in *Sahara Reporters*, August 6, 2010.

38. See "UI Council Pleads for Religious Tolerance," in *ThisDay*, August 25, 2010.

39. See Sunday Saanu, "Post-Mortem of UI's averted Religious Riot," at www.ui.edu.ng/religiousriot.

40. See "Christian, Muslim Clerics Admonish Nigerians on Peaceful Co-existence," in *News Agency of Nigeria*, March 12, 2012.

41. Interview conducted by the author in Lagos, Nigeria on October 14, 2011.

42. I propose that this religious integration takes place quite naturally when and where religious leaders are not seeking cultural and political domination for the religious groups they lead.

Chapter 7

1. It is worth noting that many religious leaders do not like the word "tolerance" because it suggests that one religion is as good as any other, or moral relativism. So, it should be noted that tolerance does not imply moral relativism but the idea that people cannot and should not be forced into religious communities and there should be no state-sanctioned religious discrimination where there are people of different religious traditions. In other words, the state should treat Christianity and Islam equally.

2. This would be true in any highly religious society.

3. The other potential explanations are poverty, political repression, and reform of Catholic teaching on religious liberty and democracy that occurred at the Second Vatican Council (1962–1966). Gill conducts probit regression analysis and cites descriptive evidence to back up this claim. He measures the degree of religious competition, the key independent variable of interest, as the percentage increase in what he calls "the non-Catholic proselytizing faiths" between 1900 and 1970 (Gill 1998: 105). He defines proselytizing faiths (i.e., CPs) as evangelicals, marginal Christian sects, and Spiritists (ibid.). These are Christian denominations that actively sought to convert Catholics and non-Christians to their brands of Christianity. Gill's dependent variable, whether Catholic bishops took a pro-, neutral, or anti-authoritarian stance, is built on an extensive review of the literature (Smith 1979; Levine 1981; Cardenal 1990; 1992; Martin 1990; and the US Army *Area Handbook Series*), drawing most heavily on the work of Scott Mainwaring and Alexander Wilde (1989).

4. See "How My Views Have Changed," in *The Cresset* 2014 (Volume LXXXVII, No. 3, pp. 16–21).

5. These indicators include infrastructure quality, infant life chances (low infant mortality), literacy, democracy, and political rights (Alsesina et al. 2003: 14).

6. We need only think of India at independence and the creation of Pakistan as a state for Muslims in 1947. Muslims were victims of violence in parts of India and Hindus were victims of violence in what became Pakistan. A mass exodus and a humanitarian crisis of immense proportions was the result. Pakistan and India have been in conflict almost continuously since Pakistan came into being. At times the tensions have run so high that many feared an extremely destructive military encounter between the two countries over contested land and other matters. Pakistan has also been home to religious extremist movements, including the Taliban and its own home-grown Islamist movements that seek to impose their own salafist version of Islam on the entire population of Pakistan, which would almost certainly drive religious minorities out of the country (see Jalal 2014). Apparently, Osama bin Laden, founder of the global jihad movement, *al-Qaeda*, found it easy to hide in Pakistan for several years.

7. John Paden (2012: 108) also argues that there is "no clean way to break up Nigeria" and there is "no four-state solution." He writes, "proponents of confederation of ethnic groups need to be aware of the negative international experience of such arrangements." In my view, we could easily replace ethnic groups with religious groups.

Bibliography

Abadie, Alberto. 2004. *Poverty, Political Freedom, and the Roots of Terrorism.* Cambridge, MA: Harvard University Press and NBER.

Afrobarometer Briefing Paper, No. 3. 2002. "Islam, Democracy, and Public Opinion in Africa." Afrobarometer Public Opinion Survey.

Ahanotu, A. M. 1992. *Religion, State and Society in Contemporary Africa: Nigeria, Sudan, South Africa and Zaire.* Berkeley and Palo Alto, CA: Joint Center for African Studies.

Ahlstrom, Sydney. 2004. *A Religious History of the American People.* New Haven, CT: Yale University Press.

Akyol, Mustafa. 2011. *Islam Without Extremes: A Muslim Case for Liberty.* New York: W. W. Norton.

Alesina, Alberto, Arnaud Devleeschauwer, William Easterly, Sergio Kurlat, and Romain Wacziarg. 2003. "Fractionalization." *Journal of Economic Growth* 8: 155–194

Aliaga, Fernando. 1989. *La Iglesia en Chile: Contexto hisorico.* Santiago: Ediciones Paulinas.

Almond, Gabriel A., and Sidney Verba. 1963. *The Civic Culture: Political Attitudes and Democracy in Five Nations.* Princeton, NJ: Princeton University Press.

Alpers, Edward. 2000. "East Central Africa." In *The History of Islam in Africa*, Nehemia Levtzion and Randall Pouwels (eds.), 303–325. Athens: Ohio University Press.

Alvarez, Michael, Jose Ceibub, Fernando Limongi, and Adam Przeworski. 1996. "Classifying Political Regimes." *Studies in Comparative International Development* 31, no. 2 (summer): 3–36.

Aminzade, Ron, and Elizabeth Perry. 2001. "The Sacred, Religious, and Secular in Contentious Politics: Blurring the Boundaries." In *Silence and Voice in the Study of Contentious Politics*, Ron Aminzade, et al. (eds.), 155–178. Cambridge: Cambridge University Press.

Anderson, Allan Heaton. 2013. *To the Ends of the Earth: Pentecostalism and the Transformation of World Christianity.* New York: Oxford University Press.

Anderson, G. H. 2002. "World Christianity by the Numbers: A Review of the *World Christian Encyclopedia* 2nd Ed." *International Bulletin of Missionary Research* 26: 128–130.

Anderson, John. 2003. *Religious Liberty in Transitional Societies: The Politics of Religion.* Cambridge: Cambridge University Press.

Anderson, John. 2004. "Does God Matter and if So, Whose God? Religion and Democratization." *Democratization* 11, no. 4: 192–217.

An-Na'im, Abdullahi. 1992. "Islam and National Integration in the Sudan." In *Religion and National Integration in Nigeria: Islam, Christianity and Politics in the Sudan and Nigeria*, John Hunwick (ed.), 11–37. Evanston, IL: Northwestern University Press.

Appleby, R. Scott. 2000. *The Ambivalence of the Sacred: Religion, Violence, and Reconciliation.* Lanham, MD: Rowman and Littlefield.

Arat, Zehra. 1991. *Democracy and Human Rights in Developing Countries.* Boulder, CO: Lynne Rienner.

Armstrong, Karen. 2007. "Religious Basis of Islamic Terrorism: The Quran and Its Interpretations." *Studies in Conflict and Terrorism* 30, no. 3: 229–248.

Banchoff, Thomas. 2007. *Democracy and the New Religious Pluralism.* New York: Oxford University Press.

Banchoff, Thomas. 2008. *Religious Pluralism: Globalization and World Politics.* New York: Oxford University Press.

Barrett, David B., George T. Kurian, and Todd M. Johnson (eds.). 2001. *World Christian Encyclopedia* (2nd ed.). Oxford: Oxford University Press.

Barton, Greg. 2002. *Abdurrahman Wahid: Muslim Democrat, Indonesian President.* Honalulu: University of Hawaii Press.

Bates, Robert. 1981. *Markets and States in Tropical Africa.* Berkeley and Los Angeles: University of California Press.

Bathily, Abdoulaye, Mamaoudou Diouf, and Mohammed Mdodj. 1995. "The Senegalese Student Movement from its Inception to 1989." In *African Studies in Social Movement and Democracy,* Mahmood Mamdani and Ernst Wamba-dia-Wamb (eds.), 369–408. Dakar: Codesrie.

Baur, John. 1990. *The Catholic Church in Kenya: A Centenary History.* Nairobi: St. Paul Publications Africa.

Beatty, Kathleen Murphy, and Oliver Walter. 1989. "A Group Theory of Religion and Politics: Clergy and Group Leaders." *The Western Political Quarterly* 42, no. 1: 129–146.

Belloni, Roberto. 2004. "Peacebuilding and Consociational Electoral Engineering in Bosnia and Herzegovina." *International Peacekeeping* 11, no. 2: 334–353.

Beneke, Chris. 2006. *The Religious Origins of American Pluralism.* New York: Oxford University Press.

Berger, Peter. 1967. *The Sacred Canopy: Elements of a Sociological Theory of Religion.* New York: Doubleday.

Berhman, Lucy. 1970. *Muslim Brotherhoods and Politics in Senegal.* Cambridge, MA: Harvard University Press.

Boix, Carles, and Luis Garicano. 2002. "Inequality, Democracy and Country-Specific Wealth." Unpublished paper. Department of Political Science, University of Chicago.

Bollen, Kenneth. 1980. "Issues in Comparative Measurement of Political Democracy." *American Sociological Review* 45, no. 2 (June): 370–390.

Bose, Sumantra. 2002. *Bosnia after Dayton: Nationalist Partition and International Intervention.* Oxford: Oxford University Press.

Bratton, Michael, Robert B. Mattes, and E. Gyimah-Boadi. 2005. *Public Opinion, Democracy and Market Reform in Africa.* Cambridge: Cambridge University Press.

Bratton, Michael, and Beatrice Liatto-Katundu. 1993. "Preliminary Assessment of Political Attitudes of Zambian Citizens." MSU Working Papers on Political Reform in Africa. East Lansing: Michigan State University.

Bratton, Michael, and Nicholas Van deWalle. 1997. *Democratic Experiments in Africa.* Cambridge and New York: Cambridge University Press.

Brown, L. Carl. 2000. *Religion and State: The Muslim Approach to Politics.* New York: Columbia University Press.

Bruce, Steve. 2006. "Did Protestantism Create Democracy?" In *Religion, Democracy and Democratization,* John Anderson (ed.), 3–20. London and New York: Routledge.

Bruce, Steve. 2002. *God Is Dead: Secularisation in the West.* Oxford: Blackwell.

Campbell, John, and Asch Harwood. 2011. "Judging Nigeria's Election Season: Can the New Government in Abuja Overcome Nigeria's Many Challenges?" *Foreign Affairs*

(April). Accessed November 26, 2014. http://www.foreignaffairs.com/articles/67736/john-campbell-and-asch-harwood/judging-nigerias-election-season.

Campbell, John. 2013. *Nigeria: Dancing on the Brink* (Second Edition). Lanham, MD: Rowman and Littlefield.

Cardenal, Rodolfo. 1990. "The Catholic Church and the Politics of Accommodation in Honduras." In *Church and Politics in Latin America*, Dermot Keogh (ed.), 187–204. London: Macmillan.

Cardenal, Rodolfo. 1992. "The Church in Central America." In *The Church in Latin America 1492–1992*, Enrique Dussel (ed.), 243–270. Maryknoll, NY: Orbis Books.

Cassanova, Jose. 1994. *Public Religions in the Modern World*. Chicago: University of Chicago Press.

Chaves, Mark, and Phillip Gorski. 2001. "Religious Pluralism and Religious Participation." *Annual Review of Sociology* 27 (August): 261–281.

Chlovy, Gerard. 1991. *La religion en France de la fin du 18eme siecle a nos jours*. Paris: Hachette.

Clark, Andrew Francis. 1999. "Imperialism, Independence, and Islam in Senegal and Mali." *Africa Today* 46, no. 3–4: 149–167.

Clark, John, and David Gardinier. 1997. *Political Reform in Francophone Africa*. Boulder, CO: Westview Press.

Collier, Paul, and Anke Hoefller. 2004. "Greed and Grievance in Civil War." *Oxford Economic Papers* 56, no. 4: 563–595.

Constantin, Francois. 1995. "The Attempts to Create Muslim National Organizations in Tanzania, Uganda and Kenya." In *Religion and Politics in East Africa*, Holger Bert Hansen and Michael Twaddle (eds.), 19–31. Athens: Ohio University Press.

Coppedge, Michael. 1997. "Modernization and Thresholds of Democracy: Evidence for a Common Path and Process." In *Inequality, Democracy and Economic Development*, Manus Midlarsky (ed.), 177–201. New York: Cambridge University Press.

Coppedge, Michael, and Wolfgang H. Reinicke. 1991. "Measuring Polyarchy." In *On Measuring Democracy: Its Consequences and Concomitants*, Alex Inkeles (ed.), 47–68. New Brunswick, NJ: Transaction.

Coulon, Christian. 1981. *Le marabout et la prince*. Paris: Pedone.

Creevey, Lucy. 1985. "Muslim Brotherhoods and Politics in Senegal 1985." *The Journal of Modern African Studies* 23, no. 4: 715–721.

Crone, Patricia. 1980. *Slaves on Horses: The Evolution of the Islamic Polity*. Cambridge: Cambridge University Press.

Cruise-O'Brien, Donald. 1971. *The Mourides of Senegal: The Political and Economic Organization of an Islamic Brotherhood*. Oxford: Clarendon.

Cullen, Trevor. 1994. *Malawi: A Turning Point*. Edinburgh: Pentland Press.

Curry, Thomas, J. 1986. *The First Freedoms: Church and State in America to the Passage of the First Amendment*. Oxford: Oxford University Press.

Dahl, Robert A. 1971. *Polyarchy: Participation and Opposition*. New Haven, CT: Yale University Press.

Davie, G. 2000. *Religion in Modern Europe: A Memory Mutates*. Oxford: Oxford University Press.

Deng, Francis. 1992. "A Three Dimensional Approach to the Conflict in the Sudan." In *Religion and National Integration in Nigeria: Islam, Christianity and Politics in the Sudan and Nigeria*, John Hunwick (ed.), 39–62. Evanston, IL: Northwestern University Press.

Diamond, Larry. 1999. *Developing Democracy: Toward Consolidation*. Baltimore and London: The Johns Hopkins University Press.

Diamond, Larry (ed.). 1994. *Political Culture and Democracy in Developing Countries.* Boulder, CO: Lynne Rienner.

Dickson, K. A. 1995. "The Church and the Quest for Democracy in Ghana." In *Christian Churches and the Democratization of Africa,* Paul Gifford (ed.), 261–275. Leiden, Netherlands: E. J. Brill.

Diouf, Mamadou. 2013. "Introduction: The Public Role of the 'Good Islam': Sufi Islam and the Administration of Pluralism." In *Tolerance, Democracy, and Sufis in Senegal,* Mamadou Diouf (ed.), 1–35. New York: Columbia University Press.

Dogan, Mattei, and Dominique Plenassy. 1984. *How to Compare Nations: Strategies in Comparative Politics.* Chatham, NJ: Chatham House.

Dolan, Jay P. 1972. "Immigrants in the City: New York's Irish and German Catholics." *Church History* 41, no. 3: 354–368.

Dolan, Jay P. 1985. *The American Experience: A History from Colonial Times to the Present.* Notre Dame, IN: University of Notre Dame Press.

Doornbos, Martin. 1995. "Church and State in Eastern Africa: Some Unresolved Questions." In *Religion and Politics in East Africa,* Holger Bert Hansen and Michael Twaddle (eds.), 260–269. Athens: Ohio University Press.

Driessen, Michael. 2014. *Religion and Democratization: Framing Religious and Political Identities in Muslim and Catholic Societies.* New York: Oxford University Press.

Duverger, Maurice. 1955. *The Political Role of Women.* Paris: UNESCO.

Easterly, William, and Ross Levine. 1997. "Africa's Growth Tragedy: Policies and Ethnic Divisions." *The Quarterly Journal of Economics* (November): 1203–1250.

Eckstein, Harry. 1988. "A Culturalist Theory of Political Change." *American Political Science Review* 82: 789–904.

Ehteshami, Anoushiravan. 2006. "Islam, Muslim Polities, and Democracy." *Democratization* 11, no. 4: 90–110.

Ellis, Stephen, and Gerrie Ter Haar. 2004. *Worlds of Power: Religious Thought and Political Practice in Africa.* Oxford: Oxford University Press.

Esposito, John L., and John O. Voll. 1996. *Islam and Democracy.* New York: Oxford University Press.

Esteban, Joan, and Laura Mayoral. 2011. "Ethnic and Religious Polarization and Social Conflict." UFAE and IAE Working Papers; 857.11. Barcelona: Unitat de Fonaments de L'Analisi Economica.

Falola, Toyin. 1998. *Violence in Nigeria: The Crisis of Religious Politics and Secular Ideologies.* Rochester, NY: University of Rochester Press.

Fearon, James D., and David Laitin. 2003. "Ethnicity, Insurgency, and Civic War." *American Political Science Review* 87, no. 1 (February 2003): 75–90.

Fenton, Elizabeth. 2011. *Religious Liberties: Anti-Catholicism and Liberal Democracy in Nineteenth Century U.S. Literature and Culture.* Oxford: Oxford University Press.

Filali-Ansary, Abdou. 2001. "Muslims and Democracy." In *The Global Divergence of Democracies,* Larry Diamond and Marc. F. Plattner (eds.), 37–51. Baltimore, MD: The Johns Hopkins University Press.

Finke, Roger, and William Sims Bainbridge. 1985. "A Supply-Side Reinterpretation of the Secularization of Europe." *Journal for the Scientific Study of Religion* 33: 230–252.

Finke, Roger, and Laurence Iannoccone. 1993. "The Illusion of Shifting Demand: Supply-Side Explanations for Trends and Change in the Religious Market Place." *Annals of the American Association of Political and Social Science* 527: 27–39.

Fish, M. Steven. 2011. *Are Muslims Distinctive?: A Look at the Evidence.* New York: Oxford University Press.

Fishman, Robert. 2004. *Democracies Voices: Social Ties and the Quality of Public Life in Spain.* Ithaca, NY: Cornell University Press.

Flannery, Austin (ed.). 1992. *Vatican Council II: The Conciliar and Post-Conciliar Documents.* Grand Rapids, MI: William B. Eerdmans.

Flis, Andzej. 2000. "The Catholic Church and Democracy in Modern Europe." In *Religion and Politics: East-West Contrasts from Contemporary Europe*, Tom Inglis, Zdzislaw Mach, and Rafal Mazanek (eds.), 31–48. Dublin: University College Dublin Press.

Fox, Jonathan. 2008. *A World Survey of Religion and State.* Cambridge and New York: Cambridge University Press.

Fox, Jonathan. 2011. "Out of Sync: The Disconnect Between Constitutional Clauses and State Legislation on Religion." *Canadian Journal of Political Science* 44, no. 1: 59–81.

Freedom House. 1989. *Freedom in the World: The Annual Survey of Political Rights and Civil Liberties 1989–1990.* New York: Transaction.

Freedom House. 2002. *Freedom in the World: The Annual Survey of Political Rights and Civil Liberties 2001–2002.* New York: Transaction.

Freedom House. 2014. *Freedom in the World: The Democratic Leadership Gap.* New York and Washington, DC: Freedom House.

Freston, Paul. 2001. *Evangelicals and Politics in Asia, Africa and Latin America.* Cambridge: Cambridge University Press.

Gambari, Ibrahim. 1992. "The Role of Religion in National Life: Reflections on Recent Experiences in Nigeria." In *Religion and National Integration in Nigeria: Islam, Christianity and Politics in the Sudan and Nigeria*, John Hunwick (ed.), 85–99. Evanston, IL: Northwestern University Press.

Geddes, Barbara. 1999. "What Do We Know about Democratization after Twenty Years?" *Annual Review of Political Science* 2: 115–144.

Geertz, Clifford. 1973 (2000). *The Interpretation of Cultures.* New York: Basic Books.

Gelb, Alan. H. 1988. *Oil Windfalls: Blessing or Curse.* Washington, DC: World Bank Publications.

Gellar, Sheldon. 2005. *Democracy in Senegal: Tocquevillian Analytics in Africa.* New York: Palgrave Macmillan.

Gertzel, Cherry, et al. 1984. *The Dynamics of the One-Party State in Zambia.* Manchester, NH: Manchester University Press.

Gifford, Paul. 1998. *African Christianity: Its Public Role.* Bloomington: Indiana University Press.

Gifford, Paul. 2009. *Christianity, Politics, and Public Life in Kenya.* London: Hurst.

Gifford, Paul (ed.). 1995. *Christian Churches and the Democratization of Africa.* Leiden, Netherlands: E. J. Brill.

Gill, Anthony. 1998. *Rendering unto Caesar: The Catholic Church and the State in Latin America.* Chicago: University of Chicago Press.

Gill, Anthony. 2002. "Religion, Democracy and Political Attitudes in Latin America: Evidence from the World Values Survey." Paper presented at conference: *Politik und Religion*, Frankfurt (Oder).

Gill, Anthony. 2006. "Weber in Latin America: Is Protestant Growth Enabling the Consolidation of Democratic Capitalism?" In *Religion, Democracy and Democratization*, John Anderson (ed.), 3–20. London and New York: Routledge.

Gill, Anthony. 2008. *The Political Origins of Religious Liberty.* Cambridge and New York: Cambridge University Press.

Gould, Andrew. 1999. *The Origins of Liberalism: Church, State and Party in Nineteenth-Century Europe*. Ann Arbor: University of Michigan Press.

Gordon, M. M. 1964. *Assimilation in American Life: The Role of Race, Religion and National Origins*. Oxford: Oxford University Press.

Greene, M. Louise. 1970. *The Development of Religious Liberty in Connecticut*. New York: Da Capo Press.

Greenstein, Fred, and Michael Lerner. 1971. *Personality and Politics: Problems of Evidence, Inference and Conceptualization*. Chicago: Markham.

Griswold, Eliza. 2010. *The Tenth Parallel: Dispatches from the Faultline Between Christianity and Islam*. New York: Farrar, Strauss, and Giroux.

Griswold, Eliza. 2008. "God's Country." *Atlantic Monthly* (March). Accessed November 25, 2014. http://www.theatlantic.com/magazine/archive/2008/03/god-s-country/306652/.

Gura, Philip. F. 1982. "The Contagion of Corrupt Opinions in Puritan Massachusetts: The Case of William Pynchon." *The William and Mary Quarterly* 39, no. 3: 469–491.

Guth, James, Ted Jelen, Lyman Kellsedt, Corwin Smidt, and Kenneth Wald. 1988. "The Politics of Religion in America: Issues for Investigation." *American Politics Quarterly* 16: 357–397.

Gutierrez, Gustavo. 1988 (1971). *A Theology of Liberation*. Maryknoll, NY: Orbis Books.

Hackett, Rosalind. 1998. "Charismatic/Pentecostal Appropriation of Media Technologies in Nigeria and Ghana." *Journal of Religion in Africa* 28, no. 3: 258–277.

Hall, John. 1985. *Powers and Liberties: The Causes and Consequences of the Rise of the West*. Harmondsworth, UK: Penguin.

Halliday, Fred. 1994. "The Politics of Islamic Fundamentalism: Iran, Tunisia and the Challenge to the Secular State." In *Islam, Globalization and Postmodernity*, Akbar Ahmed and Hastings Donnan (eds.), 91–113. London and New York: Routledge.

Hamburger, Phillip. 2004. *Separation of Church and State*. Cambridge, MA: Harvard University Press.

Harris, Frederick. 1999. *Something Within: Religion in African American Political Activism*. New York: Oxford University Press.

Hastings, Adrian. 1979. *A History of African Christianity*. Cambridge: Cambridge University Press.

Hastings, Adrian. 1996. *The Church in Africa 1450–1950*. Oxford: Oxford University Press.

Hatch, Nathan O. 1989. *The Democratization of Christianity*. New Haven, CT: Yale University Press.

Haynes, Jeff. 1995. "Popular Religion and Politics in Sub-Saharan Africa." *Third World Quarterly* 16, no. 1: 89–108.

Haynes, Jeff. 1996. *Religion and Politics in Africa*. Nairobi and London: East African Educational Publishers.

Haynes, Jeff. 1998. *Religion in Global Politics*. New York: Longman.

Hefner, Robert. 2000. *Civil Islam: Muslims and Democratization in Indonesia*. Princeton, NJ: Princeton University Press.

Hefner, Robert. 2005. Introduction in *Remaking Muslim Politics: Pluralism, Contestation, Democratization*, Robert Hefner (ed.). Princeton, NJ: Princeton University Press.

Hill, Richard. 1959. *Egypt in the Sudan, 1820–1881*. Oxford: Oxford University Press.

Hirschman, Albert. 1970. *Exit, Voice and Loyalty: Responses to Decline in Firms, Organizations, and States*. Cambridge, MA: Harvard University Press.

Hirschmann, David. 1991. "Women and Political Participation in Africa: Broadening the Scope of Research." *World Development* 19: 1679–1697.

Hoffman, Louis. 2004. "Cultural Constructs of the God Image and God Concept: Implications for Culture, Psychology and Religion." Unpublished manuscript.

Holbrook, Allison, and Jon Krosnick. 2010. "Social Desirability Bias in Voter Turnout Reports: Tests Using the Item Count Technique." *Public Opinion Quarterly* 74, no. 1: 37–67.

Horowitz, Donald. 1985. *Ethnic Groups in Conflict.* Berkeley and Los Angeles: University of California Press.

Hoschild, Adam 1998. *King Leopold's Ghost.* New York: Houghton Mifflin Company.

Hsu, Becky, Amy Reynolds, Conrad Hackett, and James Gibbon. 2008. "Estimating the Religious Composition of All Nations: An Empirical Assessment of the World Christian Database." *Journal for the Scientific Study of Religion* 47, no. 4: 478–493.

Human Rights Watch. 2013. "Leave Everything to God: Accountability for Inter-Communal Violence in Kaduna and Plateau States, Nigeria." New York: Human Rights Watch.

Hunter, Brian (ed.). 1993. *The Statesman's Year-Book. 130th Edition.* New York: Macmillan.

Hunter, Shireen. 2001. "Religion, Politics and Security in Central Asia." *SAIS Review* 21 (Summer/Fall): 65–89.

Huntington, Samuel P. 1991. *The Third Wave: Democratization in the Late Twentieth Century.* Norman: University of Oklahoma Press.

Huntington, Samuel P. 1996. *The Clash of Civilizations and the Remaking of World Order.* New York: Simon and Schuster.

Iannaccone, Laurence R. 1991. "The Consequences of Religious Market Structure: Adam Smith and the Economics of Religion." *Rationality and Society* 3: 156–178.

Imo, C. 2008. "Evangelicals, Muslims, and Democracy." In *Evangelical Christianity and Democracy in Africa,* T.O. Ranger (ed.), 37–66. New York: Oxford University Press.

Inglehart, Ronald. 1988. "The Renaissance of Political Culture." *American Political Science Review* 82: 1203–1230.

Inglheart, Ronald, et al. (eds.). 2004. *Human Beliefs and Values: A Cross-Cultural Sourcebook on the 1999–2002 Values Surveys.* Mexico City: Siglo XXI Editores.

Isichei, Elizabeth. 1995. *A History of Christianity in Africa: From Antiquity to the Present.* Grand Rapids, MI: William B. Eerdmans.

Jalal, Ayesha. 2014. *The Struggle for Pakistan: A Muslim Homeland and Global Politics.* Cambridge, MA: Harvard University Press.

Jenkins, Phillip. 2002a. "The Next Christianity." *Atlantic Monthly* 290, no. 3: 53–68.

Jenkins, Phillip. 2002b. *The Next Christianity: The Coming of Global Christianity.* New York: Oxford University Press.

Jenkins, Philip. 2003. *The New Anti-Catholicism: The Last Acceptable Prejudice.* New York: Oxford University Press.

Jenkins, Philip. 2006. *The New Faces of Christianity: Believing the Bible in the Global South.* New York: Oxford University Press.

Johnston, Douglas. 1994. "Beyond Power Politics." In *Religion: The Missing Dimension of Statecraft,* Douglas Johnston and Cynthia Sampson (eds.), 3–7. Oxford: Oxford University Press.

Johnson, Todd M. and Brian Grim (eds.). 2008. *World Religions Database.* Leiden/Boston: Brill.

Juergensmeyer, Mark. 2003. *Terror in the Mind of God: The Global Rise of Religious Violence* (Revised). Berkeley and Los Angeles: University of California Press.

Kaba, Lansine. 2000. "Islam in West Africa: Radicalism and the New Ethic of Disagreement, 1960–1990." In *The History of Islam in Africa,* Nehemia Levtzion and Randall Pouwels (eds.), 189–208. Athens: Ohio University Press.

Kaigama, Ignatius A. 2006. *Dialogue of Life: An Urgent Necessity for Nigerian Muslims and Christians*. Jos, Nigeria: Fab Educational Books.

Kalyvas, Stathis. 1996. *The Rise of Christian Democracy in Europe*. Ithaca, NY: Cornell University Press.

Karanja, John. 2008. "Evangelical Attitudes Toward Democracy in Kenya." In *Evangelical Christianity and Democracy in Africa*, Terrence O'Ranger (ed.), 67–94. New York: Oxford University Press.

Karatnycky, Adrian (ed.). 2002. *Freedom in the World: The Annual Survey of Political Rights and Civil Liberties 2001–2002*. New York: Freedom House.

Karl, Terry Lynn. 1997. *The Paradox of Plenty: Oil Booms and Petro-States*. Berkeley and Los Angeles: University of California Press.

Kasozi, A. B. K. 1995. "Christian-Muslim Inputs into Public Policy Formation in Kenya, Tanzania and Uganda." In *Religion and Politics in East Africa*, Holger Bert Hansen and Michael Twaddle (eds.), 223–246. Athens: Ohio University Press.

Kedourie, Elie. 1994. *Democracy and Arab Political Culture*. London: Frank Cass.

Keller, Edmond. J. 1999. "Political Institutions, Agency and Contingent Compromise: Understanding Democratic Consolidation and Reversal in Africa." *The National Political Science Review* 7: 96–115.

Kokole, Omari. 1995. "Idi Amin, the Nubi, and Islam in Ugandan Politics 1971–1979." In *Religion and Politics in East Africa*, Holger Bernt Hansen and Michael Twaddle (eds.), 45–58. Athens: Ohio University Press.

Kukah, Matthew. 1993. *Religion, Politics, and Power in Northern Nigeria*. Ibadan, Nigeria: Spectrum Books.

Kukah, Matthew. 1995. "Christians and Nigeria's Aborted Transition." In *Christian Churches and the Democratization of Africa*, Paul Gifford (ed.), 225–238 Leiden, Netherlands: E. J. Brill.

Kukah, Matthew, and Toyin Falola. 1996. *Religious Militancy and Self-Assertion*. Avebury, UK: Ashgate.

Kymlicka, W., and Norman, W. (eds.) 2000. *Citizenship in Diverse Societies*. Oxford: Oxford University Press.

Laakso, Markku, and Rein Taagepera. 1979. "Effective Number of Parties: A Measure with Applications to Western Europe." *Comparative Political Studies* 12, no. 1: 3–27.

Laitin, David. 1986. *Hegemony and Culture: Politics and Religious Change among the Yoruba*. Chicago: University of Chicago Press.

Lane, Robert. 1959. *Political Life: Why People Get Involved in Politics*. Glencoe, IL: Free Press.

Lawrence, Bruce. 1989. *Defenders of God: The Fundamentalists Revolt Against the Modern Age*. San Francisco: Harper and Row.

Leege, David C. 1993. "Religion and Politics in Theoretical Perspective." In *Rediscovering the Religious Factor in American Politics*, David C. Leege and Lyman A. Kellstedt (eds.), 3–25. Armonk, NY: M. E. Sharpe.

Lemarchand, Rene. 1970. *Church and Revolution in Rwanda*. New York: Praeger.

Lenski, Gerhard. 1963. *The Religious Factor: A Sociologist's Inquiry*. New York: Anchor Books.

Levine, Daniel. 1981. *Religion and Politics in Latin America: The Catholic Church in Venezuela and Colombia*. Princeton, NJ: Princeton University Press.

Lewis, Bernard. 2003. *The Crisis of Islam: Holy War and Unholy Terror*. New York: The Modern Library.

Liddle, R. William. 1992. "Indonesia's Threefold Crisis." *Journal of Democracy* 3: 60–74.

Liddle, R. William. 1999. "Indonesia's Democratic Opening." *Government and Opposition* 34: 94–116.

Lijphart, Arend. 1977. *Democracy in Plural Societies: A Comparative Exploration.* New Haven, CT: Yale University Press.

Lijphart, Arend. 2004. "Constitutional Design for Divided Societies." *Journal of Democracy* 15, no. 2: 96–109.

Linz, Juan, and Alfred Stepan. 1996. *Problems of Democratic Transition and Consolidation: Southern Europe, South America and Post-Communist Europe.* Baltimore: The Johns Hopkins University Press.

Lipset, Seymour Martin. 1959. "Some Social Requisites for Democracy: Economic Development and Political Legitimacy." *American Political Science Review* 53: 69–105.

Lipset, Seymour Martin. 1960. *Political Man.* New York: Doubleday.

Loimeier, Roman. 2007. "Nigeria: The Quest for a Viable Religious Option." In *Political Islam in West Africa,* William F. S. Miles (ed.), 43–72. Boulder and London: Lynne Rienner.

Longman, Timothy. 1995. "Christianity and Democratization in Rwanda: Assessing Church Responses to Political Crises in the 1990s." In *The Christian Churches and the Democratization of Africa,* Paul Gifford (ed.), 188–204. Leiden, Netherlands: E. J. Brill.

Lyman, Princeton, and J. Stephen Morrison. 2004. "The Terrorist Threat in Africa." *Foreign Affairs* (January–February). Accessed November 26, 2014. http://www.foreignaffairs.com/articles/59534/princeton-n-lyman-and-j-stephen-morrison/the-terrorist-threat-in-africa.

Mahmud, Sakah Saidu. 2013. *Sharia or Shura: Contending Approaches to Muslim Politics in Nigeria and Senegal.* Lanham, MD: Lexington Books.

Mainwaring, Scott, Guillermo O'Donnell, and Samuel Valenzuela (eds.). 1992. *Issues in Democratic Consolidation: The New South American Democracies in Comparative Perspective.* Notre Dame, IN: University of Notre Dame Press.

Mainwaring, Scott, and Alexander Wilde. 1989. *The Progressive Church in Latin America.* Notre Dame, IN: University of Notre Dame Press.

Marshall, Ruth. 2009. *Political Spiritualities: The Pentecostal Revolution in Nigeria.* Chicago and London: University of Chicago Press.

Martin, David. 1978. *A General Theory of Secularization.* New York: Harper and Row.

Martin, David. 1990. *Tongues of Fire: The Explosion of Pentecostalism in Latin America.* Cambridge: Basil Blackwell.

Martineau, Harriet. 1837. *Society in America.* New York: Saunders and Otley.

McClymond, M. J. 2002. "Making Sense of the Census: What 1,999,563,838 Christians Might Mean for the Study of Religion." *Journal of the American Academy of Religion* 70: 875–890.

McGreevy, John T. 2003. *Catholicism and American Freedom.* New York and London: W. W. Norton.

McLoughlin, William G. 1971. *New England Dissent 1630–1833: The Baptists and the Separation of Church and State.* Cambridge, MA: Harvard University Press.

Mecham, Lloyd J. 1966. *Church and State in Latin America: A History Politico-Ecclesiastical Relations.* Chapel Hill: University of North Carolina Press.

Menocal, Maria Rosa. 2002. *The Ornament of the World: How Muslims, Jews and Christians Created a Culture of Tolerance in Medieval Spain.* Boston and New York: Back Bay Books.

Meriboute, Zidane. 2009. *Islam's Fateful Path: The Critical Choices Facing Modern Muslims.* London: I. B. Tauris.

Micklethwait, John, and Adrian Wooldridge. 2009. *God Is Back: How the Global Rise in Faith Is Changing the World.* New York: Penguin.

Minkenberg, Michael. 2007. "Democracy and Religion-Theoretical and Empirical Observations on the Relationship Between Christianity, Islam and Liberal Democracy." *Journal of Ethnic and Migration Studies* 33(6): 887–909.

Milbrath, Lester, and M. L. Goel. 1977. *Political Participation: How and Why Do People Get Involved in Politics?* Chicago: Rand McNally College.

Miles, William. 2000. "Religious Pluralism in Northern Nigeria." In *The History of Islam in Africa,* Nehemia Levtzion and Randall Pouwels (eds.), 209–226. Athens: Ohio University Press.

Miller, Donald, and Tetsunao Yamamori. 2007. *Global Pentecostalism: The New Face of Christian Engagement.* Berkeley and Los Angeles: University of California Press.

Montalvo, Jose G., and Marta Renyal-Querol. 2003. "Religious Polarization and Economic Development." *Economic Letters* 80, no. 2: 201–210.

Munck, Gerardo, and Jay Verkuilen. 2002. "Conceptualizing and Measuring Democracy: Evaluating Alternative Indices." *Comparative Political Studies* 35, no. 1 (February): 5–34.

Munocal, Maria Rosa. 2002. *The Ornament of the World: How Muslims, Jews and Christians Created a Culture of Tolerance in Medieval Spain.* New York: Little and Brown.

Ndegwa, Stephen. 1996. *The Two Faces of Civil Society: NGOs and Politics in Africa.* West Hartford, CT: Kumarian Press.

Nelson, Hart M., and Michael Blizzard. 1975. "Why Do Pastors Preach on Social Issues?" *Theology Today* 32, no. 1: 56–73.

Njoroge, Lawrence. 1999. *A Century of Catholic Endeavor: Holy Ghost and Consolata Missions in Kenya.* Nairobi: Pauline Publications.

Noonan, John T. 1998. *The Lustre of Our Country: The American Experience of Religious Freedom.* Berkeley and Los Angeles: University of California Press.

Norris, Pippa, and Ronald Inglehart. 2004. *Sacred and Secular: Religion and Politics Worldwide.* Cambridge: Cambridge University Press.

Nzunda, Matembo, and Kenneth R. Ross. 1995. *Church, Law, and Political Transition in Malawi 1992–1994.* Lanham, MD: International Scholars.

O'Brien, Donal B. Cruise. 1995. "Coping with the Christians." In *Religion and Politics in East Africa,* Holger Bert Hansen and Michael Twaddle (eds.), 200–221. Athens: Ohio University Press.

Oded, Arye. 2000. *Islam and Politics in Kenya.* Boulder, CO: Lynne Rienner.

Ohadike, Don. 1992. "Muslim-Christian Conflict and Political Instability in Nigeria." In *Religion and National Integration in Nigeria: Islam, Christianity and Politics in the Sudan and Nigeria,* John Hunwick (ed.), 101–122. Evanston, IL: Northwestern University Press.

Oliver, J. Eric. 2001. *Democracy and Suburbia.* Princeton, NJ: Princeton University Press.

Oliver, Roland. 1965. *The Missionary Factor in East Africa.* London: Longmans.

Olsen, Mancur. 2000. *Power and Prosperity: Outgrowing Communist and Capitalist Dictatorships.* New York: Basic Books.

Oxhorn, Phillip D. 1995. *Organizing Civil Society: Popular Sectors and the Struggle for Democracy in Chile.* College Station: Pennsylvania State University Press.

Paden, John. 1972. *Religion and Political Culture in Kano.* Berkeley and Los Angeles: University of California Press.

Paden, John N. 2005. *Muslim Civic Cultures and Conflict Resolution: The Challenge of Democratic Federalism in Nigeria.* Washington, DC: Brookings Institution Press.

Paden, John. 2008. *Faith and Politics in Nigeria: Nigeria as a Pivotal State in the Muslim World.* Washington, DC: United States Institute of Peace Press.

Paden, John. 2012. *Postelection Conflict Management in Nigeria: The Challenges of National Unity.* Arlington, VA: George Mason University School for Conflict Analysis and Resolution.

Peel, J. D. 1967. "Religious Change in Yorubaland." *Africa: Journal of the International African Institute* 37, no. 3: 292–306.

Peel, J. D. 2000. *Religious Encounter and the Making of the Yoruba.* Bloomington, IN: Indiana University Press.

Pestana, Carla Gardina. 1991. *Quakers and Baptists in Colonial Massachusetts.* Cambridge: Cambridge University Press.

Pew Research Center. 2006. *Spirit and Power: A 10-Country Study of Pentecostals.* Washington, DC: Pew Forum on Religion and Public Life.

Pew Research Center. 2010. *Tolerance and Tension: Islam and Christianity in Sub-Saharan Africa.* Washington, DC: Pew Forum on Religion and Public Life.

Pew Research Center. 2012. *The Global Religious Landscape: A Report on the Size and Distribution of the World's Major Religious Groups as of 2010.* Washington, DC: Pew Forum on Religion and Public Life.

Philpott, Daniel. 2004. "The Catholic Tradition and Comparative International Politics." Unpublished paper delivered at the annual meeting of the American Political Science Association, Chicago, IL.

Philpott, Daniel. 2007. "Explaining the Political Ambivalence of Religion." *American Political Science Review* 101, no. 103: 505–525.

Phiri, Isaac. 2001. *Proclaiming Political Pluralism: The Churches and Political Transitions in Africa.* New York: Praeger.

Phiri, Isabel. 2008. "President Frederick Chiluba and Zambia: Evangelicals and Democracy in a 'Christian' Nation." In *Evangelical Christianity and Democracy in Africa,* Terrence O' Ranger (ed.), 95–130. New York: Oxford University Press.

Pierson, Paul Everett. 1974. *A Younger Church in Search of Maturity: Presbyterianism in Brazil from 1910 to 1959.* San Antonio, TX: Trinity University Press.

Pinkney, Robert. 2003. *Democracy in the Third World.* Boulder, CO: Lynne Rienner.

Pipes, Daniel. 1983. *In the Path of God: Islam and Political Power.* New York: Basic Books.

Pirouet, M. Louise. 1980. "Religion in Uganda Under Amin." *Journal of Religion in Africa* 11, no. 1: 13–29.

Posner, Daniel N. 2004. "Measuring Ethnic Fractionalization in Africa." *American Journal of Political Science* 48, no. 4 (October): 849–863.

Posner, Daniel N. 2005. *Institutions and Ethnic Politics in Africa.* Cambridge and New York: Cambridge University Press.

Przeworski, Adam, Michael Alvarez, Jose Ceibub, and Fernando Limongi. 1997. "What Makes Democracies Endure?" In *Consolidating the Third Wave Democracies,* Larry Diamond, Marc Plattner, Yun-han Chu, and Hung-Mao Tien (eds.), 295–311. Baltimore, MD: The Johns Hopkins University Press.

Putnam, Robert. 1993. *Making Democracy Work: Civic Traditions in Modern Italy.* Princeton, NJ: Princeton University Press.

Putnam, Robert. 2000. *Bowling Alone: The Collapse and Revival of American Community.* New York: Touchstone.

Quinn, Charlotte, and Frederick Quinn. 2003. *Pride, Faith and Fear: Islam in Sub-Saharan Africa.* Chicago: University of Chicago Press.

Rabushka, Alvin, and Kenneth A. Shepsle. 1972. *Politics in Plural Societies: A Theory of Democratic Instability.* Columbus, OH: Charles E. Merrill.

Raison-Jourde, Francois. 1995. "The Madagascan Churches in the Political Arena and their Contribution to the Change in Regime 1990–1992." In *Christian Churches and the Democratization of Africa*, Paul Gifford (ed.), 292–311. Leiden, Netherlands: E. J. Brill.

Ramet, Pedro (ed.). 1990. *Catholicism and Politics in Communist Societies*. Durham, NC, and London: Duke University Press.

Reeber, Michael. 1993. "Islamic Preaching in France: Admonitory Addresses or Political Platform?" *Islam and Christian-Muslim Relations* 4, no. 2: 210–222.

Riker, William. 1962. *The Theory of Political Coalitions*. New York: Greenwood.

Rittgers, Ronald. 2004. *The Reformation of the Keys: Confession, Conscience, and Authority in Sixteenth Century Germany*. Cambridge, MA: Harvard University Press.

Roberts, Dana L. 2008. *Converting Colonialism: Visions and Realities in Mission History*. Grand Rapids, MI: Eerdmans.

Roberts, Keith. 1984. *The Sociology of Religion*. New York: Praeger.

Robinson, David. 2000. *Paths of Accommodation: Muslim Societies and French Colonial Authorities in Senegal and Mauritania*. Athens: Ohio University Press.

Rose, Richard. 2002a. "Does Islam Make People Anti-Democratic? A Central Asian Perspective." *Journal of Democracy* 13, no. 4: 8–37.

Rose, Richard. 2002b. "How Muslims View Democracy: Views of Central Asia." In *How People View Democracy*, Larry Diamond and Marc E. Plattner (eds.), 143–152. Baltimore: The Johns Hopkins University Press.

Rose, Leo E., and D. Hugh Evans. 1997. "Pakistan's Enduring Experiment." *Journal of Democracy* 8, no. 1 (January); 83–96.

Roy, Olivier. 1994. *The Failure of Political Islam*. Cambridge, MA: Harvard University Press.

Rudolph, Lloyd, and Susanne Rudolph. 1987. *In Pursuit of Lakshmi: The Political Economy of the Indian State*. Chicago: University of Chicago Press.

Rudolph, Susanne. 1997. "Introduction: Religion, States and Transitional Civil Society." In *Transitional Religion and Fading States*, in Susanne Hoeber Rudolph and James Piscatori (eds.), 1–24. Boulder, CO: Westview Press.

Schattschneider, E. E. 1960. *The Semisovereign People: A Realist's View of Democracy in America*. New York: Holt, Rinehart and Winston.

Schatzberg, Michael G. 2001. *Political Legitimacy in Middle Africa: Family, Fatherhood, Food*. Bloomington: Indiana University Press.

Scully, Timothy R. 1992. *Rethinking the Center: Party Politics in Nineteenth and Twentieth Century Chile*. Palo Alto, CA: Stanford University Press.

Seewald, Peter. 2010. *Light of the World: The Pope, the Church, and the Signs of the Times*. New York: The Catholic Truth Society.

Sen, Amartya. 2006. *Identity and Violence: The Illusion of Destiny*. New York: W. W. Norton.

Sepulveda, Juan. 1988. "Pentecostalism and Popular Christianity." *International Review of Mission* 78, no. 309: 80–88.

Shadid, Anthony. 2002. *Legacy of the Prophet: Despots, Democrats, and the New Politics of Islam*. Boulder: CO: Westview Press.

Siavoshi, Sussan. 2002. "Between Heaven and Earth: The Islamic Republic of Iran." In *Religion and Politics in Comparative Perspective: The One, The Few, and the Many*, Ted Jelen and Clyde Wilcox (eds.), 125–137. Cambridge: Cambridge University Press.

Simon, David. 1999. "An Investigation into the Economic Sources of Political Participation in Zambia's Third Republic." PhD Dissertation, Department of Political Science, University of California Los Angeles.

Sisk, Timothy. 2011. "Introduction: Religious Leaders, Conflict and Peacemaking." In *Between Terror and Tolerance: Religious Leaders, Conflict, and Peacemaking*, Timothy D. Sisk (ed.), 1–8. Washington, DC: Georgetown University Press.

Sklar, Richard. 1997. "Crises and Transitions in the Political History of Independent Nigeria." In *Dilemmas of Democracy in Nigeria*, Paul Becket and Crawford Young (eds.), 15–44. Rochester and London: University of Rochester Press.

Smith, Brian H. 1979. "Churches and Human Rights in Latin America: Recent Trends in the Sub-Continent." *Journal of Interamerican Studies and World Affairs* 21, no. 1: 89–127.

Smith, Brian H. 1982. *The Church and Politics in Chile: Challenges to Modern Catholicism*. Princeton, NJ: Princeton University Press.

Smith, Christian. 2000. *Christian America? What Evangelicals Really Want*. Berkeley and Los Angeles: University of California Press.

Smith, Christian (ed.). 1996. *Disruptive Religion: The Force of Faith in Social Movement Activism*. New York: Routledge.

Smith, David, and Alex Inkeles. 1974. *Becoming Modern: Individual Change in Six Developing Nations*. Cambridge: Cambridge University Press.

Sobrino, Jon. 1991. *Jesus the Liberator*. Maryknoll, NY: Orbis Books

Soroush, Abdolkarim. 2000. *Reason, Freedom, and Democracy in Islam*. Oxford and New York: Oxford University Press.

Spaulding, Jay. 2000. "Precolonial Islam in the Eastern Sudan." In *The History of Islam in Africa*, Nehemia Levtzion and Randall Pouwels (eds.), 117–130. Athens: Ohio University Press.

Sperling, David, and Jose Kagabo. 2000. "The Coastal Hinterland and the Interior of East Africa." In *The History of Islam in Africa*, Nehemia Levtzion and Randall Pouwels (eds.), 273–302. Athens: Ohio University Press.

Stark, Rodney. 1992. "Do Catholic Societies Really Exist?" *Rationality and Society* 4: 261–271.

Stark, Rodney, and William Sims Bainbridge. 1985. *The Future of Religion: Secularization, Renewal and Cult Formation*. Berkeley: University of California Press.

Steigenga, Timothy. 2001. *Politics of the Spirit: The Political Implications of Pentecostalized Religion in Costa Rica and Guatemala*. New York: Lexington Books.

Stepan, Alfred. 2000. "Religion, Democracy and the Twin Tolerations." *Journal of Democracy* 11, no. 4: 37–57.

Stepan, Alfred. 2001. *Arguing Comparative Politics*. Oxford: Oxford University Press.

Stepan, Alfred. 2013. "Stateness, Democracy, and Respect: Senegal in Comparative Perspective." In *Tolerance, Democracy, and Sufis in Senegal*, Mamadou Diouf (ed.), 205–238. New York: Columbia University Press.

Stepan, Alfred, Juan Linz, and Yogendra Yadav. 2011. *Crafting State-Nations: India and Other Multinational Democracies*. Baltimore and London: Johns Hopkins University Press.

Stepan, Alfred, and Graeme Robertson. 2003. "An Arab More Than a Muslim Electoral Gap." *Journal of Democracy* 14, no. 3 (July): 30–44.

Stokes, Anson Phelps. 1950. *Church and State in the United States*. New York: Harper.

Teets, Jessica. 2014. *Civil Society under Authoritarianism: The China Model*. Cambridge and New York: Cambridge University Press.

Temple, Arnold. 1991. "Should the Church Meddle in Politics?" *Mindolo World* 2: 8–12.

Tessler, Mark. 2002. "Islam and Democracy in the Middle East: The Impact of Religious Orientations on Attitudes Toward Democracy in Four Arab Countries." *Comparative Politics* 34, no. 3 (April): 337–354.

Thompson, A. 1848. *A Historical Sketch of the Origins of the Secessionist Church.* Edinburgh: A. Fullerton.

Throup, David, and Charles Hornsby. 1998. *Multi-Party Politics in Kenya.* London: James Currey.

Tocqueville, Alexis de. 1969. *Democracy in America,* J. P. Mayer (ed.). Garden City, NY: Doubleday.

Toft, Monica, Daniel Philpott, and Timothy Shah. 2011. *God's Century: Resurgent Religion in Global Politics.* New York: W. W. Norton.

Triaud, Jean-Louis. 2000. "Islam in Africa under French Colonial Rule." In *The History of Islam in Africa,* Nehemia Levtzion and Randall Pouwels (eds.), 169–188. Athens: Ohio University Press.

Trigg, Roger. 2014. *Religious Diversity: Philosophical and Political Dimensions.* Cambridge and New York: Cambridge University Press.

Trimingham, J. Spencer. 1964. *Islam in East Africa.* Oxford: Oxford University Press.

Trudeau, Pierre Elliot. 1968. *Federalism and the French Canadians.* New York: St. Martin's Press.

Tryacke, Nicholas. 1991. "The Rise of Puritanism in the Legalizing of Dissent, 1571–1719." In *From Persecution to Toleration: The Glorious Revolution and Religion in England,* Ole Peter Grell, Jonathan I. Isreal, and Nicholas Tyacke (eds.), 17–50. Oxford: Oxford University Press.

United Nations. 1999. *Human Development Report 1999.* Oxford: Oxford University Press.

Usman, Y. B. 1987. *The Manipulation of Religion in Nigeria 1977–1987.* Kaduna, Nigeria: Vanguard.

Varshney, Ashutosh. 2002. *Ethnic Conflict and Civic Life: Hindus and Muslims in India.* New Haven, CT: Yale University Press.

Vatin, J. 1982. "Revival in the Magreb." In *Islamic Resurgence in the Arab World,* A. Desouki (ed.), 246–247. New York: Praeger.

Verba, Sidney, and Norman Nie. 1972. *Participation in America: Political Democracy and Social Equality.* Chicago: University of Chicago Press.

Verba, Sidney, Norman Nie, and Jae-On Kim. 1978. *Participation and Political Equality.* Chicago: University of Chicago Press.

Verba, Sidney, Kay Lehman Schlozman, and Henry E. Brady. 1995. *Voice and Equality: Civic Volunteerism in American Politics.* Cambridge, MA: Harvard University Press.

Villalon, Leonardo. 1995. *Islamic Society and State Power in Senegal: Disciples and Citizens in Fatick.* New York: Cambridge University Press.

Villalon, Leonardo. 2007. "Senegal: Shades of Islamism on a Sufi Landscape." In *Political Islam in West Africa,* William F. S. Miles (ed.), 161–182. Boulder and London: Lynne Rienner.

Villalon, Leonardo. 2013. "Negotiating Islam in the Era of Democracy: Senegal in Comparative Perspective." In *Tolerance, Democracy, and Sufis in Senegal,* Mamadou Diouf (ed.), 239–266. New York: Columbia University Press.

Villalon, Leonardo, and Ousmane Kane. 1998. "Senegal: The Crisis of Democracy and the Emergence of an Islamic Opposition." In *The African State at a Critical Juncture: Between Disintegration and Reconfiguration,* Leonardo A. Villalon and Phillip Huxtable (eds.), 143–166. Boulder: Lynne Rienner.

Voll, John. 2000. "The Eastern Sudan, 1822 to the Present." In *The History of Islam in Africa,* Nehemia Levtzion and Randall Pouwels (eds.), 153–168. Athens: Ohio University Press.

Wald, Kenneth D. 1987. "Churches as Political Communities." *American Political Science Review* 82: 531–548.

Wald, Kenneth D. 2003. *Religion and Politics in the United States* (4th ed.). Lanham, MD: Rowman & Littlefield.

Waliggo, John M. 1995. "The Role of Christian Churches in the Democratization Process in Uganda." In *The Christian Churches and the Democratization of Africa*, Paul Gifford (ed.), 205–224. Leiden, Netherlands: E. J. Brill.

Walker, Andrew. 1983. "Pentecostal Power: The Charismatic Renewal Movement and the Politics of Pentecostal Experience." In *Of Gods and Men: New Religious Movements in the West*, Eileen Barker (ed.), 89–108. Macon, GA: Mercer University Press.

Ward, Kevin. 2005. "Eating and Sharing: Church and State in Uganda." *Journal of Anglican Studies* 3, no. 1: 99–119.

Weber, Max. 1930 (1958). *The Protestant Ethic and the Spirit of Capitalism*. London: George Allen and Unwin.

Weber, Max. 1963. *Sociology of Religion*. Boston: Beacon Press.

Whitehead, Laurence. 1997. "Bowling in the Bronx: The Uncivil Interstices Between Civil and Political Society." *Democratization* 4, no. 1: 94–114.

Wiarda, Howard. (ed.). 1974. *Politics and Social Change in Latin America: The Distinct Tradition*. Amherst: University of Massachusetts Press.

Widner, Jennifer. 1992. *The Rise of a Party-State in Kenya: From Harambee to Nyayo*. Berkeley and Los Angeles: University of California Press.

Woodberry, Robert. 2012. "The Missionary Roots of Liberal Democracy." *American Political Science Review* 106, no. 2: 244–274.

Woodberry, Robert, and Timothy Shah. 2004. "The Pioneering Protestants." *Journal of Democracy* 15, no. 2: 47–61.

World Bank. 2000. *African Development Indicators 2000*. Washington, DC: The International Bank for Reconstruction and Development.

Yong, Amos. 2010. *In the Days of Caesar: Pentecostalism and Political Theology*. Grand Rapids, MI: William B. Eerdmans.

Zakaria, Fareed. 2003. *The Future of Freedom: Illiberal Democracy at Home and Abroad*. New York: W. W. Norton.

Zaman, Muhammed Qasim. 2002. *The Ulama in Contemporary Islam: Custodians of Change*. Princeton, NJ: Princeton University Press.

Zubaida, Sami. 1993. *Islam: The People and State*. New York: I. B. Tauris.

Index

Ababakar, Atiku, 103
Abdu (interview subject in Nigeria), 80
Abuja (Nigeria), United Nations compound
  bombing (2011) in, 103
Action Congress (AC; Nigerian political
  party), 103
Act of Toleration (Great Britain, 1689), 168
Adeboye, A.E., 40
Afghanistan: religion's influence on politics
  in, 7, 11, 33, 37; Soviet occupation
  of, 37; Taliban in, 11, 28, 33, 37, 102;
  U.S. war in, 28
Afrobarometer survey: attitudes toward liberal
  democratic freedoms measured in, 84,
  86–87, 89–90, 93, 149, 154; methodology
  of, 82–84, 87, 93–94, 114–115, 121,
  148–149; nonvoting political participation
  data in, 84, 86; religious contacting data
  in, 83, 89–90, 92–94; religious identity
  data in, 83–85, 89–90, 148; religious
  observance data in, 83–84, 87, 89–90,
  92–94, 120–121, 148–149, 154; voting
  data in, 84, 87, 89–91, 149
Agnes (interview subject in Nigeria), 96
Ahmadenijad, Mahmoud, 28–29
Alesina, Alberto, 9, 55, 165
Algeria, 25
'Ali Nadwi, Sayyid Abdu'l-Hasan, 22–23, 34
All People's Party (APP; Nigeria), 103
Al Shabab, 17, 87, 109, 113
"The America I Have Seen" (Qutb), 23
Amin, Idi, 109, 111–112
The Amish, 43
Anderson, John, 37
Anglicans and Anglican Church: Anglican
  Church Missionary Society (CMS) and,
  145, 160; decolonization in sub-Saharan
  Africa and, 65; in Nigeria, 1–2, 98–99,
  102, 129, 145, 160; policies toward Roman
  Catholics in England and, 7; pro-freedom
  political activism and, 112–113; split

from Roman Catholicism and, 54–55; in
  sub-Saharan Africa as a whole, 67–68; in
  Uganda, 6, 63, 67, 109–113
Angola: Christian majority in, 60; education
  and human development levels in, 72;
  ethnic diversity in, 62, 75; mainline
  Protestants in, 70; Muslims in, 70; political
  repression levels in, 75; pro-freedom
  political activism in, 70, 72, 75; religious
  diversity in, 59–60, 62, 75; Roman
  Catholic Church in, 70
Ansaru (Islamist group in Nigeria), 102–103
anti-freedom political activism: Christianity
  and, 34–35, 37, 48–49, 65–68, 99, 164;
  Islam and, 37, 66, 68, 99; Pentecostals and,
  67–68, 99; religious diversity's impact on,
  47, 151; Roman Catholic Church and,
  34–35, 37, 164; in sub-Saharan Africa as a
  whole, 66–68
Arab Spring (2011), 27
Argentina, 6, 10, 35, 165
Ashafa, Muhammed Nurayan, 153, 161, 171

Baganda ethnic group (Uganda), 63, 110
Baghdad (Iraq), during the medieval era, 26
Baghdadi, Abu Bakr al-, 7
Banda, Hastings, 64
Bangladesh, 27–29
Belgium, 10, 53
Benedict XVI (pope), 43
Benin: education and human development
  levels in, 72; ethnic diversity in, 62,
  75; political repression levels in, 75;
  pro-freedom political activism in, 70, 72,
  75; religious diversity in, 59, 62, 75, 85;
  Roman Catholic Church in, 70
Berger, Peter, 165
Berom ethnic group (Nigeria), 145
Biafran War (1967-1970), 98
The Bible, 7, 20, 39, 50
Boko Haram, 17, 87, 102–103, 128, 148

Bolivia, 10, 165

Borno (state in modern-day northeastern Nigeria), 102

Borno (state in ninth-century Nigeria), 97

Bosnia and Herzegovina, 7, 27, 39

Botswana, 10, 62, 85

Brazil, 6, 30, 34, 41, 164

Brussels Declaration, 52

Buganda Kingdom (Uganda), 110, 112

Buhari, Muhammadu, 104

Burkina Faso, 85

Burundi: education and human development levels in, 72; ethnic diversity in, 62, 75; political repression levels in, 75; pro-freedom political activism in, 70, 72, 75; religious diversity in, 59, 62, 75; Roman Catholic Church in, 70

Cameroon: education and human development levels in, 72; ethnic diversity in, 62, 75; mainline Protestants in, 70; Muslims in, 70; political repression levels in, 75; pro-freedom political activism in, 70, 72, 75; relations between religious groups in, 104; religious diversity in, 59–62, 75; Roman Catholic Church in, 70

Cape Verde, 85

Casamance region (Senegal), 105

Catholics. See Roman Catholic Church

Central African Republic: education and human development levels in, 72; ethnic diversity in, 62, 75; mainline Protestants in, 70; Muslims in, 70; political repression levels in, 75; pro-freedom political activism in, 70, 72, 75; religious diversity in, 59–60, 62, 75; Roman Catholics in, 70

Central Asia, 25

Chad: education and human development levels in, 72; ethnic diversity in, 62, 75; mainline Protestants in, 70; Muslims in, 70, 104; political repression levels in, 75; pro-freedom political activism in, 70, 72, 75; relations between religious groups in, 104; religious diversity in, 59, 62, 75; Roman Catholic Church in, 70

Chile, 10, 34–35, 164

Chiluba, Frederick, 31, 64–65, 67–68

Christian Association of Nigeria (CAN), 101–102, 104

Christian Council of Churches (Madagascar), 64

Christianity. See also Christians; specific sects: anti-freedom political activism and, 34–35, 37, 48–49, 65–68, 99, 164; confessional diversity within, 6, 30, 54–57, 61, 83; fluidity and dynamism of, 6–7, 31–32, 48–50, 65, 156; growth of, 15–16, 51–52; inculturation and, 52; Jesus Christ's teachings and role in, 20, 39, 54; liberal democracy's compatibility with, 1–5, 7, 14, 18, 24–26, 33, 36, 48–50, 57, 64–65, 154–157, 163–164; multinational reach of, 14–15; political theologies in, 6–7, 30–36, 48–50, 54, 64, 73, 93, 96, 104–105, 110, 127–129, 143, 147–148, 151, 156, 163, 166–167, 171; prosyletization and, 15, 40–42, 56–57, 101–102, 139–140, 143, 158; religious growth axiom and, 40–42, 158; religious influence axiom and, 42–44, 158; in religiously diverse settings, 2–3, 8, 11–12, 18, 41, 48, 53–54, 56–57, 81, 93, 96, 152, 154, 158, 163–166, 168–169

Christians. See also Christianity: attitudes toward elections among, 150; attitudes toward freedom of religion among, 119–121, 123, 127–128, 136–137, 157–158, 175; attitudes toward freedom of speech among, 93; attitudes toward religious leaders among, 80, 83; attitudes toward separation of religious and political authority among, 50, 105; decolonization in sub-Saharan Africa and, 65–66; in Nigeria, 1–2, 7, 12–13, 15–18, 21–22, 30–31, 40–41, 43, 50, 60, 63, 70, 96–105, 110, 113, 116–121, 124–130, 132–148, 150–154, 157–164, 167, 169–171, 175; nonvoting political participation among, 1, 7, 20–21, 30–32, 34–37, 44, 49–51, 64–65, 67–71, 79, 82, 95, 111–113, 135, 138–142, 154, 158–159, 164, 175; political interest levels among, 118, 134–135, 175; pro-freedom political activism and, 34–37, 49–51, 64–65, 67–71, 79, 82, 95, 111–113, 154, 164; religious observance levels among, 81, 83, 114, 116–123, 133–137, 141, 150, 157, 162, 175; in Senegal, 41, 70, 105–107, 109, 116–119, 121, 175; in sub-Saharan Africa as a whole, 3–4, 16, 20–21, 25, 30–31, 42, 48–53, 56–57, 61,

64–65, 67–68, 70, 81, 157; in Uganda, 18, 21, 63, 67, 70, 95, 97, 109–114, 116–119, 121, 123, 154, 162, 175; voting and voting rates among, 116–117, 133–134, 139, 159, 175

Church of Uganda (Anglican Church in Uganda), 109–113

Clark, Andrew Francis, 107

Cold War, 66–67

Comite Islamique pour la Reforme du Code de la Famille au Senegal (CIRCOF), 108

Congo Republic: Christian majority in, 60; education and human development levels in, 72; ethnic diversity in, 62, 75; mainline Protestants in, 70; political repression levels in, 75; pro-freedom political activism in, 70, 72, 75; religious diversity in, 59–60, 62, 75; Roman Catholic Church in, 70

Congress for Progressive Change (CPC; Nigerian political party), 104

Constituent Assembly (MCA; Nigeria), 144

Côte d'Ivoire: education and human development levels in, 72; ethnic diversity in, 62, 75; mainline Protestants in, 70; Muslims in, 70; political repression levels in, 75; pro-freedom political activism in, 70, 72, 75; religious diversity in, 59–60, 62, 75; Roman Catholics in, 70

Creevey, Lucy, 107

Darhiratoul Moustarchadina wal Moustarchidaty (Islamist group in Senegal), 107

Deliverance Church (DC; Kenya), 67–68

Democracy in America (Tocqueville), 25

Democratic Party (DP; Uganda), 110

Democratic Republic of Congo: education and human development levels in, 72; ethnic diversity in, 62, 75; mainline Protestants in, 70; Muslims in, 70; political repression levels in, 75; pro-freedom political activism in, 70, 72, 75; relations between religious groups in, 104; religious diversity in, 59–60, 62, 75; Roman Catholic Church in, 70

Dialogue of Life: An Urgent Necessity for Nigerian Muslims and Christians, 153

Dieye, Cheikh Abdoulaye, 108

Diouf, Abdou, 107

Doe, Samuel, 64

effective number of religions (INTER-RD) and effective number of sub-religious groups (INTRA-RD) scores, 57–60, 62, 76–77, 84–85, 90–92, 97

Egypt, 23–24, 27

Ehteshami, Anoushiravan, 36

Ellis, Stephen, 15

El Salvador, 10, 164

Enugu (Nigeria): attitudes toward differences of opinion in, 152; attitudes toward freedom of religion in, 125, 132–133, 136–137, 143, 152, 154, 157, 164; attitudes toward liberal democracy in, 133; attitudes toward separation of religious and state authority in, 159; Christian majority population in, 1, 18, 124–125, 130, 132–139, 141–143, 157, 159; income levels in, 132; Muslims in, 125, 133–136, 139–140, 143; nonvoting political participation in, 1, 132, 138–142, 152, 159; Pentecostals in, 133–137, 143; political interest levels in, 125, 132–135, 137; religious observance rates in, 130, 132–138, 152, 154, 157, 164; Roman Catholics in, 138–139, 141–142; voting and voting rates in, 125, 132–134, 137–138, 159

Equatorial Guinea: education and human development levels in, 72; ethnic diversity in, 62, 75; mainline Protestants in, 70; Muslims in, 70; political repression levels in, 75; pro-freedom political activism in, 70, 72, 75; religious diversity in, 59, 61–62, 75; Roman Catholics in, 61, 70

Ethiopia: education and human development levels in, 72; ethnic diversity in, 62, 75; mainline Protestants in, 70; Muslims in, 70; political repression levels in, 75; pro-freedom political activism in, 70, 72, 75; relations between religious groups in, 104; religious diversity in, 59, 62, 75; Roman Catholic Church in, 70

Evangelicalism. *See also* Pentecostalism; Pentecostals: anti-freedom political activism and, 67; Christian Association of Nigeria (CAN), 102; growth of, 15; liberal democracy's compatibility with, 25, 31, 64; in Nigeria, 30, 98–100, 102, 129; prosyletization and, 41; in sub-Saharan Africa as a whole, 31, 67; in Uganda, 109

Ezekial (interview subject in Nigeria), 143

Falae, Olu, 103
Fall, Ousseynou, 108
Falola, Toyin, 101, 129, 144
Family Code (Senegal), 108
Fenton, Elizabeth, 165
Fish, Steven, 5, 87
France, 53, 108
Francis, Michael, 64
Freedom House scores, 25, 28, 74–75
"free riders" in pro-democracy movements, 24, 68–69

Gabon: education and human development levels in, 72; ethnic diversity in, 62, 75; mainline Protestants in, 70; Muslims in, 70; political repression levels in, 75; pro-freedom political activism in, 70, 72, 75; religious diversity in, 59, 62, 75; Roman Catholic Church in, 70
The Gambia: education and human development levels in, 72; ethnic diversity in, 62, 75; mainline Protestants in, 70; Muslims in, 70; political repression levels in, 75; pro-freedom political activism in, 70, 72, 75; religious diversity in, 59–60, 62, 75; Roman Catholic Church in, 70
Gellar, Sheldon, 107
Ghana: anti-freedom political activism in, 67; autocratic era in, 31, 64, 67; education and human development levels in, 72; ethnic diversity in, 62, 75; mainline Protestants in, 64, 70; Pentecostals and Pentecostalism in, 31, 67; political repression levels in, 75; pro-freedom political activism in, 64, 70, 72, 75; relations between religious groups in, 104; religious diversity in, 59–62, 75, 84–85; Roman Catholic Church in, 64, 70
Ghanouchi, Rachid, 21
Gill, Anthony, 10, 45–46, 164
Global Pentecostalism: The New Face of Christian Social Engagement (Miller and Yamamori), 32
God's Century: Resurgent Religion and Global Politics (Toft, Philpott, and Shah), 24
Gould, Andrew, 10
Grand Khadi Kanam, 153, 170–171
Great Britain. *See* United Kingdom
Guatemala, 30

Guinea: education and human development levels in, 72; ethnic diversity in, 62, 75; mainline Protestants in, 70; Muslim majority in, 25; Muslims in, 70; political culture in, 25; political repression levels in, 75; pro-freedom political activism in, 70, 72, 75; religious diversity in, 59, 62, 75; Roman Catholic Church in, 70
Gumi, Abubakar, 144

Hadith, 36, 99
Hassan (interview subject in Uganda), 80
Hausa-Fulani ethnic group (Nigeria), 63, 97–98, 145
Hefner, Robert, 21–22, 28
Hinduism, 15
Hiszbut Tarquiyyah (Islamist group in Senegal), 107
Honduras, 10, 165
Human Development Index (HDI), 71–73, 77–78
Huntington, Samuel, 25
Hussein (Muslim leader in Jos, Nigeria), 141

Ibadan (Nigeria): attitudes toward differences of opinion in, 136, 146; attitudes toward freedom of religion in, 125, 133, 137–138, 142–144, 146, 148, 151–152, 154, 157, 160, 164, 167; attitudes toward liberal democracy in, 18, 22, 71, 125, 133, 137; attitudes toward separation of religious and state authority in, 152, 159; Christians in, 125, 129, 133–137, 142–146, 148, 151, 157, 159–160, 167; income levels in, 132; Muslims in, 22, 71, 125, 129, 133–137, 141, 142–146, 148, 151, 154, 157, 159–160, 167; nonvoting political participation in, 125, 132, 137, 142–143, 159; Pentecostals in, 133–134, 137, 143, 157; political interest levels in, 132–135, 137; religious diversity in, 18, 22, 71, 124–125, 129–130, 132–138, 141, 142–146, 151–152, 154, 157, 159–160, 164; religious integration in, 18, 22, 125, 146, 152, 154, 164; religious observance rates in, 130, 132–138, 146, 151–152, 154, 157, 164; Roman Catholics in, 151; Shari'ah law and, 144; voting and voting rates in, 132–134, 137–138; Yoruba ethnic majority in, 142–144, 146

133–134, 137–138, 146–147, 150–152, 154, 158, 161–165, 168–169; religious observance rates' impact on, 29, 81, 86, 88–90, 92, 94–95, 97, 116, 120–123, 126–127, 130, 133–137, 146–148, 150, 154–156, 162, 174–175; religious segregation's impact on, 13–14, 18–19, 126; Roman Catholicism's compatibility with, 1, 4, 6–7, 9–10, 25–26, 31, 34–37, 65, 89; separation of religious and state authority in, 3, 8–9; "tipping points" regarding, 167–169

Liberia: Christians in, 60, 64, 70; education and human development levels in, 72; ethnic diversity in, 62, 75; mainline Protestants in, 70; Muslims in, 60; political repression levels in, 75; pro-freedom political activism in, 64, 70, 72, 75; relations between religious groups in, 104; religious diversity in, 59–60, 62, 75, 85; Roman Catholic Church in, 64, 70; traditional African religions in, 60

Libya, 27

Lithuania, 37–38

Lutheranism, 37–38, 65

Lwanga, Cyprian, 113

Madagascar, 64, 85

Madjid, Nurcholish, 21

Maina (Kenyan interview subject), 49

mainline Protestantism. *See also* mainline Protestants; *specific sects*: civic skills building and, 1, 4–5; colonial era missionaries in sub-Saharan African and, 52–53; liberal democracy's compatibility with, 1, 4–6, 9–10, 24–26, 31, 65, 89; movement between denominations in, 41; political theologies and, 34, 36, 49; pro-freedom political activism and, 49, 64, 67–70; social service provision and, 68

mainline Protestants: attitudes toward freedom of religion among, 119, 121, 123; in Kenya, 63–64, 68, 70; in Nigeria, 70, 100, 116–119, 133–134; religious observance rates among, 116–123; in Senegal, 70, 116–119, 121; in sub-Saharan Africa as a whole, 31, 50, 52–53, 64–65, 67–68; in Uganda, 63, 67, 70, 109–113, 116–119, 121; voting and voting rates among, 116–117, 133

Malawi: Catholic Church in, 64–65; education and human development levels in, 72; ethnic diversity in, 62, 75; mainline Protestants in, 70; political repression levels in, 75; pro-freedom political activism in, 64, 70, 72, 75; religious diversity in, 59–60, 62, 75, 84–85; Roman Catholic Church in, 70

Malaysia, 27

Mali: education and human development levels in, 72; ethnic diversity in, 62, 75; liberal democracy in, 27; Muslim majority in, 10, 27, 52, 69–70; political repression levels in, 75; pro-freedom political activism in, 69–70, 72, 75; religious diversity in, 59–60, 62, 75, 85

marabouts (Sufi leaders), 106–107, 120

Mark, Gospel of, 20

Marshall, Ruth, 6, 31–32, 40

Matthew, Gospel of, 39

Mauritania: education and human development levels in, 72; ethnic diversity in, 62, 75; mainline Protestants in, 70; Muslim majority in, 60; Muslims in, 70; political repression levels in, 75; pro-freedom political activism in, 70, 72, 75; religious diversity in, 59–60, 62, 75; Roman Catholic Church in, 70

Mawdudi, Ayyid, 7

Mennonites, 43

Middle Belt (Nigeria): increasing calls for religious tolerance in, 153, 161; Islamist groups in, 103, 147; Muslim migration to, 126, 160–161; overlap between ethnic and religious identity in, 130, 161; political theologies in, 129–130; religious diversity in, 98, 160–161, 170; violence between religious groups in, 101, 103–104, 129, 147, 160

Middle East. *See also specific countries*: colonial rule in, 23; Islam and, 25–27, 29; liberal democracy and, 25–27; religious diversity in, 15, 22

Miller, Donald, 32

Mohammed (The Prophet), 21, 40, 54, 65

Moi, Daniel arap, 31, 49, 64, 67–68

Montalvo, Jose, 55–56

Mouridiyya brotherhood of Sufism, 106–107

Mousavi, Mir-Hossein, 29

Mozambique: education and human development levels in, 72; ethnic diversity in, 62, 75; mainline Protestants in, 70; political repression levels in, 75; pro-freedom political activism in, 70, 72, 75; relations between religious groups in, 104; religious diversity in, 59, 62, 75, 85; Roman Catholic Church in, 70

Muhammediyah, 28

Munocal, Maria Rosa, 26

Museveni, Yoweri, 67, 109, 112–113

Muslims. *See also* Islam: in Arab Middle East as a whole, 25–27, 29; attitudes toward elections among, 150; attitudes toward freedom of religion among, 118–119, 121, 123, 136–137, 157–158, 174; attitudes toward freedom of speech among, 93; attitudes toward individual freedoms among, 29; attitudes toward religious leaders among, 80, 83, 106–107; attitudes toward the word "democracy" among, 86; decolonization in sub-Saharan Africa and, 65–66; in India, 15, 27; in Indonesia, 11, 22, 27–29; in Kenya, 27, 63, 68–70; in Mali, 10, 27, 52, 69–70; in Nigeria, 1, 12–13, 15–18, 22, 27, 29, 31, 40–41, 52, 60, 63, 65, 69–71, 80, 97–105, 110, 113, 116–119, 121, 124–130, 132–148, 150–154, 157–164, 167, 169–171, 174; nonvoting political participation among, 1, 21–24, 27–28, 37, 66, 68, 99, 138–141, 158–159, 174; political interest levels among, 118, 134–135, 174; religious observance rates among, 29, 81, 83, 114, 116–123, 133–135, 141, 150, 157–158, 162, 174; in Senegal, 11, 18, 25, 41, 52, 70, 95, 97, 105–109, 113–114, 116–121, 123, 138, 154, 162, 174; in sub-Saharan Africa as a whole, 3–4, 16, 22, 25, 48–52, 56–57, 60–61, 64–65, 81, 157; in Sudan, 15, 52, 65, 70; in Uganda, 70, 80, 109–113, 116–119, 121, 174; voting and voting rates among, 116–117, 120, 133, 138

Nahdatul Ulama (NU), 28

Namibia: Christian majority in, 60; education and human development levels in, 72; ethnic diversity in, 62, 75; mainline Protestants in, 70; political repression levels in, 75; pro-freedom political activism in, 70, 72, 75; religious diversity in, 59–60, 62, 75, 85; Roman Catholic Church in, 70

Nasser, Gamal Abdel, 23

National Christian Coalition (Zambia), 31

National Council of Churches of Kenya (NCCK), 64

National Resistance Movement (Uganda), 112

National Supreme Council of Islamic Affairs (NSCIA; Nigeria), 104

The Netherlands, 10

Nicaragua, 10, 164

Niger: education and human development levels in, 72; ethnic diversity in, 62, 75; mainline Protestants in, 70; Muslim majority in, 52, 70; political repression levels in, 75; pro-freedom political activism in, 70, 72, 75; religious diversity in, 59–60, 62, 75; Roman Catholic Church in, 70; Sufism in, 60

Nigeria. *See also specific cities and states*: Anglicans and Anglican Church in, 1–2, 98–99, 102, 129, 145, 160; anti-innovation legalist movements in, 54, 99–100, 105; attitudes regarding separation of religious and state authority in, 29, 50, 105, 152, 159; attitudes toward differences of opinion, 119, 136, 146, 152, 174; attitudes toward freedom of religion in, 115–116, 119–121, 125–126, 132–133, 136–138, 142–144, 146, 148, 152–154, 157–158, 160, 164, 167, 174–175; Biafran War (1967-1970) in, 98; Boko Haram in, 87, 102–103, 128, 148; British colonial rule in, 63, 98; census data in, 58, 97; Christians in, 1–2, 7, 12–13, 15–18, 21–22, 30–31, 40–41, 43, 50, 60, 63, 70, 96–105, 110, 113, 116–121, 124–130, 132–148, 150–154, 157–164, 167, 169–171, 175; constitution in, 103; education and human development levels in, 72; elections in, 103–104, 148; ethnic diversity and identity in, 62–63, 75, 96–98, 103, 129–130; Hausa-Fulani ethnic group in, 63, 97–98, 145; Igbo ethnic group in, 63, 98; Islamist movements in, 102–103, 128, 147; Kanuri ethnic group in, 97; liberal democracy and, 13, 17–19, 71, 87, 97, 115–116, 121–122, 126–128, 130, 132, 147, 152, 157, 162–163, 168, 174–175; mainline Protestants in, 1–2, 70, 98–100, 102, 116–119, 129, 133–134, 145, 160; map of religions by region, 124; map of religious violence by region, 128; Muslims